# The Impossible City

THE

# Impossible City

A HONG KONG MEMOIR

# Karen Cheung

RANDOM HOUSE
NEW YORK

Published in the United States by Random House, an imprint and
division of Penguin Random House LLC, New York.

RANDOM HOUSE and the HOUSE colophon are registered trademarks
of Penguin Random House LLC.

LIBRARY OF CONGRESS CATALOGING-IN-PUBLICATION DATA
Names: Cheung, Karen, author.
Title: The impossible city : a Hong Kong memoir / Karen Cheung.
Other titles: Hong Kong memoir
Description: New York : Random House, [2022]
Identifiers: LCCN 2021027512 (print) | LCCN 2021027513 (ebook)
| ISBN 9780593241431 (hardcover) | ISBN 9780593241455 (ebook)
Subjects: LCSH: Cheung, Karen. | Hong Kong (China)—Social life
and customs—21st century. | Hong Kong (China)—Social
conditions—21st century. | Hong Kong (China)—History—21st
century. | Hong Kong (China)—Biography.
Classification: LCC DS796.H753 C44 2022 (print) |
LCC DS796.H753 (ebook) | DDC 951.2506/12092 [B]—dc23
LC record available at https://lccn.loc.gov/2021027512

LC ebook record available at https://lccn.loc.gov/2021027513

PRINTED IN THE UNITED STATES OF AMERICA ON ACID-FREE PAPER

randomhousebooks.com

2  4  6  8  9  7  5  3  1

First Edition

*To my Hong Kong friends, wherever you are*

# Preface

If you had asked me when I was eighteen what I thought of Hong Kong, I would have told you that I was ambivalent. Hong Kong was a place in which I just happened to find myself. The chaotic streets where dripping water from air conditioners was always sliding down my hair; the thick summer air steeped with the scent of fried peppers stuffed with fish paste; the view of the fabled harbor where a mountain ridge peeks out behind jagged buildings—this was merely the setting for the messy childhood I was trying to navigate and survive. I was shuttled between separated parents in two different cities, between a private school and a conservative public school, between my father's good mood and his explosive temper. I had no identity yet—I was not an immigrant or a third-culture kid or even a Hong Konger.

I was not a Hong Konger because I did not yet know what that meant. I was born in Shenzhen, a neighboring Chinese city where my parents met, and arrived in Hong Kong before I turned one. My father's side of the family moved to Hong Kong from Hoiping in China in the 1950s, and my grandmother brought with her pagan superstitions and archaic village phrases. My mother is from Wuhan and to this day she cannot speak my mother tongue—Cantonese, the southern Chinese language spoken in Guangdong Province and Hong Kong—without an accent, swerving back to Mandarin after a few sentences. My Singapore-raised brother and I conversed in English. But my family never thought of this as an emigration story; I've never even heard anyone refer to themselves as a Hong Konger. It did not seem important, then, to give a name or a narrative to what we were.

When I was four, my small city went from being a British colony to Chinese property. At the time of the historic event, known as the handover, literature and media depicted Hong Kong as at the intersection of clashing identities, but the truth was worse: We had no identity. The only thing that could be called a Hong Kong identity was the fact that we had some neat colonial buildings but also bamboo scaffolding and great Chinese food in our dai pai dongs. We defined ourselves in negatives—not Communist, no longer colonial subjects. The fact that we had rule of law, which exists in a great many other countries, became the basis for an entire collective identity. It would take a few decades of experimentation before each of us would come to define this identity for ourselves.

My childhood was set in an old, sluggish neighborhood in To Kwa Wan, Kowloon, near a decommissioned airport and a walled city turned park. Dark gaming arcades frequented by truant kids were juxtaposed with restaurants that served steaks seasoned with too much tenderizer; the cluttered façades of public housing stood next to glossy private apartment blocks with their own clubhouses and pools. Across from stores run by ethnic-minority families, theater companies put on plays in a former cattle slaughterhouse.

When the typhoons hit in the summer, we'd tape huge crosses on our windows to keep them from shattering; when a plane flew overhead, we'd stick fingers in our ears. This was my kingdom. I did not understand any of the evening news on every night at dinner, nor did I venture out much to Hong Kong Island or the New Territories. I stayed mostly in libraries, cramming myself with English literature and Chinese history, so I could score well enough to earn a coveted university place in Hong Kong. I lived inside television shows, books, and, later, the internet.

When I was sixteen, I had a sort-of crush on a boy from a different school, sort-of because it wasn't so much that I wanted to date him as that I wanted to be him. We never met, but he blogged about Jim Jarmusch, Frank Sinatra, and tattoo parlors. He was what I thought then to be the epitome of cool. He later went on to film school in London. I read his blog religiously because I was so bored with my life in Hong Kong. I daydreamed about going to gigs, seeing art house cinema, having intellectually stimulating conversations, and being in the midst of the next great literary movement. I could not find any of this at home. My classmates and I were brought up on the belief that nothing was more important than securing a job that would eventually buy us a flat, a basic human right that had become nearly impossible for my generation, and these jobs were usually soul sucking. Hong Kong's brand of capitalism makes it easy to live in a place and never engage with it.

I thought that when I eventually became an adult I would be one of those people who power-walked in heels across the bridge of the International Finance Centre in the central business district. The building is an altar of marbled floors, luxury shops, and office workers in Brooks Brothers ties—

a sleek, phallic tower that thrusts into the thick mist guarding the night sky. My father told me that it was normal we did not know our neighbors, because no one knows their neighbors. I had bought into all the clichés that the adults told me about my city: that it was an apolitical cultural desert inhabited by go-getters who have no real values except becoming rich. But I did not know yet that this is a place where parallel universes coexist, and you could live your entire life here without ever pulling back the curtains on the other Hong Kongs.

Hong Kong is a subtropical city with over seven million people, an oft-quoted factoid that previously existed in my head in abstraction. I understood what that meant only when I left the city for the first time, on an exchange semester in Glasgow. On the main street of the Glasgow city center on a Saturday, I almost had a panic attack. *Where is everyone? Is this it?* There was less than a tenth of the crowd I would see back home. Hong Kong pulses with a sort of frenzied energy, and speaks the language of alienation and impatience. It's difficult to walk on the street, any street, in Hong Kong Island and Kowloon without accidentally touching someone. My favorite sign in the city is located at the airport, next to the platform for inter-terminal trains: "Relax, train comes every two minutes." In public parks there are boards that list activities you are not allowed to partake in: *No skateboarding; no lying on benches.* We pretend to have four seasons when really we have two: sweaty and less sweaty.

Hong Kong is also a city of many hills: the higher the altitude, the more expensive the apartments—the most literal of class metaphors. The whole of Hong Kong is only a little over a thousand square kilometers in size, but its three regions, Hong Kong Island, Kowloon, and the New Territories, are marked by geographical stereotypes and differences. Hong Kong Island, the area first colonized by the British, is responsible for the common mischaracterization of Hong Kong as an "island." Across the Victoria Harbour are Kowloon and the New Territories, both part of a landmass that connects to China. Then, appearing as either specks on a map or taking up so much space you wonder why you have never heard of these places before, are the outlying islands, over two hundred of them—tourist attractions, abandoned villages, or settlements where life is idyllic and swampy.

Historically, Kowloon has had a flourishing Chinese community. In To Kwa Wan, I don't recall ever running into a single white person. When I moved over to Hong Kong Island for university, I saw English-speaking expats everywhere, mostly from Britain or America or Australia. Ethnic Chinese make up over 90 percent of the population in Hong Kong. There are also significant Filipino, Indonesian, and Indian communities, known as the ethnic minority—families that have been here since the colonial era, or recent immigrants or refugees, or domestic workers. The term that expats and English-language publications sometimes use to refer to Kowloon is "the dark side." This classist and racist description stereotypes the traditionally Chinese and South-Southeast Asian enclave as a gritty underbelly; it has no equivalent in the Chinese language. The inhabitants of Kowloon and Hong Kong Island sometimes imagine the New Territories to be miles of uninterrupted nature, deserted train stations and unpaved tracks, and minimal human activity, but the lives of most New Territories residents revolve around malls and residential blocks.

In university, before I found the universe I eventually wanted to belong to, I lived for a while in the "cosmopolitan city" version of Hong Kong, populated mostly by exchange students, international school graduates, and expats who moved to Asia to teach English or find themselves. I learned to see my hometown through their eyes, to become a tourist in my own city. Their paradise is Lan Kwai Fong, a bar-infested slope of drunk men and Jell-O shots. They spent weekends hiking up the Dragon's Back or cannonballing into water from junk boats, and thought the city was so beautiful. Locals here still nursed colonial hangovers and were nice to them. They loved our dumplings and roast meat and noodles, and the fact that it takes only a short train or ferry ride to get out of the city and be surrounded by trees and reservoirs. Our public railway stops are clean and the trains are mostly on time. The good expats ate chicken feet, tried to learn Cantonese, and followed the news enough to make political jokes. It isn't that the Hong Kong they lived in wasn't real; it's that they inhabited one universe in many that existed here, and they only ever wanted to get to know that one.

Through them, I understood why I had been ambivalent about this place as a child. It takes work not to simply pass through a place but instead to become part of it. I did not try to understand why the people hit the streets every year on July 1, the anniversary of the handover, because I never thought I would stay here. Instead, I ached over descriptions of young writers showing up at one another's indie bookstore readings in New York, guitarists and photographers who shared pints together in Camden in London. I did not know enough about the place I grew up in, did not know these scenes exist here in their own form. That there are people here who can talk about jazz and no-wave cinema but also about the history of blues music in Hong Kong; communities I would want to be part of and give back to.

I moved out of home at the age of eighteen, the first step in a gradual and inevitable process of estrangement from my family. Instead, the city slowly became my family. I found a place of many secrets that reveal themselves to you only when you are ready. I found that there were quiet corners everywhere—urban gardens with ponds, outlying islands like Peng Chau, late-night tram rides from one end of Hong Kong Island to another, small bookstores where the booksellers offer their customers tea and a paperback they know we would enjoy. I also found a universe populated by underground musicians in industrial buildings, anarchists who run a vegetarian restaurant, and zinemakers and poets who write in both Chinese and a bastardized English. We haunted the smoky staircases of warehouses, the public waterfront, restaurants on the top floor of wet markets, drinking till three A.M. after protests and chatting about art, politics, and life.

When the occupation movement took place in 2014, I was away from Hong Kong for a study-abroad semester, and missed the protests entirely. A year later, I began working as a reporter at a local news start-up. I wanted an excuse to let myself finally get to know this place on a more intimate level. I met student leaders who had been guiding crowds through tear gas while I was far away from home. I learned about the many nefarious forces that dictate every seemingly insignificant change to our local neighborhoods, interviewed queer activists and community workers serving elderly populations, and covered the clashes on the streets. I loved looking around me, finally understanding. By the time I left my reporting job to work for nonprofits, I was in a long-term relationship and my mental health was not a total disaster. I was starting to plan a future in Hong Kong.

Then came the protests in 2019.

On June 8, one day before the first major protest against an extradition bill that could send "criminals" in Hong Kong to China, my partner and I were dancing in a warehouse to a Singaporean emo band. The next day, we joined hundreds of thousands on the street, all dressed in white, united against the bill. I thought it would be another one of those protests where we showed up for an afternoon, patted ourselves on the back, and went home to our lives. But for the rest of the year, we marched in the suffocating heat, ran away from street battles in neighborhoods we previously barely visited, and watched kids decking themselves in protest gear of hard hats and cellophane wrap. The fractures left behind by the previous protest movements tore open. On the streets, in the restaurants, and in the privacy of our homes, we cheered and grieved together. The government remained unmoved, the police attacked residents like we were their sworn enemies, and Beijing lost patience.

In the years leading up to 2019, I had been so singularly focused on trying to rebuild my relationship with the city that I had forgotten it never belonged to us in the first place. For a short window in my adulthood, I thought I had found Hong Kong, when really it was already fading away, one authoritarian decree at a time. Hong Kong is a city that is always dying. Mainstream media had pronounced Hong Kong dead as early as 1995, and every few months or years some political commentator who suddenly remembered we existed would pen a new obituary. But we've never been as dead as when the national security law was enacted on the last day of June in 2020, a few months after the pandemic put an end to the protests. The law itself was a weapon for Beijing to silence dissent in Hong Kong, but it also marked the turning point for a total crackdown that soon infiltrated all aspects of life. We had known all along that this would be the Communist Party's script, but the speed with which developments came was so startling that it sometimes felt like payback for our petulance during the protests. Within a year, the government would find ways to rid itself of all opposition lawmakers and district councillors, shut down the city's biggest pro-democracy newspaper, and promote former cops to top political positions.

The day after the national security law was enacted, a gray banner that lay between tram tracks read, "I really fucking love Hong Kong" 我哋真係好撚鍾意香港. The photograph went viral, as a sort of declaration of love toward the place everyone told us was now disappearing. The catchphrase accompanied cute protest artwork, playlists of local music, stories of random acts of kindness by Hong Kongers. But did we *really* fucking love Hong Kong? The timing of the statement felt almost ironic, like we were describing an abusive partner on their deathbed, and you couldn't talk about how much they suck. I knew that my own attachment to this place was rooted in sentimentality, that the community spaces and grassroots organizers I had found in my early adult years were the exception rather than the rule. Even before the national security law and subsequent government crackdown, Hong Kong had been a difficult place to live in, with its high rents, inaccessible mental health care, and intolerance for nonconformist arts. This is all by design: If you could not even survive here, perhaps you would never have time to make this place feel like home. But maybe this is what it means when we say we love this place—we recognize all of its imperfections, and still refuse to walk away.

In Hong Kong we speak often of moments of awakening when one becomes political—from student to organizer, homemaker to activist, cabdriver to protester. Many of these moments involve landmark protests, either witnessing or participating in them: in 2003, 2005, 2010, 2014, 2019. Each of us experienced small moments when we decided we no longer wanted Hong Kong to be only a background for our personal dramas: running to work, ordering takeaway and eating at our desk, going home to our families. But when we read about Hong Kong, it can seem as though the place exists only when our protests make the headlines, that our lives are defined by nothing but our politics. We fall back on sound bites like how we protest because we want to "preserve our way of life." But what does that way of life look like? Why are we still trying to fight for it rather than choosing to flee? Why are we defying the advice of our parents and grandparents who tell us to run because they remember what life was like in China under Communist rule? Why are we not the ambivalent, apolitical generation that our leaders want us to be?

I came of age alongside a city that had just escaped the shadow of colonial rule. We were told we had until 2047 before China would resume total control. I was brought up on the myth that these fifty years would be a liminal space where we could construct our identity, not British anymore and not quite China yet. We had dreams of how we wanted this place to be. During the 2019 protests, an online thread that went viral described what Hong Kong people would want to do if the city truly belonged to us: make desserts using locally farmed produce; become a teacher on East Asian and Hong Kong history; make a film about the local experience. These things may not sound like much, but if you had asked a Hong Konger thirty years ago, during the colonial era, they would have talked about building businesses and buying multiple properties.

My generation had over twenty years to imagine different possibilities in the face of new economic realities, and seek out a local identity. But we wrote about these dreams precisely because of their increasing impossibility: our farmers have been evicted from their homes for large-scale housing projects, our classrooms and cinemas censored. By 2020, our future in Hong Kong had been made so uncertain by the crackdown that those dreams have been cut short, or forced to morph into different forms. It was clear we would not have our fifty years.

This book documents the years between 1997 and 2020, that space when so much felt possible. In each of these chapters, I take a personal narrative as an entry point into a different side of Hong Kong, and detail how we tried to build a sense of belonging amid all the challenges of survival. There are stories about sleeping on couches and living with twenty-two roommates; wrestling with depression at a time of collective political trauma; evading tear gas—and the allies and comrades we found in the process. Each chapter deals with a different but related subculture, historical moment, or facet of life in Hong Kong; the first half of the book leans more toward memoir, and the second half reportage and cultural criticism. While the book is generally chronological, the chapters themselves often end in 2019, when a protest movement imbued these topics with a new urgency; hence time sometimes rewinds or speeds up, and characters reappear or are resurrected across chapters.

I could not write a book purely about protest. I was burnt out from writing the genre of personal-political essays that turned the camera lens toward myself, from incessantly describing moments of crisis through my limited experience of them. By the time the demonstrations against the extradition bill began, I was no longer working as a reporter. I walked an uncomfortable line between protester and writer, and was spared the worst of the violence that my journalist peers had to witness firsthand. I certainly lacked the distance that could allow me to theorize the city I call home. I mention this because it has always mattered to me whether the storyteller or artist is part of or merely passing through a place. Physical, cultural, and interpersonal proximity does not always mean a person is well-placed to write about the spirit of a political moment, either; in fact, sometimes it could mask and deceive.

I don't include stories of underage protesters risking their lives to fight China, or profiles of protest leaders. It is not a narrative of how "their parents came here to escape from the Communist Party, they're protesting because their freedoms are threatened, they're leaving because they lost hope." There is little colonial history; there are enough books about that period. Instead, I write about my favorite places in Hong Kong, what it was like for me to grow up in this city, and the stories of the writers and journalists and artists and musicians and activists in my generation. The way we lived.

This book is about the many ways a city can disappear, but also the many ways we, its people, survive. It is a portrait of life in a particular time and space. A story about how we uncovered a Hong Kong that had existed here all along—a place where we, against all odds, made a home.

I did not want to write a book about Hong Kong. But I had thought we would have thirty more years to build a body of stories, to archive our way of life so that it would be remembered after 2047. Then the walls began closing in, and we were running out of time. I didn't want to write about this place after everything had already disappeared, when I would have only me and my unreliable memory to reconstruct how I remembered this place. And so I wrote you this. Documenting disappearances is a defeatist line of work: I can never write fast enough to keep up with the changes of my hometown. Nothing survives in this city. But in a place that had never allowed you to write your own history, even remembrance can be a radical act.

# Contents

# Author's Note

This book is a work of nonfiction. Personal accounts have been reconstructed through research, photographs, texts, and diary entries, but memories are inevitably distorted by the myths we tell ourselves. Names have been changed for privacy and safety, except in instances where the full names of interviewees appear.

Because I wanted to accurately depict Hong Kong as it is experienced by its people, units of measurement as well as vocabulary and word choice have not been converted or adapted in the book, nor do conversions appear in the body of the text. For reference, 1 kilometer is equivalent to around 0.62 miles, and 1 U.S. dollar is 7.8 Hong Kong dollars. British terms have been kept; any remaining bastardization of Englishes is the author's fault.

# The Impossible City

# A Map of Hong Kong, 2021

## WESTERN DISTRICT

If all of Hong Kong were razed to the ground and I could save but one place, it would be Western District. Sai Wan, or 西環, as it is also known, is on the western shore of Hong Kong Island, between the dried seafood stores of Sheung Wan and the hilly terrains of Mount Davis, and down the slope from the University of Hong Kong where I studied law and literature. I moved here when I was eighteen for university. I often tell people that I grew up in Sai Wan, because it was the first place in Hong Kong whose stories I wanted to learn, and where I found the freedom to make my own stories. Away from the shadow of my family, I finally felt like I had control over the trajectory of my life.

In Western District, I found a home in my roommates who shared bunk beds with me in tiny flats, the lady at the laundromat who reminisced about Beatlemania in Hong Kong, the diner that always left me an extra bowl of soup, the fellow residents who cracked open beers and booed the Chinese national anthem during a Hong Kong versus China football match. During typhoon season, I headed down to the strip of salt-drenched promenade called the Praya to watch the sea crash into the shore. On weekday mornings at the cargo dock, ships unloaded their freight, and trucks drove in to tow the goods away, but in late afternoon the technically off-limits pier transformed into a utopian space where all the suffocating rules governing public gatherings in Hong Kong no longer applied.

Every evening for a year, my flatmate Kit and I would take our puppy to the pier and let her off the leash as residents rode their bikes, smoked next to ship containers graffitied with obscenities, and cast their fishing lines into the water. Dog owners were regulars at this pier; so were housewives and university students and retired blue-collar workers and even a police officer. We exchanged news about our favorite restaurants in the area and held secret barbeques on winter nights with the seafarers stationed at the pier. It was one of the few waterfronts in the city not bounded by railings, no security guards to pull back anyone who just wanted to see the sea.

西環 is one of the oldest districts in Hong Kong, made up of three smaller areas—Sai Ying Pun, Shek Tong Tsui, and Kennedy Town. Sai Ying Pun literally means "western encampment" because British troops were stationed here in the early colonial days. Kennedy Town was named after the governor Sir Arthur E. Kennedy, and Shek Tong Tsui was once renowned for its brothels. If you're walking home late at night down Hill Road, you might see an apparition of Anita Mui in a cheongsam, still waiting for Leslie Cheung to meet her in the afterlife. Hong Kongers will tell you that it's boring to love Western District. There is little unexplored terrain left in the area, few new places to discover. But my own memories are folded within the space. Here—outside the China Liaison Office, a barricaded building with a wavering five-star flag, housing the top Chinese officials that are in charge of this place—is where I was pepper-sprayed at a protest for the first time. And most who live here have never been inside No. 1 High Street, the outpatient psychiatric clinic that has been doling out antidepressants and sleeping pills to me for the past half-decade.

Western District was the first place that felt real to me, and not like some strange simulation populated with faceless, only vaguely there human beings. My flatmate tutored the son of our convenience-store lady, who was always trying to remind me, when I pointed to a pack of Lucky Strikes at three in the morning, that I had said I was quitting smoking. The dog owners remembered my puppy's quirks and brought her favorite treats. When my building overcharged its residents for maintenance, some of them banded together to kick out the apparently corrupt building management committee, which was tight-knit with the pro-Beijing district councillor. "The roots of a civil society have to start here. If you go into ideologies, residents may not easily understand that. It could be too detached from the realities of their lives," the organizer told me. Community activists set up book exchange booths and fought to keep ancient trees from being cut down by the government. The administrator and founder of a Facebook group for Western District residents would later be the photographer at my wedding. The residents of this neighborhood gave me a community, and in return, I promised to write its stories.

In 2015, I began anxiously documenting the changes in

Western District. The train line was extended to the district in late 2014, and the accessibility suddenly made the neighborhood prime real estate. The auto-repair shops streaked with grease, grocers with bags of chips dangling from a rod, and stores selling red-capped jars of fermented sauces have been replaced by cafés with white minimalist décor. Bars and bougie restaurants moved in along with the expats, multiplying the late-night noise complaints in the district and hastening the gentrification. Families who had lived in the area for decades suddenly found their weekend dinner spot taken over by coffee shops selling matcha egg tarts, the patrons of which were mostly Instagram influencers and white couples walking Shibas. In a couple of years, it would look nothing like the place I once called home.

Three months after the national security law in Hong Kong came into effect, my partner and I went to the pier on a blazing Saturday afternoon to take wedding photographs. I wore a cheap white dress and combat boots. My partner wore a navy suit that came from a pro-protest tailor. My hair became tangled in the wind. We struck ridiculous poses before mustard-colored shipping containers. This was where we'd had our first kiss four years ago. In the photographs, the skyline floats above the water against a background of gradient blue, hazy like a mirage.

Whenever I'm in my neighborhood, I don't see a city always on the cusp of death, only a place where, for the first time, I felt like I belonged. I loved 西環 before I learned to love Hong Kong, before I learned that you could love a place so desperately you would do anything to save it, even when you no longer recognize it.

## The Tourist Map

You're living somewhere in Southeast Asia. You aren't sure how you ended up here. The recession hit just when you graduated, rendering your university degree in marketing obsolete: There are no jobs. You hear there are programs that can take you to Asia; you can teach English there, no qualifications necessary. Everything is a tenth of the price back home. You find cheap tickets to Hong Kong over the summer. *It's so cyberpunk, you'd love it,* your mate, a fellow teacher, says.

On the first day here, you have a yum cha lunch at the Lin Heung Kui teahouse in Sheung Wan, which your local guide assures you is the *authentic experience.* Aunties push trolleys stacked with little bamboo steamers of white buns, blood-orange char siu spilling between their lips. On the top deck of the tram that slides itself from east to west then back again on Hong Kong Island, the humid wind runs its fingers through your hair. The tram takes you past light boxes with bulbs in the shape of a foot with a smiley face, narrow doorways that reveal steep stairs, boutiques fronted by mannequins with cursed expressions, property agencies and loan offices, and buildings that have been boarded up and stamped with the name of a developer. This neighborhood has become more expensive since the train station opened, the guide explains. This construction is for an upscale housing project that will attract few buyers and remain vacant for another decade or so. In Central, up two grueling slopes, you're surrounded by drunken men in Hawaiian shirts downing shots and shouting in English. *But I don't want to go where the tourists are,* you tell the guide. *Actually, they're not tourists—they live here,* he says.

You hike up to Victoria Peak, stopping to snap selfies before a panoramic view of the undulating skyline obscured by swaths of smog. After an hour on a hiking trail, you end up at a slick futuristic mall shaped like a shallow bowl at the top of a hill, with a *Forrest Gump*–themed restaurant and a gelato store that sells ice cream for dogs. You notice how much you're sweating, so you route the rest of your trip around your proximity to convenience store air-conditioning. You take the star ferry across the Kowloon, ogling the skyscrapers, the reflection of the fuchsia and navy lights scribbled across the water. The ferry rumbles to a stop at the dock. *Wait, it's already over?* The ride lasted only five minutes. *It's the reclamation,* the guide says apologetically. *Hong Kong has a land problem.*

At Yau Ma Tei, steaming clay pots of rice drench the air with the scent of salted fish. You snap photos of neon lights, butchers slaughtering animals in plain sight deep within wet markets, goldfish surfing in plastic bags, karaoke performers loitering at street corners. The Chinese pavilion entrance of Temple Street, with its emerald tiles and red pillars. *Snap.* The breathless rows of low-rises with paint peeling off the walls. *Click.* Fruit markets, bamboo scaffolding, graffiti. *Flash.* At Chungking Mansions, you're inundated by the steaming trays of colorful curries, foreign currency exchange shops, and budget motels. Wong Kar Wai's *Chungking Express,* the 1994 film of canned pineapples, painful longing, and drug dealers, is your favorite film—it's why you want to visit Hong Kong, really. As you navigate the labyrinth, you hum "California Dreamin' " under your breath.

Tomorrow you can go to a cha chaan teng, the guide tells you. *A local café. French toast with syrup, milk tea, satay beef noodles.* You misunderstand what he means by *café.* The next morning, you walk into a diner with a green tiled floor and trays of glistening yellow pastries. You share a table with middle-aged men in thin white shirts and construction workers, and after you finish your breakfast of thin pink slices of ham atop vermicelli soup, you fish out a copy of *Fragrant Harbour* and start reading. But that doesn't last very long. The restaurant is too loud and bustling to read even with head-phones on, and soon you feel eyes boring into you. Your empty plates have been whisked away and the auntie pushes the white slip of paper with your bill scrawled in blue ball-point pen toward you for the third time. You sigh and get up to pay at the door.

You visit a few more spots on your Hong Kong must-see list in the *Lonely Planet* guide—Duddell's, Stanley, a fish market—but none of them feel like the *real* Hong Kong. By the end of the week, you've run out of steam. Where are the roadside restaurants doling out fresh plates of stir-fried clams, the hand-painted signs hanging over storefronts? You feel nostalgic for something you can't quite name. Hong Kong feels like a city that's past its prime.

## The Coffee Shops

Hong Kong is a city without coffee shops, the son of a Tai-wanese culture critic once declared. What he meant wasn't that there were literally no cafés in Hong Kong, but that the city lacked spaces where one could chat and read for an af-ternoon. "I think Hong Kong people lack culture; by cul-ture I don't mean theatre or dance or music or art exhibitions, but a kind of lifestyle. . . . Hong Kong people are always hurrying somewhere. If they meet at a restaurant, coffee shop, or bar, it's so that they can check off that item on their calendar, to show that they've completed the task. Even when they're in the middle of one meeting, they're already thinking about the route to get to the next."

I was seventeen when I read this passage for the first time, in a book that had collected these letters between the critic and the son. It was a chapter that stuck with me, because in my formative years, I felt a deep yearning for these coffee shops I had never been in, only read about in books—cafés in Paris frequented by writers, or a fictional coffeehouse in Greenwich Village where a group of six friends would discuss their latest relationship problems. Hong Kong did have literal coffee shops, of course: In my adolescence, my friends and I sometimes studied at Starbucks or Pacific Coffee if the local library was full. On holidays, we sat for long afternoons at board-game cafés in Mong Kok, where we drank stale bubble tea and I developed a lifelong aversion to the card game Uno. I wasted away the hours of my youth at these cafés, but these weren't what the critic's son meant.

The "coffee shop culture" he spoke of is similar to the concept of the third place, spaces outside of work and home that are conducive to conversation, accessible, and warm. Hong Kong needs such spaces more than any other city: We lack both public and private space. The city is known for rents higher than New York, London, or San Francisco for apartments half the size. Hong Kongers on average enjoy less than three square meters of open space per person, well under that of Tokyo, Singapore, or Seoul residents, and over-tourism floods the streets and leaves us claustrophobic. We retreat to the malls, the central structure of every neighborhood around which urban life is organized. It's where we find restaurants, cinemas, supermarkets and department stores, drugstores, ice-skating rinks, and, most significantly, free air-conditioning in a city with unbearably hot summers—but even there, security guards are employed to put you in your place if you dare sit on the floor or at the cement border surrounding fake shrubbery. The existence of third places didn't seem possible here in this city designed to be an amusement park for real estate overlords.

But in my early twenties, I found them. They aren't coffee shops, although sometimes they serve rank coffee like it's an inside joke. One of the first I frequented was Hong Kong Reader, a "social activism bookstore" selling mostly philosophy, local political theory, and translated leftist literature, located on the seventh floor of a nondescript building in the busiest shopping district of Mong Kok. Its cofounder Daniel Lee and his two partners had considered opening a coffee shop, but ultimately decided on a bookstore when they realized that few Hong Kongers saw coffee shops as cultural spaces. (The co-founders once witnessed students at a café storming off after the owner said they didn't have Monopoly.) Hong Kong Reader is modestly sized, with only three small desks and a stained orange couch, but since it opened in the 2000s, hundreds of events have taken place in the venue: discussions on feminism in China, Hong Kong localism, Brexit. These "upstairs bookstores" are a mainstay of Hong Kong's cultural scene, selling niche titles in cheap tong lau units since the 1950s; they're also rare community spaces where lingering and idling is encouraged.

Across the harbor in Wan Chai, a few blocks away from the red-light district, is Foo Tak Building, a "vertical arts village" that houses an independent community radio station, a literary magazine, a grassroots media outlet, an experimental art space, and other creative initiatives. The elevator is erratic and impatient, closing mere moments after it opens, and its interior is violently decorated with stickers of a protest pig meme made popular on a local forum, and slogans like "Return the land to the people" and 齊上齊落. The top floor of the slim building houses Art and Culture Outreach, a bookstore that stocks zines, albums, and books by Hong Kong creators. The units have hosted joint events and shown films that could not be screened in the cinema as the political climate deteriorated, such as *Liu Xiaobo: The Man Who Defied Beijing*. The owner and managers of the building lease out the units to artists and creators for nominal rent, a valiant effort to circumvent the greatest obstacles to the development of arts and alternative culture in Hong Kong: money and space.

But two neighborhoods down from the bookstore, in a little alley not far from the business district in Central, it's past last call for drinks at Club 71. Audaciously named after the half-million-strong protest march on July 1, 2003, the bar welcomed scores of activists, journalists, and artists but eventually succumbed to unaffordable rents during the coronavirus pandemic. It was my favorite watering hole. "Financially, I really couldn't hang on," owner Grace Ma said in an interview. "It's time to move on, I want to do something else." In its last month of operation, the bar was so packed that patrons had to stand in the park outside, sloshing down the foaming beers. On one of those nights, I took a seat amid the loud crowds. I had spent so much of my twenties at the happy hours here, trying to get the attention of Ah So the cat, strumming the guitar on the wall that's always out of tune, and watching Grace tell me under the drunken yellow lights that she knows my face, but she's forgotten my name again. I didn't slide up to talk to the staff behind the bar, and my partner and I slipped away after two beers. I'm always bad at goodbyes.

## "The New Brooklyn"

At the table outside Bound, a tattoo artist smokes a cigarette as he chats with one of the owners of the coffee shop and bar at Prince Edward. The artist rocks a full sleeve and a mess of curls underneath a panama hat. He gave me my first ink when I was eighteen and unaware of his indie music fame. In the years since, I've run into him at live houses and seen him perform onstage at the music festival Clockenflap. His two kids are here, too, engrossed in some inexplicable game, and call out "Dad!" every now and then to summon him.

Bound lies on a street of old apartment buildings, diners, laundromats, and a co-living space that markets itself as a "quiet cross-section of East meets West and old meets new" in the "urban jungle," where a single bed costs upward of HK$8,550. The interior deco at Bound is a millennial photographer's wet dream: a neon sign bearing the traditional Chinese characters for "New Romance" fixed on the wall above the bar, a worn Mac DeMarco tour poster carelessly plastered on the back door, turquoise lighting that casts a *Moonlight*-esque hue on its patrons. Even its bathroom looks like part of a film set, with its rose-colored tiles and mirrors suited to an eighties hair salon.

At Bound, the playlist swerves from local shoegaze band White Wave to Kendrick Lamar and Radiohead. It's a mecca for local musicians, artists, and photographers; the venue has held after-gig parties for overseas indie outfits such as Bo Ningen. Fotan Laiki, a Hong Kong trap artist with an underground following, worked behind the bar for a bit. Bound's barista Jessica, who later starred in a film as herself (a deadpan unsuccessful district council candidate who couldn't care less she lost), pours craft beer out of a nozzle and glares at the Instagrammers.

For two years, my writer friends and I hung out at the back of the dimly lit café every other weekend, discussing pitches over Americanos while nursing hangovers. We were all in our twenties or early thirties, young and immersed in different facets of subculture. We wrote about electronic music and dance parties, photographers who resisted the aesthetics of dense building façades that stack against each other, publishers operating outside of the Chinese-controlled book industry, queer filmmakers and artists. My friends and I were idealistic, enamored with the idea that we could take it upon ourselves to document Hong Kong's cool. Our fuel was Bound's coffee and, when the sun sank, cocktails and beers. It's still a favorite spot of local creatives, although it has since been renovated, and these days my visits have been sporadic. The space reminds me of a time when I was hopeful, and the fact that I've never felt quite that hopeful again ever since. Shortly before the protests of 2019, the group broke up.

To the northwest is Sham Shui Po, an old working-class neighborhood known for its flea market and computer center. Nestled within Sham Shui Po's tong lau tenement buildings are subdivided units, small apartments made even smaller so the space can be shared by multiple families. For a long time it was known in the popular imagination as a "gritty" city space, packed to the brim with cheap eats and fabric stores. In 2016, a multinational street brand paired up with a nonprofit arts organization to bring street artists to Sham Shui Po, splattering paint onto walls and shop shutters. At the time, a cultural critic started arguing publicly on social media with the event organizers: He worried that the art would gentrify the area, thus pushing up rents in one of the poorest neighborhoods in Hong Kong.

By 2020, Sham Shui Po had gained a reputation for being a new "cultural center," and *Time Out* dubbed it one of "the world's ten coolest neighborhoods." Taglines such as "Sham Shui Po Is the New Brooklyn" caught on and were printed onto pens, and critics and artists began examining the phenomenon in earnest. A rough tally showed that around a dozen cafés opened in just a year in Sham Shui Po, concentrated around Tai Nam Street. A cup of coffee on Tai Nam Street goes for more than what a filling plate of chive dumplings costs at Yuen Fong Dumplings a few streets away.

My favorite record shop in the city, White Noise Records, moved from the second floor of an unassuming building in Prince Edward, where they rarely got any foot traffic, to a ground-level store in Sham Shui Po. In summer 2020, my friend Lok and I spend the late afternoon browsing records at White Noise. *I feel like I'm gentrifying Sham Shui Po by just existing,* I say as we enter, nodding a brief hello at the owner, Gary, whose face is obscured by a mask and the usual cap pulled over his head. The store has been busier, Gary says, but flocks of giggling young "hipsters" taking pictures of the store cat and checking in on Instagram haven't exactly upped sales.

But the most violent gentrifier is our government. In the name of progress, down goes the Edinburgh Place Ferry Pier. The Wedding Card Street in Wan Chai is turned into a "high street" of "sidewalk cafés and gourmet restaurants." Kwun Tong, the industrial building epicenter in East Kowloon that used to house illegal dance studios, live houses, and band practice spaces, is now predominantly offices, and artists have moved farther out to disused factories in other parts of Kowloon. In the mad pursuit for revitalization, even neon signs, our most iconic aesthetic, haven't made the cut and are taken down. Decades-old cha chaan teng give way to chains that are cheap manufactured imitations of nostalgia for tourists, who cling on to this fantasy of old Hong Kong even as everything else fades away for the people inhabiting this city. Individuality and character on the streets are erased so as to conform to a specific idea of beauty. An aesthetic that has no room for those who have no spending power to indulge in the new shops that charge sixty dollars for a ginger tea. But you can't fight back. Remember, you don't get to elect your own government.

## The Other Front Line

I am and have always been a city girl in all the worst ways: squeamish about insects, grumpy about inconvenience, good with being alone amid crowds of people. It is easy to be a city girl from Hong Kong, because that is presumed: When books and movies depict Hong Kong, they tend to feature only the cityscape of Kowloon and Hong Kong Island. The third main region is the New Territories, which stretch over 80 percent of Hong Kong. In university, I asked my friend Jack if I could visit him in Tuen Mun, a new town in the west of the New Territories. *I've never been,* I told him, excited at the prospect of visiting a new neighborhood. He looked baffled, then annoyed. *You know we don't ride cattle to get around, right?* he said. *It's just a residential area, there's nothing there, really.* We met at a mall, a whirlwind of shoppers carrying suitcases. He took me to a park where elderly women sang cheesy Chinese tunes and old men sat around a gray stone table playing chess. We lay underneath a tree, reading books. That evening, on the way to dinner, we passed by a movie theater named the Paris London New York Milano Cinema.

"The New Territories—it's the forgotten narrative of Hong Kong, because it doesn't have the architecture or cityscape with traces of colonial characteristics," said my friend SP, who is from Sheung Shui. "You won't really think it's that special. But we're here."

The popular imagination of the New Territories is dominated by its villages: in rural areas surrounded by wetlands or hills, on small islands that require short ferry rides, or even at the end of off-beaten tracks not far from urban areas. In total, there are more than six hundred rural villages in Hong Kong. In contrast to the high-rises that are synonymous with the city, village houses are usually three stories, surrounded by quiet paths and plenty of open space.

Between 2009 and 2011, a village in Yuen Long in the New Territories called Choi Yuen Tsuen became the subject of a series of protests when villagers refused to move away on the orders of the government. The village was to be demolished for a new high-speed train to China, and the rights of the villagers were not protected, as they were considered non-indigenous—a legal designation that reflected not ethnic or cultural differences but the vested interests of powerful rural families in Hong Kong. Artists, activists, and villagers held festivals with music performances and film screenings amid semi-derelict houses and fields. Some of them later clashed with land officers and the police, but Choi Yuen village was nonetheless eventually demolished in the name of "development," and the villagers relocated.

But the major orbits of activity in the New Territories are not villages, but semi-urban "new towns." In the second half of the twentieth century, the Hong Kong government built large-scale housing projects known as new towns in the New Territories. While the New Territories encompass village houses, farmland, country parks, bicycle trails, and light rail, the region is also home to mega malls for the middle class, with major chain boutiques and cosmetic shops popular with tourists from China, who can take a train into Hong Kong and get off at one of the new towns.

A short while after the village protests, clashes of a very different nature would take place in the New Territories. Demonstrations in Hong Kong over the past decade have been concentrated around the government offices areas— a stretch on Hong Kong Island that was a designated march route. But even before 2019, when protests erupted in neighborhoods all across Hong Kong, the New Territories were no stranger to rallies. In the early 2010s, Hong Kongers in the New Territories protested traders from mainland China who took day trips to the city and hauled back suitcases full of milk formula. After the milk formula scandal in China, when babies became affected by Chinese-made powdered milk tainted with the chemical melamine, demand for safe formula in Hong Kong spiked. The New Territories are geographically the closest to mainland China, connected through a railway to the two border checkpoints in Shenzhen, and the malls in new towns became choked with small-time traders and tourists from mainland China. Shops that catered to Hong Kong residents made way for pharmacies stocked with milk formula. The streets of Sheung Shui, the northern town only one train station away from the border, are especially affected: They are now populated by pharmacies, and their traditional marketplaces have disappeared.

Residents head downstairs to buy a pen from their local stationery shop only to find that the shop has closed down.

Taking place alongside the political struggle in the city over the past decade is a slower, more subtle economic and cultural transformation. These days, our landlords would not bat an eyelash when renting out shops to profitable pharmacies or cafés, or tearing down one building to make way for another mainland Chinese capital–backed enterprise. Our pop stars and filmmakers have ditched the Hong Kong market in favor of the lucrative billion-strong audience in China, making art for them rather than us; our politicians with vested business interests bow at the feet of new money from the motherland, and continually vote for policies that work against their own people. Hong Kong's capitalism perpetuates an endless reproduction of wannabe oppressors, and with the help of government policies and Chinese money, we—consumers and residents and small-business owners and future landlords—devour ourselves until there is nothing left.

Even though the New Territories is a "forgotten narrative," protests at these new towns inspired a slogan that would later be heard at every demonstration. The slogan is derived from protests in the New Territories that took place in response to mainland traders, and were then known as the "reclaim" movement. International leftists often attribute the rise of localism to a surge in right-wing ideology propelled by pure xenophobia. But in the beginning, these residents weren't angry at mainland Chinese people or about the then-still-abstract notion that China could take away Hong Kong's freedoms whenever they wanted to. They were angry that the combination of overtourism, lack of policies to protect small businesses, and a government that was not elected by the people had made their neighborhood disappear. By the time of the 2019 protests, the slogan had permeated the public consciousness and taken on new life, scrawled onto the back of bus seats and onto discreet park benches. And then, after the national security law was enacted, the government called the eight words secessionist, and declared it banned altogether.

## A Map, Erased

I didn't want to include a map in this book, to hold your hand through the harbor and stilt houses, the alleys and hilltops. I won't be able to reclaim our history, but maybe I could reconstruct our geography. Maybe I can map out the city on my own terms, and write about my districts, my streets, my buildings. But every time I turn around to look back, a street corner has changed and something has vanished: a tree sliced down, a shop shuttered, a protest slogan on the side of the road crudely covered. Hong Kong is a place always on the verge of mutilation.

In spring 2016, community activists screened the film *Ten Years* in dozens of locations across the city simultaneously, after mainland China censored mentions of the movie in the media because of its rebellious undertones. My partner laid a piece of newspaper down on the pavement of Hill Road, and we made ourselves comfortable amid a slope packed with my fellow neighbors in Western District. The dystopian film, which is made up of five shorts and had a limited run in local cinemas, imagined what Hong Kong's political situation would be like in a decade. The screen was far away and the sound was choppy, but I still cried. In the second short, a couple desperately archives what remains of a post-

apocalyptic Hong Kong, labeling jars and preserving speci-
mens until they eventually turn themselves into relics, too.

A few years later, months after my engagement photographs, the government closed my pier off to the public,
depriving residents and dogs of a beloved public space. My
university removed the boards where students had once been
able to voice their opinions on political issues. The pro-
democracy district councillors resigned after the government
threatened to disqualify them. At least half of the shops I
used to frequent were now gone. Western District became
instead another piece of Hong Kong I was forced to mourn.

It didn't take ten years for the political situation in Hong
Kong to become similar to the way it is depicted in the film.
By 2021, we had national security police in Hong Kong.
Our legislature is now almost entirely dominated by pro-
China "patriots." The justice department appeals until the
courts mete out the harsh punishments the government
wants for anyone who dares to speak up or take part in protests. Journalists have been arrested, teachers barred from
their profession for having views that deviated from the government's official narrative. Political activists are jailed or in
exile, and friends are making plans to leave. It is not Hong
Kong that has died, but the imagination of the place we were
promised in 1997.

There are many ways of talking about loss in this city.
Decades ago, around the time of the handover, scholar Ackbar Abbas wrote a seminal text about Hong Kong as a space
defined by disappearance. These days, when we talk about
disappearance, we are often referring to the protest-free
streets, the disbanded political parties or activists who have
vanished, words that have become forbidden. But the map of
Hong Kong was transforming long before the major protests

of 2014 and 2019. Western District, Sham Shui Po, and Sheung Shui may have succumbed to different gentrifying forces, but their stories are one and the same. Our community spaces never stood a chance in a place with no rent control or democratic recourse, where everything always goes to the highest bidder. For the past few years, we've been bracing ourselves for not only the devastating consequences of political oppression, which determines who gets arrested and what bills are passed, but also the redrawing of maps and stifling of communities.

Look closer at this street corner: The sun is setting. The newspaper stand packs up the dailies and puts away the cartons of eggs. Students with laptops in their arms shuffle out of the cha chaan teng. Elderly couples and their poodles take a stroll by the pier. You can still hear the uproar of the crowds that once gathered on the steep slopes for film screenings, festivals, protests. The florists at the wet market put away the last lilies. The last tram slots itself into the station. And then the scene dissolves again. Maybe you can't save this place; maybe it isn't even worth saving. But for a moment, there was a sliver of what this city could have become. And that is why we're still here.

# PART I

# 1997

Summers in Hong Kong always heave with rain, but on this first of July, the downpour feels deliberate, overdone. The water is charging down the steps, drenching our concrete pavements, dripping from the banyan trees. The observatory hoists the black rainstorm signal, to warn us of tumbling landslides. It is too neat a metaphor, but still we're pointing to the sky, mumbling to ourselves: It's crying.

I am four years old. After my parents' separation, my mother and little brother move to Singapore. They live in a property overlooking the East Coast beach, where I would later spend my summers rollerblading and sitting on the back of my mother's bike. They won't return, and neither will my father and I move there as he had promised. I'd grow up as if I were a single child. But I don't know that, not yet. My grandmother is seventy, and her post-retirement project is me. When I'm running a fever late in the middle of the night, she places a damp cloth over my head, takes me to the doctor first thing in the morning, *so you don't get brain damage,* she says. When I fall over, she buries a silver ring inside the yolk of a boiled egg, wraps a cloth around it, then rubs it over my bruises to help blood circulation.

Our days are quiet, uneventful. I attend a kindergarten near my family's tong lau home in To Kwa Wan, humming along to "Descendants of the Dragon" with the rest of my class, its Chinese nationalist sentiments lost on me: *In the Ancient East there is a dragon, / her name is China / In the Ancient East there is a people, / they are all the heirs of the dragon.* While I'm at school, my grandmother goes to the wet market at a municipal building with a red apple painted on its façade. The market stinks of chicken feathers and animal carcasses. She puts on the Cantonese opera song 《鳳閣恩仇未了情》 and makes soy sauce chicken wings, steamed pork cakes, clear broths that have been boiling away all day: dinner for me and her four aging children. Then we make the trip back to Villa Athena in Ma On Shan, a ten-tower upscale housing estate on a road lined with trees and overlooking the Tolo Harbour, where we live with my father.

My father drives us home in his silver BMW, a new car that mirrors the swagger of the young businessman he is then, the child of Chinese immigrants who came to Hong Kong with nothing. Above us, a slice of moon is impaled upon the dark trees, away from the city lights and skyscrapers. I fall asleep on the leathery seats I would later associate with the scent of money, or I sing along to the Teresa Teng songs my father plays on the stereo system. Teresa Teng is the Taiwanese goddess of song. "If I hadn't met you, where would I be now?" she sings over the speakers in 《我只在乎你》.

My father can't speak Mandarin properly even after decades of working in China, even after marrying a Chinese woman, but he knows the words to all of Teresa's songs. Her voice coos from our cassette players, on the radio in a cab, at the local grocer's in Hong Kong. Beijing called her songs "spiritual pollution" and banned her music in the 1980s, but despite this, people throughout Hong Kong, China, and Taiwan are smitten by her, united not in politics but at least by a love for Teresa Teng.

We crawl through the Tate's Cairn Tunnel's beige interior as the line of lights above us makes ghostly imprints on the windshield. For the few minutes it takes to cross, my heart races. I'm always scared that we'll be trapped there forever, that we won't emerge, or that the world will look different when we're finally at the other end.

Across Hong Kong, an anxious mood has punctured the smog. Near my grandmother's flat is the old Kai Tak Airport, which would be decommissioned in a year's time. We can see airplanes from my grandmother's window, taking Hong Kongers far away from here, to Canada, to the United States, to Australia. Every takeoff sends tremors that make the windows shiver, long piercing whistles like a kettle going off. They're leaving for a new life somewhere before the handover, before Communist China takes hold of the city. I'm oblivious to it all. My grandmother takes me to the waterfront park, where I play with grasshoppers and on slides. We have banana splits at the clubhouse at our apartment block, which is guarded by a statue of the goddess Athena herself. Gran buckles me onto the stallion on the merry-go-round inside the Ma On Shan mall, and her gaze follows me as I go up and down and around, become one with the constellation of bright lights.

It's June 29, 1997. On TVB, the anchor Keith Yuen announces solemnly: Thirty more hours till Hong Kong is handed back to China. The handover ceremony is taking place at midnight on July 1; Prince Charles and Tony Blair would be in attendance, as would Jiang Zemin and Li Peng. At Tiananmen Square, where less than a decade ago students were killed asking for democracy, Beijingers are waving little handheld flags with the Hong Kong bauhinia flower stamped onto it, celebrating our return. It's raining near the Hong Kong–China border in Sheung Shui, where my friend SP is holding a Chinese five-star flag to welcome the motherland. When she tells me this two decades later, I'm astonished. How do you love a mother you have never known?

My family is watching the evening news broadcast over steamed fish. The Chinese army is getting ready to crawl into the city. A police spokesperson says they will try their best to accommodate peaceful protests, but that Hong Kong will not tolerate "illegal" ones. Chris Patten, the last governor of Hong Kong, is at an English Gothic cathedral in the affluent, Westernized area of Mid-Levels for a final mass. Pro-democracy protesters have pitched their tents near the Wan Chai Pier under the watchful gaze of the police. They camp out there until the handover ceremony at the convention center just a kilometer away. Journalists take their place, mounting their cameras, notebooks ready. Veteran reporter Yuen Chan is at the ceremony, reporting for ATV, a major television station in Hong Kong, and later she writes: "The whole thing seemed strangely devoid of passion. The players just went through the motions. Some soldiers marched, some bands played. . . . Everyone clapped. The territory of Hong Kong and 6.5 million people were handed over from one sovereign power to another. It left me cold."

It is midnight, and the hostile sky is collapsing under the storm. The Chinese state media calls it the "washing away of the century-long humiliation due to colonialism." Prince

Charles says, "We shall not forget you, and we shall watch with the closest interest as you embark on this new era of your remarkable history." At the ceremony in the Wan Chai Convention Centre, the British flags are lowered. Chris Patten boards a yacht and sails out of the harbor. We are on our own now. No longer controlled by our colonial masters, and not yet subsumed by our postcolonial lords.

The queen's portrait is taken down. "God Save the Queen" is swapped for "March of the Volunteers." A few government institutions are renamed, and all mentions of "royal" and "crown" are scrubbed. But for months, even years, the only visible changes are ceremonial. It is the beginning of what the British and the Chinese promised us: one country, two systems. English remains an official language, and we can keep speaking our southern Chinese dialect of Cantonese for now. A separate territory under one sovereignty, with the right to preserve our independent judiciary and capitalist systems. In twenty years, the Chinese will tell us that this is not a right, but a privilege that could be taken away if we misbehave. The chief executive is the leader of the city now rather than the British governor, but ordinary residents still do not have the right to vote them into office democratically, although our constitution assures us that we could in the future. For now, they promise that it will be "Hong Kong people administering Hong Kong"—that our way of life will be unchanged for fifty years.

Post-handover, my life is exactly the same. In the mornings I eat salted pork and century egg congee and fried dough sticks from the shop run by the family of a kindergarten classmate. After class I watch Japanese anime cartoons on the 4:00 P.M. children's show on TVB, licking artificial orange powder off my fingers from the two-dollar packets of cheesy ring snacks. My aunt and I play slot machines with fake coins at the local game arcade, and trade the tickets for plush toys that are knockoff Disney cartoon characters. I stare out the window at Ma On Shan into a body of water connected to the South China Sea. I speak on the phone with a faraway mother who is desperate for my love, who wants to get to know me. My father makes plans to move to Farm Road near To Kwa Wan so we can be closer to the family home. Every Saturday we eat at a fish ball noodle place that also serves Cantonese casseroles and stir-fries, a typical Hong Kong restaurant that makes you wash your own cutlery. On name days we buy cakes from the local bakery, cakes with too much cream and topped with an array of bright preserved melons, "Happy Birthday" shakily written in chocolate sauce.

Across the city, artists try to mark the historical event in their own ways. Fruit Chan releases *Made in Hong Kong,* a grim realist film about wayward teenagers forgotten in the story of the city. Hong Kong was meant to be about the "Lion Rock spirit": *We use our hard work to write Hong Kong's own legend / That will go down in history forever,* goes the theme song for the eponymous popular television series about the grit of ordinary Hong Kongers. They had come from nothing, but they will persevere and succeed. All they have to do is push on. But in Chan's film, the characters are working-class, from broken families, and with no economic future. A sense of homelessness perpetuates throughout—an allegory for Hong Kong's political abandonment, as scholar Esther Cheung notes. She writes: "The disbanded soldiers, illegal immigrants, and prostitutes from the mainland depicted in Chan's later films played no part in the grand narrative of

Hong Kong as an economic miracle." *I do whatever I want; it's so freeing,* the protagonist Autumn Moon says. But the true price of freedom, we learn, is death. The film opens with one suicide and ends with another; most scenes are in grave-yards, public housing estates with faint lighting, ghostly hospital corridors. Hong Kong has always been obsessed with the notion of its own death. *Fifty years left,* we say in 1997.

At the Hong Kong Arts Centre, curator Oscar Ho has put together a show called *Museum 97: History, Community, Individual.* This is where the myth of Lo Ting, a half-fish half-man figure, is first introduced. According to the exhibition, Hong Kongers are descendants of ancient merpeople that dwell near Lantau Island. The writers Leung Man Tao and Dung Kai Cheung drew from the histories of the Tanka boat people in Hong Kong and that of mainland China to construct a fresh narrative. "Serving two masters from two opposing sides, and making a living from the precarious existence between the two domains, was effectively the role of the Hong Kong comprador, a role so critical to the formation of Hong Kong culture," Oscar Ho writes. "Whenever I see waves lapping on the shore, I think of the Lo Ting being chased, casting about helplessly for a home."

The creators of the myth ask: Who is it that perpetuated the idea of Hong Kong history being the development of a fishing village to an international city? The act of mythmaking, of creating an alternate history, is to assert sovereignty over your own story, when politically you've had no say over your own future at all—when the handover was forced onto you. The people of Hong Kong had been stripped of the right to self-determination, with no seat at the table when the negotiations for our fate took place. You are *Asia's world* city, an *international financial center,* an *inalienable part of China,* the government tells us, the foreign press tells us, Beijing tells us. But if we cannot rewrite our origin story, can we at least reimagine our future?

One evening, two months after the ceremony, my family and I are staring at the news on the television, rapt. A speeding car, a drunk driver, a tunnel in Paris. A princess scorned in love, adored by her country and its former colonies, constantly pursued by the paparazzi—now dead. My aunt was unrattled by the handover, but Diana's death shakes her. *Such a lovely woman, so graceful and elegant, always doing charity work, she'll be terribly missed,* as though she knew Diana personally. On the screen: a tiara on a blond head, pearl earrings, a wistful smile. This is one of my earliest memories: our affinity for all things British, our lingering colonialism. Many years later, my brother tells me his first memory is being in Wuhan, where my mother grew up, and my father delivering a loud commentary to her and her parents about how underdeveloped the place looked compared to Hong Kong. My brother had unwittingly remembered our smug superiority over China, which was still taking its first steps toward prosperity.

At the mouth of the Tate's Cairn Tunnel on the way home, I sing along to Teresa Teng's songs, belting almost aggressively to drown out my prayers: *Please please please let us make it out of here.*

I am there, too, amid these historic events, but no one sees me. I'm there with my mushroom haircut and my lunch box of apples and crackers, pining after my classmate's silver bracelets. I'm buying small tubes of bubblegum-hued plastic from the snack shop across the road from Gran's, trying to make bubbles that feel sticky and featherlight on my fingertips, so precarious that one wrong jab and they deflate. I'm climbing onto the second deck of the red-topped un-air-conditioned buses, the sun that bursts from between the buildings beating down on my arms.

My parents are shouting over the phone, and sometimes I quietly pick up the third line in the flat to listen in. I'm being taken on a plane to Singapore for the summer, to a mother I think of as a stranger. The night before, I stay up till late, chatting with my grandmother. I ask her if she wants souvenirs, so I could make the trip a mission. *I don't think you can take durians onto the plane,* she says, *but maybe an ointment made from essence of flies* for her creaking arthritis. *And dried mango snacks.* I do not want to go, even if it's just for two weeks. I am a child, and children are helpless. They do not get to write their own story, not yet. But it is early. The promise of life is the promise that soon I can be anything I want.

It is raining, again. We are reaching the end of the tunnel. At the vanishing point, the edges of a storm are protruding into the sky. Suddenly we are thrust out into the open; we've made it out alive. The world looks different. We are at a new beginning again. For now, everything is possible.

# Festivities

We are sitting around the dinner table: my grandmother, my two uncles, my aunt, my father, and me. The tong lau smells like soy sauce. The furnishings in our ancestral home are still in the style of the 1960s: great mahogany chairs, steel bed frames, and a showerhead right next to the toilet bowl. It hasn't been renovated since my aunts and uncles grew up here, to the soundtrack of the Beatles on the radio and the clang of mahjong tiles. The faint red glow from the shrine to our household gods, just steps away from the display of fruit offerings and incense to Guan Yin, goddess of mercy.

It is another festival, another occasion for the family to gather. My grandmother's four children don't like one another much, but they put up with this for her. She brings out plates of food, hurrying back and forth between the kitchen and the table, her jade bangle jiggling against her bony wrist.

My grandmother is in every single one of my childhood memories, the only reliable presence in my life. She slept on the bed next to me for all eighteen years, a small woman who was already seventy by the time I was born. When my father loses his temper, she steps in between us to protect me.

When I have my heart broken over a crush and I secretly sob in bed, she can always hear me even after she's become mostly deaf. When I have classmates over to my father's place, she checks in every fifteen minutes to see if we have enough food, offers to order us Pizza Hut, brings us bags of chips.

My grandmother isn't supposed to love me this much. She had three boys, a girl, and a stillborn. My father is the youngest, the most doted on. My aunt is the only one in the pack who did not receive a higher education, because my gran is a woman from the heungha, and she would not pay for a girl to go to school. When my mother took my brother to Singapore after my parents' separation, my grandmother took over the task of raising me. No one expected my grandmother and me to grow this close, two girl-women separated by seven decades, trying to survive my father's erratic outbursts.

The only time I am afraid of my grandmother is during festivities. These days follow their own fevered logic, prescribe a mythical set of rules. It does not occur to me that these rules my grandmother religiously adheres to could be what outsiders call our "traditions," because I have never had a different way of life. I have always lived amid these festivals and gods, and I know no other truth: You light an incense stick on the anniversary of the death of your great-grandparents, even if you never met them. You make your way back to the dinner table on these days no matter how far away you have moved from your family, physically or emotionally. You return to watch Grandmother cook triangles of rice wrapped in long strips of lotus leaves in a tall metal vat above the gas stove for hours, unfazed by the heat.

·  ·  ·

My father was born in Hong Kong in the late 1950s. After an uneventful childhood in To Kwa Wan—chasing typhoons, being bitten by a stray dog, and turning up the music on the radio—he studied social sciences at the Chinese University of Hong Kong. He then worked as a trader of electronics and as a middleman between foreign companies and China in the 1980s and '90s, when China's business environment was still a rugged terrain that required experienced guides. He wears button-up shirts and black pants, his oily hair slicked back; he walks with a slight limp, the result of bad bones and football injuries. His glasses are always sliding down his bulbous nose.

My mother is from Wuhan, China, born at a time when the place was still a backwater, when girls were worthless, 多餘; she was thrown into the river as a child by her father, but saved by her grandmother. She barely finished primary school. My father met my mother when she was a waitress in Shenzhen, on one of his regular business trips to the neighboring Chinese city. She is tall where my father is stocky, with high, proud cheekbones. After only a few months of courtship, they married. My mother was exactly a zodiac cycle younger than he was: twelve years.

I was born in 1993 in Shenzhen, when my mother was twenty-four. A year later, my brother was born in Hong Kong. My family let out a sigh of relief. I inherit my father's uneven eyes, bone-related problems, and insomnia; my brother and I both have fleshy noses, what we later call the Cheung nose. By this time, my father has amassed enough of a fortune to move out of the family's ancestral home in To Kwa Wan.

First we live in Shatin, in a private housing estate called Golden Lion Garden, which has a view of Lion Rock, the symbolic summit of the Hong Kong middle-class dream. We move to Ma On Shan, another New Territories suburb, after repeated hauntings at Golden Lion, seen by multiple members of my family: a ghost mother and child who lurked in the corner of our living room, melancholic but not resentful. My family say I have a third eye; I cry everywhere, pointing at phantoms. My aunt takes me to her Buddhist sifu and converts me to the religion.

The family lore is that my father had been attracted to my mother for her shapely nose, which in face reading meant she was auspicious for his business. In return, he saved her from making ends meet in Shenzhen, working extra shifts to send money back to her family in then-rural Wuhan. But this practical arrangement did not last. By the time I am four, my parents are no longer living together. They both had explosive temperaments, and fought all the time. My mother moves to Singapore. There are vague plans for my father to follow her over, but he never does.

My mother has to fend for herself in a strange new land where she has no friends, no employable skill. She could take one child—that seems fair. She picks the son, the male heir, more bargaining power. Sometimes, I think about my mother when I watch the period dramas that are on television every evening, about women in ancient China that would be banished into the "cold palace" after they fell out of favor with the emperor. My mother's cold palace is the eternal-summer island of Singapore. And I am the abandoned child.


Every summer, my parents make me spend weeks in Singapore with my mother and brother. The trips are hell for everyone involved. I feel no attachment to the person I am supposed to call my mother; the only mother figure in my life is my grandmother. I cry and beg to be taken home to Hong Kong. I count down the seconds in an hour, the number of hours in the days, the days I have left until I can get on a plane. I cry again when they put me on the phone with my grandmother, until I throw up. To shut me up, my parents buy me new phones, the latest iPod, shoes and cosmetics, everything they did not have as a kid.

On one of these afternoons in Singapore, locked inside my bedroom as a punishment for crying, I look out the window to the sandy beaches of East Coast, and then twenty-seven floors down at the concrete pavement, and I know I want to jump. This is the beginning of what I would learn, twenty years later, is called *suicidal ideation,* intrusive thoughts that would follow me around in life, thoughts that sometimes become more than thoughts.

I finally stop crying on these trips when I am fourteen. But even then, I plot and devise summer plans that make it impossible for me to be in Singapore: I schedule music theory classes in July, join dance competitions that force me to stay and practice over the break. I still cannot explain what made these trips feel so traumatic as a child, only that there is a string tying me to my grandmother, and as the string stretches and eventually snaps from the distance, something in my body unravels and I can no longer function.

Nobody knows exactly how old my grandmother is, not even she herself. Her date of birth on her Hong Kong identity card is fake: many Chinese immigrants of that era did the same so that they could be of optimal working age, whether that was younger or older. She no longer remembers what her real birthday is. She believes she was born in the year of the dog, meaning she must have been born somewhere in the vicinity of 1922. She has wiry, permed hair that makes her head look like a cauliflower, dyed an unnatural black color every few months before it fades back to gray. For as long as I've known her, she has worn only light flower blouses she picks up from roadside boutiques for less than twenty Hong Kong dollars.

My paternal family is from Hoiping in Guangdong Province. She and my grandfather had an arranged marriage, and came to Hong Kong in the 1950s. My grandmother is a woman of secrets, divulging little about herself or the rest of the family to me. I know that she never learned to read but taught herself basic words all the same; that she was a factory worker in her youth and raised her children single-handedly. But she never shared stories about my father, and was a woman of few words. Perhaps she thought I was not old enough to understand. Instead, she would say, *Have you eaten?* and *Are you full?*, even though I had never grown up hungry. She would later take the secrets of my father's infidelity to her deathbed.

The village fortune-teller told my grandmother that she would have an awful son who would be born during winter. That awful son was apparently my father. He also said she would live only until the age of sixty. But she defied the odds and survived a bout of violent illness in her sixties. My aunt believes it was because of the good fortune my grandmother had accumulated from being a selfless woman during her lifetime. After my grandmother recovered, she became vegetarian, not for health reasons, but in hopes of amassing more good fortune so that the gods would spare her. It worked. In her seventies, she lived to meet her two and only grandchildren, and I got to grow up with a grandmother.

Every Lunar New Year, my grandmother is up before the first light breaks across the sky. First, she heads downstairs to burn offerings at the side of the road for our ancestors. Then she is at the flower market for all the new year essentials—narcissus plants resting in water, a handful of mandarins. She takes the double-decker bus home and hauls her purchases up the five flights of stairs in our walk-up building, all by herself, with the kind of inhuman strength only grandmothers possess.

A stalk of peach blossoms guards the doorway of our tong lau family home, raining wispy petals onto visitors. The buds drip over an arching network of branches; red ribbons are wrapped around the bark of the trunk to keep it from toppling over its own weight in the porcelain vase. The tree bears inedible green peaches smaller than the top of a pinky finger, tiny fruits I would mangle and crush in childish delight. The red lanterns I made from stapling lai sees together dangle from the ceiling. At dinner, Grandmother makes abalone and lettuce, steamed fish, char siu, dried "vegetable" that resembles matted clumps of hair.

I wear half-rimmed glasses, a red coat, and a jade pendant around my neck, which is supposed to break my fall and shatter in my place during accidents. By the time I am fourteen, I'm well versed enough in the new year taboos to navigate the next fifteen days: unwritten traditions that are still followed by families across Hong Kong, rarely explained and never questioned. I know I should never say the word *death,* which sounds easy until you consider that 死啦 is just a gentle way of saying "fuck" in Cantonese. I know which of my family members are experiencing lunar year eclipses in their zodiac signs, indicating disruptions in their planetary cycles, and they should maybe steer clear of buying property or getting married. I dutifully bathe in pomelo leaves and place my red packet money underneath my pillows. I wear articles of clothing in the lucky color red every day. I wash my hair just before the first day of new year, so I would not risk washing away my luck afterward.

I never challenge my grandmother on these rules. They are Chinese customs passed down through thousands of years, and even if we sometimes disagreed with China's politics, their culture has had a staying power, from British-ruled Hong Kong till today. The legacy of Chinese culture is thousands of years old and so deeply rooted within us that it is impossible to deny we are their people, or at least that's what the official line in China is. I thought these traditions were what made me *Chinese,* until a mainland Chinese girl told me years later that much of these customs were purged by Mao during the Cultural Revolution, and anyway they were not practiced homogeneously across China; *you southern Chinese are the most superstitious,* she says.

My grandmother inherited Taoist traditions from her ancestors. She was a young girl during the Second Sino-Japanese War in the 1930s; it was against her instincts to challenge the rules when she had so little to gain, so much to potentially lose. She lived her entire life making sure to never tempt fate. She passed on all of these instincts to her children.

My aunt is the family mystic. In her twenties, she worked as a secretary at a clinic, until she quit during a prolonged period of depression. She has been unemployed since, living in the same tong lau flat all her life, where she makes me eggs marinated in tea leaves and soy sauce. By the time I was born, she had started giving divination readings to her other brothers. She committed to a life of being a devout Buddhist, removing garlic and onions from her diet—they are said to give you bad breath that could invite evil spirits. She utters quick incantations when I accidentally squash an ant with my elbow, so that the insect can reincarnate as a human in its next life.

My aunt studied face reading and purple star astrology, an ancient divination practice. She could recite our family's history with divination as well. She tells me that my mother went to a fortune-teller when my brother and I were born. I imagine a low stool before a balding man in a thin white shirt, a hand over her nose to block out the smoke bruising the air, fortunes told and lives ruined over a small oak table that laid out a complex chart scrawled with Chinese characters. *He told her that neither of her kids will be filial. She believes that no matter how much love she offers you both, she'll die alone.* My aunt's own reading supported this theory. *Your mother has buckteeth and a short chin,* she tells me. *That means her fortune in the later part of her life is terrible.*

My father's tragic flaw is his unwavering faith in superstitions. He adheres to every rule of the festivities, believing that one misstep would cost him his success in business, which already seems too good to be true. Every time our family gathers for festivals, my father consults my aunt about his wealth in the next few months. But after my father's business begins to fail, her predictions become static. *I see fortune at the end of your path,* she always says. Later, my aunt admits to me that she told my father this because he would curse at her if she told him she thought the stars showed that he should let go of his business.

My father holds on to his business, trusting that his persistence will be rewarded, even as he loses more and more money every year. Eventually, he loses the savings that would have guaranteed a comfortable retirement life, had he quit earlier on. Between my father and my mother, my family's story has become a series of self-fulfilling prophecies.

I am ten. My father screams at me about something I no longer remember, could not remember because he screams often. My grandmother opens the door to my aunt's bedroom in the tong lau to see the old bunk creaking as my body shakes. I look away and start peeling layers of paint off the frame of the bed.

*Don't cry during new year, it's unlucky,* she says softly. She does not ask why I am upset. *I say, stop crying,* more abrasively this time. The angrier she becomes, the harder I sob. Then she pulls out a match, strikes the side of the box until it catches fire, and waves it under my face. She isn't trying to hurt me, but maybe it will scare me enough that I'll stop. In the fleeting glow from the fire burning at the match's head, I can see from the expression on her freckled face that this pains her as much as it does me.

It is the only time she is ever mad at me.

The day before tomb-sweeping day, I sit next to my grandmother, folding hundreds of small yuanbaos out of thin beige paper squares with a perfect slab of silver and gold at their centers. We make a tube shape, tuck the two corners into a trapezoid. We could do this in three seconds. Now they are the shape of the ingot currency used in ancient and imperial China; money for our ancestors in the underworld.

The next day, Gran and I take a bus to Fanling in the New Territories. In our metal trolleys and bags are roast meat, incense sticks, flimsy watches, and rings made of glossy paper. We trek up the Wo Hop Shek cemetery with our offerings, stopping every fifteen minutes so my grandmother can catch her breath. She is already in her eighties. Firecrackers rip through the air near us every few minutes. We build a small fire at our grave and burn the offering in small batches at a time, my eyes watering from the smoke, and her flowery blouse rippling gently in the wind. When we are done, we walk back down, my fingers laced through her drier, bonier ones, leaving a gap between our palms as if they were a cage for a soft secret we shared between us.

My grandfather was apparently a drunk gambler who left my grandmother to raise their children, and my great-grandmother insulted and abused her every day. Still, my grandmother insists on making the trip to the gravesite, even though with each year that passes each step takes more effort on her part.

In the last few years of her life, Gran loses most of her hearing. She still calls me every other day. *Have you had dinner yet?* she asks.

*Yes, hours ago,* I say.

*What?*

*Yes!* I practically scream.

*Okay, okay,* she says.

*Sorry for shouting.*

*What?*

But she never once forgets the birthdays and death anni-

versaries of any of my ancestors, the great-uncles of her husband, the family she married into. She slips out of the flat
when the night sky begins to crack with light, and burns
offerings in a great red tin with dozens of half-moon slits. It
is her way of remembering, of honoring them, of being filial
to people who did not deserve it.

Even in her nineties, my grandmother's routine has not
changed. She gets up early from my father's flat, walks a kilometer to the Red Apple wet market, climbs five flights of
stairs up her tong lau with bags of groceries, and begins
making dinner in the afternoon.

My father doesn't eat with us. Instead, he has her pack
leftovers in boxes and bring it over to his flat, a few streets
away at Farm Road, since my gran and I would return there
every evening to sleep anyway. Then he says he's getting sick
of her food, because her taste buds are dead and her cooking
is "inedible." She starts bringing him takeaway from fast-food
restaurants. One evening, I find her in the living room at my
father's, muttering to herself. She accidentally bought a ginseng chicken set from the Maxim's fast-food restaurant for
him. *Your father hates ginseng, he'll never eat it,* she says, putting
her fanny pack back on. Her tone is light, but for a moment
we're both quiet: We can already hear him yelling.

Because I'm sixteen and still a jerk, I don't offer to go
down for her. I choose the most unhelpful response: become
annoyed at her, too. *You've been spoiling him his whole life.
That's why he's like this.*

At night, my father terrorizes us. He opens the door to
our bedroom at two in the morning and barks out instruc-
tions for my grandmother to run an errand for him at the

pharmacy the next day. He plays loud music with no regard for anyone's sleep schedule but his own. The windows tremble from the noise. If I tell him to turn it down, he says, in a booming baritone: *Liar, you can't hear it. I've been monitoring the frequency levels, and the music can't reach you through two doors.* Two years later, I move out.

I don't worry about being unfilial: that I could be struck by lightning because I have not been grateful enough to my family. But sometimes, I worry that I'm mean, that it has something to do with genetics or upbringing or it doesn't matter, I'm just mean. How else could you explain it, the way I am so terrible to the only person who loves me, except that I am incapable of kindness? Every day I tell myself that I'll make an effort to change, that I'll remember to be nice to Gran tomorrow. I try, really try, until maybe six P.M., and then I forget all about it. And then I'll say, *Ugh, Grandma, stop nagging.*

*Filial:* to respect your elders, to care for the senior members of your family in their old age. In school, my Chinese culture teacher tells an old tale about how even if your father had stolen a goat, you could not turn him over to the authorities; you could only try to persuade him to do the right thing and confess. I am unconvinced, repulsed, but then relieved. It gives me a framework under which I can finally explain my family's dysfunctional tendencies. My family aren't shitty people; they just have little incentive to try with me and my brother, since they are conditioned to believe that fate and traditions guarantee our loyalty to them.

Before I learn about it in class, I hear it from my family, who wield the term at me like a weapon. *You're not filial,* they say, when I try to tell them that I think my father is being emotionally abusive. *He just has a bad temper. He doesn't mean it. He gave you so much. You have no choice but to forgive him.*

*You're not filial,* they say, after I move out when I am eighteen, to get away from my father. *You're not filial,* after I get into an argument with my grandmother on my twenty-first birthday. On the way home, she falls while getting off the bus and hits her head. I am not there when this happens. My aunt, who is supposed to be looking after her that day, says my grandmother slipped because she's upset with me. Everyone in the family takes turns leaving me angry messages on my birthday, squarely placing the blame on me.

*You're not filial,* my family say, as I'm in the hospital for depression, because I am "making my grandmother worry." *You're not filial,* they say, when I don't move in to take care of my father after he loses his eyesight, because I am in recovery from depression and trying to hold down a job. *You're not filial,* when I don't send a monthly allowance back to my family, because I am still paying off my school debt and can barely afford my living expenses.

I blame Confucianism, the ancient concept in Chinese philosophy from which filial piety arises. After the confusion of my childhood, I love grand, overarching structures that make sense of otherwise randomized behavior. I want to call it *Confucianism* rather than *abuse.* I do not want to admit that every culture has its own explanation for breeding toxic families, or that it is an abuser's tactic to confuse cause and effect, motivation and legitimization. That if we were in a society that did not have the convenience of pretending that portraying victims as villains for rejecting abuse is justified through a thousands-year-old dictum, we would simply call it *gaslighting.*

Still, I don't cut off contact with them. I have no choice. My grandmother wants to see me there at the festivities, at the dinner table.

I have abandonment issues. I learn this only in my adulthood, in therapy, after a series of failed relationships. What this means is that I am constantly paranoid that I will lose someone I love, and sometimes, because I think I will be abandoned anyway, I sabotage myself enough to make it happen. If you are my friend and you leave Hong Kong, I may never forgive you. If you are my lover and you leave my bedside to go out in the middle of the night, whether it's for an emergency or for a pack of cigarettes, and I wake up alone, I will automatically assume that you will never come back.

Having abandonment issues is a part of my borderline personality, which includes symptoms like suicidal ideation. But I don't need therapy to tell me where this came from. All the women in my family were abandoned: my mother, my aunt, me. Neither of my parents wanted me. My mother chose the boy, and my father had no idea what to do with me: When my brother is around, my father is suddenly animated, talking about football and action movies. To me he would say, *You're lucky that corporal punishment is outlawed in Hong Kong.*

During holiday breaks in Singapore, my parents often took my brother and me to a bookstore and told us to stay there while they went off to shop on their own. They didn't leave us with a cellphone. My brother and I would make a game of it at first, browsing through the different sections, flipping through the comics and the books, playing hide-and-seek ourselves. But by the second hour we would look at each other nervously, unsure if our parents were ever going to return. We never knew when they would come back, so we could only ever use the bathroom in turns, in case we missed them and they decided they didn't really need to have kids after all. *They'll be back when I count to a hundred,* we'd say. I'd count to five hundred, then a thousand.

Another time, when I was around eight, my parents left me in the car alone because they had a craving for spicy food. My brother loved chilies from a young age, but I could not handle spice at all. So the three of them went off to get spicy food at a mall while I sat in the air-conditioned vehicle for half an hour, staring at the shoppers and passersby. For a year afterward, I slowly trained up my spice levels so when they asked me to join them, I could triumphantly announce that I was now the spice queen, but they never went out for spicy food together again.

Should I keep going? I have so many of these stories. My family says it's a sign of my spitefulness and selective memory, the fact that I still hang on to all of this.

My grandmother wanted me when neither of my parents did. She fed me, bathed me, loved me. But anyone raised by a grandparent knows of that watershed moment, when you become old enough to realize that the shrunken skin and eggshell hair on the person you love is an indicator that they are old, and old people tend to die. You start counting down the days, and everything in life aches with the loss that is to come. My grandmother never intended to abandon me, but when the day came, she had no choice.

There is a story by Zhu Ziqing, one that every Hong Kong student doing the local Chinese curriculum had to read in school. The title is "My Father's Back," and it describes a scene at a train station, just before the narrator is to leave town. His father, who is sending him off, insists on getting mandarins for him, even though he is old and it is physically strenuous for him to make the journey to the vendor's stall and back. The narrator stares at his father's back, hobbling across the train platform to buy mandarins for his son. I loved this story because it was not didactic, did not prescribe me with a code of conduct or go on at length about the virtues of filial piety. It focused on the father's love rather than what the son should do in return for that love; reminded me that love from our parental figures can manifest in small, everyday gestures. And then, maybe, we would want to stop being mean.

In September 2016, I have my last conversation with my grandmother where she is lucid. It is at our family dinner for the mid-autumn festival. Earlier that day, Grandmother walked to the bakery to get me a cake roll, even though she is over ninety and has to walk up and down the five flights of stairs at the tong lau to get anywhere. She's been getting the same cake roll for me for years—Swiss roll, milk-flavored cream—ever since I mentioned in passing that I liked them. She wants me to have something to take home, since home no longer means where she is.

After dinner, grandmother tries to walk me to my minibus stop. My partner and I just started dating, and I am waiting for him to pick me up. *Go home,* I tell her. *It's getting late.*

"得啦，都話送你去車站囉," she says. I suddenly feel irritated: I am not a kid anymore. *Just go, please. I'll be fine.*

The next time I see her, she is in the hospital after a stroke. My aunt found her paralyzed on the steel-framed bed in the tong lau. She never gets up again.

·   ·   ·

I spend Christmas inside a funeral parlor at Hung Hom. My grandmother doesn't look peaceful today, the way they always make dead people look in films; instead, she is disorienting, unrecognizable: as though the mortuary beautician had accidentally emptied the contents of their makeup bag onto her face. In the picture they pick of her, though, she is smiling, serene. It must be from around twenty years ago, but she looks the same, only with fewer gray hairs and wrinkles. Twenty years ago I was still a toddler; she would strap me to her back at daybreak, wiping sweat off her forehead in the kitchen marred with tar-colored stains, while she poured bubbling chicken broth over white pasta in the shape of Osmanthus flowers.

I look at her and think, *You're not supposed to die.* My family and I had made plans to send her to a nursing home, sure that she would be discharged. She may never make a full recovery from her stroke, we thought, but she would still be around. I always forgot that she was already ninety-four, ninety-five, whatever her age was. Her condition had been stable, but she choked over lunch one day and the water never left her lungs. It triggered an inflammation and she died a day later.

I find myself worrying about the most trivial of matters. Is my black underwear going to show underneath the white funeral clothes? Is there WiFi at the funeral parlor? Is it all right that my brother and I swear every couple of sentences, so long as we do it in a different language? The two of us sit in front of the furnace, folding yuanbaos. We pretend it is a chore, but we are just grateful to be given something to do. And so we watch as the molten roses shed their petals of ashes one by one, disappearing into a bed of incense sticks that once stood like candles on a birthday cake.

We learn that there are loads of things we aren't allowed to do. We can't take the white clothes we had on for the ceremony home; we have to throw them away on the side of the road. We can't say thank you if someone comes; we are only supposed to say, "Your kindness is appreciated." We have to eat the sweets they give us, for good luck. After we cremate her, we are not to look back. My brother is the last male descendant left in the family line. He is on his knees for hours during the ceremony. I am spared, because I am a girl. When we pay our last respects, Gran's sons and grandsons get to stand in the first row, out of tradition, and I'm relegated to the second.

My father thinks someone's put a curse on our family. *Look at the facts: I'm broke, you're depressed, and your grandma's gone,* he says. *I could go to someone, to get the voodoo lifted.* There is always something new to blame, something paranormal that could absolve him of guilt, so he doesn't have to accept that life is a cesspool that can't always be fixed by prayers or talismans. My father is still muttering about villain hitters—women who could be hired to curse your enemies—who work underneath the overpass next to Times Square at Causeway Bay. A life trapped between past traditions and future prophecies has left my family with nowhere else to turn, no way out in the present. I flag down a cab outside the funeral parlor to make my escape.

After my grandmother passed away, the last thread between my family and me breaks. I never return to the dinner table again.

There is a mid-autumn festival gig underneath an overpass in Kowloon. On the makeshift stage, the musicians play amid stacks of speakers. Dozens of us sit on the floor, snacking or smoking up or listening to the music in a meditative pose with our eyes closed. A few dogs strut around and sniff our bags for food. My throat is aching from tonsillitis, and still I ask my friend Tomii if he could roll me a cigarette. Tomii is a musician, but he isn't performing tonight. We slice through one of the mooncakes I brought with a Swiss knife.

These guerrilla shows, organized by the city's underground artists and anarchists, are a holiday tradition for those who have found a family among their peers. The police arrive, but miraculously leave without shutting it down. I don't know the organizers personally, so I'm invited to one of these secret guerrilla gigs only when a friend plays, but whenever I go, I feel more at home than I ever had at the tong lau, where my family has sat in silence since Gran died. Ever since I moved out, I've spent so many festivals trying to parasite off other friends' 家庭溫暖, inviting myself over to their families' for dinner, or swaying to live music with friendly strangers at a warehouse or playground.

My father calls me. "You know, the other night I could really feel your grandmother's presence. I think she's watching over me." As always, he leaves me a music riddle. *Hey, who's the musician that looks kinda like Patti Smith but isn't Patti Smith, with the album title that references the ocean?* I figure it out within seconds: PJ Harvey, *Stories from the City, Stories from the Sea.* We don't talk about his new girlfriend, his plans to move to Zhuhai in Guangdong Province, his health. I put my phone away and drink some more beers, then get up to dance among the music with my friends.

I am always mistaking kindness and community for home. The friends I've made since secondary school and university have taught me that loving relationships of mutual care do not have to be an anomaly. They are supportive, kind, and they show up for me; best of all, they do not expect anything from me that I cannot give. But even your best friends may not be the people you want at your two reserved seats in the auditorium during your graduation ceremony, or the ones to walk you down the aisle. And no matter how much I revel in these parasocial relationships in the alternative art scenes and with the people in my neighborhood, they could never be stand-ins for family that promise to always be there. Sometimes the only people who can do this for you are the people you could never walk away from, however unbearable it is to stay. And this is why we return, again and again, to homes that are abusive; better that than to be unmoored, to have no home at all.

At Wong Tai Sin, devoted Hong Kongers queue up for hours outside the temple, desperate to offer the first joss sticks to the gods on the first day of the new year. Coils of incense hang from the door of the temple. An illegal fireworks display erupts in the sky of Yuen Long, and the flower markets crawl with people in red coats and scarves, holding ridiculous inflatable animals. The cinema screens Chinese New Year films with rambunctious characters and over-the-top plots. Grocery shopping becomes unbearable because supermarkets insist on playing festive songs with clashing cymbals.

Feng shui books fly off the shelf. A fortune-teller-influencer's m-shaped forehead and ponytail is ubiquitous at this time of the year, smiling grimly at me on subway ads. A lion dances through my office building to offer luck, and we are given lettuce scraps to stuff into our red packets. This is just before the Covid-19 pandemic hits, although we are already wearing masks. No one here has forgotten the devastation of SARS.

I've been avoiding new year celebrations since Gran died. Everywhere in the city, I see traces of this holiday that is meant to symbolize family harmony. Our family has been broken ever since we lost Gran. We have all become unraveled. No one took up the mantle of calling everyone else up, asking for their availability on winter solstice. Her sons rarely cook for themselves, let alone whip up eight dishes every festival.

The weekend before Lunar New Year, my partner and I watch Edward Yang's *Yi Yi*. We still don't have a television, so we balance my twelve-inch MacBook on the lid of the record player and turn off the lights in the flat. In the first few scenes, the grandmother has a stroke. Throughout the movie, everyone in the family takes turns talking to her by her bedside. The granddaughter thinks the stroke is her fault, because she forgot to take out the trash. "Is it because you still haven't forgiven me? Why have you still not woken up yet?" the granddaughter asks in a scene. I pause the movie to catch my breath.

For a while, I would see grandmother-granddaughter pairings in my building and think, *Do you even fucking realize how lucky you are to have an old person?*

My neighbor and friend K, one of the shopkeepers at Mount Zero Books, tells me that he's been studying purple star, the same divination practice my aunt consulted. He says that a sifu has predicted Hong Kong would be facing bad luck in the coming years, and that everyone should carry their passports with them at all times, just in case we need to flee. This is four months before the national security law is announced.

On the eve of Lunar New Year, I have dinner with my fellow family-less friends. Outside the detention center at

Lai Chi Kok, where dozens of protesters charged with riot-ing are held, a group of elderly Hong Kongers gather in a show of solidarity.

Musician Wong Hin Yan performs an oldie with his gui-tar as the silver-haired supporters sing along.

拋開愛慕 飽遭煎熬 早知代價高
絲方吐盡 繭中天蠶 必須破籠牢

Outside the fenced gates, they wave the lights from their phones against a black revolutionary flag, the slogan now outlawed. This is a night meant for family reunion. These grandparents, parents, aunties, and uncles want the prisoners to know they are not alone.

My father tries to call me at work. I don't pick up, because I'm exhausted. It's the third anniversary of my grandmother's death. He leaves me a voice message instead. *Your grandmother died resenting you, because you weren't filial,* he says. I know this isn't true, because I was the only one she recognized when I approached her hospital bed. My aunt had muttered then, *Her grandkids are the only ones she cares about; the rest of us mean nothing to her.* She, too, later sends me a voice message in the middle of the workday. *Don't forget that you've been Buddhist since you were a child. In Buddhism, there is karma: cause and ef-fect. You'll bear evil children, if you're unfilial.*

Tolstoy says every unhappy family is unhappy in its own way; the Chinese say every family has their own litanies they find difficult to utter. The first time I talked about my family in therapy, my counselor asked me if I knew what dissocia-tion was. *Imagine your soul suddenly zooming so far out that you could see yourself from a distance, standing in that scenario, like you're on the set of a movie,* she said. *The way you talked about your family, it was like you were describing stories that had happened to someone else. There were characters; a beginning, middle, end. But you don't tell me how you feel, where you are when all of this is happening.*

How else could I make sense of these episodes happening within the walls of a place I had called home, that were more fantastical than the soaps I saw on television? The moments of conflict have no resolution, no grand finale where the family gathers on a rooftop for a barbeque at the end of the series, talking about how they loved each other despite all the tribulations. They are messy, unsatisfying, ludicrous even. When my partner and I first started dating, I secretly recorded a fight my parents were having at the airport, when my mother threw a fork across the table and my father bellowed so hard that the guards had to come and ask us to leave. My partner had never questioned the veracity of the stories I told him, and still, I sent it to him and said, *See, I'm not lying. This is what they do.*

Another saying, we're full of them: 家醜不可外揚, my grandmother had said. Shame within the family cannot be shared with outsiders. There is so much I want to say: secret lovers and half-siblings, a stint in a Chinese jail for a poor business decision, a history of mental health conditions, severe physical scars on a family member left behind by a freak incident. There are obvious gaps in this narrative. But I can give you only these fragments, memories that are mine.

No one has visited our ancestors' grave in years, not since Gran left us. She isn't buried with the rest of our family; she has only a small plaque at a memorial garden. On tomb-sweeping day, I circle the grounds trying to find her, but get lost amid the rows of numbers assigned to each of the deceased, death at its most methodical and yet abstract. The family grave still sits at Wo Hop Shek, now covered in dust.

My father and I don't talk anymore. My mother and I are distant: We have never spent more than a few months in the same city for over two decades. But in recent years she will ask me for updates about work and my partner, and say, *I know that we failed as parents.* Sometimes I respond to her text and she won't reply for another two months, as though she's forgotten that she initiated the conversation. During festivities, she will send me a text: *Happy holidays?*

For all the distance I put between my family and me, there are still aftershocks in my body I could not walk away from: a deformed hip that doctors tell me my parents should have noticed, a series of mental health conditions, addictions that arose from self-medicating and which I'm trying to kick. I've found families in the form of friends that babysit you through your depression, a partner that builds a home alongside you, the people in a place that refuse to give up on you. I know only this: that you cannot demand obedience and devotion if you have not earned it, even from the people closest to you.

I have not been back to To Kwa Wan in almost two years. When I take a bus that drives through the old streets of my childhood, I still see the ghost of my grandmother, slowly making her way home with red plastic bags of groceries. If I close my eyes, I can hear my father, my aunt, my uncles, gently calling me by my Chinese name, in the now-quiet tong lau flat, dinner table unmade. No one answers.

# Parallel Universes

哭啊 喊啊 叫你媽媽帶你去買玩具啊
快 快拿到學校炫耀吧 孩子 交點朋友吧
—草東沒有派對,《大風吹》

My father and I are at a registration booth set up in the covered playground of a public primary school in Ho Man Tin, a neighborhood in Kowloon. I'm in a pink-and-white-striped frock, my collarbone-length hair tied back neatly, a smile twitching on my lips. My father is clutching my papers in a clear plastic folder, already impatient. We are here because I had been sent to take one elite primary school entrance test after another, tests that I swore I had done well on, but all the letters in the mailbox say *I'm sorry to inform you . . .* This is the nondescript, non-elite school guaranteed by the central allocation system. My father isn't happy.

We sit down at a table. The air is sticky and heavy. A teacher looks at my Shenzhen birth certificate. She mutters, loud enough for both of us to hear: *Another one from mainland China.*

My father grits his teeth. He puts his fancy ballpoint pen

back into his shirt pocket. Then he turns to me and says, *We're leaving.*

Two weeks later, my father gives me a call when I'm at my grandmother's apartment. *This international school—they said they'd take you,* he says. *It's a lot more expensive, but do you want to?* I hesitate; it feels like a trick question, because I don't have any other offers from schools. *It's so grand, you'd love it. You can learn more about Singapore, too; your mother would approve,* he says. The school is run by Singaporeans, stocked with Singaporean teachers, and admits children of Singaporeans in Hong Kong.

I press the red receiver deeper into my left ear, my elbows resting on a plastic table cover with a print of bright fruits. The table cover stinks like an ancient pair of sandals. I don't know what *grand* looks like, so I imagine crisp lace tablecloths, bathrooms that smell of roses, and I'm almost giddy with excitement. *Yes yes yes,* I say, not understanding what it means.

On the first day of school in September 1999, my grandmother gets up at five to make me macaroni in soup. She combs my hair into high pigtails and clips shiny butterfly barrettes onto each of them. She pulls the uniform over me, a gray overall dress with a white rounded collar. Then she puts me on a bumpy school bus ride, and I fall asleep with drool sliding down the window. After an hour the bus pulls into a gray building stamped with a red Tetris-block school logo, on a slope in the lush light-dappled Aberdeen.

The campus is a sprawling, monumental affair: It has a plaza, an indoor basketball court, an auditorium, music and dance studios, a library, an indoor pool, and other floors for classrooms, which come with a stretch of mini gardening plots right in front of them. Every morning the whole school gathers in the gymnasium to sing the Singapore national anthem and recite the pledge: *We, the citizens of Singapore, pledge ourselves as one united people,* whether or not the pupils are in fact Singaporeans.

Everywhere I turn, I hear a language that I cannot understand. I attended a local pre-school that taught only basic English, and no one in my family, apart from my brother, whom I barely see, is fluent in the language. Cantonese, my mother tongue, is forbidden on the campus—in Chinese class, we learn Mandarin and simplified characters instead of the traditional characters used in Hong Kong. My classmates have been friends since kindergarten, swapping Singlish-tinged inside jokes that reference afternoons spent at their parents' Mid-Levels flats. Their parents are lawyers, bankers, company directors, and regional heads, affluent Hong Kongers or Singaporean expats.

At the first parent-teacher meeting, Mrs. G, my class teacher, tells my father to get me a private English tutor. My father is confused. *I thought the point of me paying this much money is that you are going to teach her,* he says.

In English class, Mrs. G yells, *Freeze!* Everyone obliges, bringing their flinging arms into a halt, withdrawing breaths and farts. We're strewn across different corners of the classroom, which is decorated with notice boards featuring photos of each of us; under the cutout of my face, there are no gold stars. I am still trying to catch up. It feels as though we're swimming, and everyone glides through the water easily and does laps around me while I struggle to float. I don't even stick my head underwater, in case I forget to come up for air.

I don't notice the class has stopped moving, gone quiet. *Can I go to the toilet?* I say. It's still one of the only complete sentences I can say in English. *Don't you know what* freeze *means?* she asks, and laughs. I do know what *freeze* means: water turning into ice in the fridge. The class laughs. They later call me *toilet queen,* even though I never again ask to go to the bathroom in her class. Instead I hold in the tremors of my bladder in my seat, trying not to spill. To distract myself, I tear off the corners of my textbooks and put the pieces in my mouth, drench them with my saliva. Here in this classroom, I would forget how to speak, then learn it all over again. I chug the language, not pausing even when it clogs my lungs.

I did not know what to expect at the school, and no one in my family could have prepared me for it, not the mannerisms of the upper-middle-class nor the way the international school culture isolates you from the rest of Hong Kong. My primary school is one of the country-specific international schools that target expatriates from certain nationalities, or parents looking for school diplomas compatible with those of other countries. On the secondary school level, the largest international school body is the English Schools Foundation, established in 1967 to govern schools in Hong Kong that offer, "without regard to race or religion, a modern liberal education through the medium of the English language." *Our mission is to inspire creativity and nurture global citizens and leaders of the future,* its website says. Other international schools include the local chapter of the United World Colleges, a global international school network, and British boarding or prep schools that have opened branches in Hong Kong.

International school students make up only about 7 percent of the primary and secondary student population, with over forty thousand students in total in the 2020–21 school year. These schools were initially set up to offer schooling to the children of our colonizers; they still, to some degree, serve the expat and non-Chinese population in Hong Kong. In the postcolonial era, however, most cater to a nouveau riche and upper-middle-class Chinese population; a significant percentage of their students come from well-off Hong Kong families. The schools are still required to admit at least 70 percent non-local students, but almost half of the fifty-four international schools in the city do not meet that rule. One international school admitted more than 75 percent local students.

For all their talk about global citizenship, international schools show little interest in engaging local communities except on superficial levels, usually in the form of volunteering excursions. But kids who are meant to one day go to expensive American universities don't need to learn about Hong Kong. The physical cityscape of Hong Kong exists but for your amusement. You need to know only enough so that when you are an adult, you can make clever memes about which section of the minibus to sit in so that the driver can hear you when you need to alight, or what spice level of broth to get at our most beloved noodle joint.

My father's decision to send me to the school was made out of wounded pride, and like most decisions he made relating to my upbringing, he had given it little thought—even though annual school fees are an average of fifty thousand Hong Kong dollars a year. But at the time, we were rich. After his business started failing, my father bitterly called it my decision to go to the school, saying that it cost him a fortune. He never quite forgave me for it.

.    .    .

The early years of primary school are a dissociative daze. I'm on the other side of the glass, and no one can hear me no matter how hard I bruise my fists. I check out book after book from the library: The Boxcar Children, Nancy Drew, Betsy-Tacy, *The Secret Garden,* Harry Potter, and everything by Jacqueline Wilson, looking up every word I don't know with the pocket electronic dictionary Instant-Dict. A teacher writes on my report card that I've been doing well in school, complimenting especially my writing compositions. It's the first time anyone ever tells me that I'm good at anything. I buy notebooks and scribble them with stories about soup fairies and a magic boarding school that feels vaguely like the plot of a book I've just read. Someday, *someday,* I'll speak so well the words will come as I beckon them, falling like Tetris blocks to fill up a blank space.

In my third year, I'm finally fluent enough to make friends. I eat snacks with my classmates on the bumpy school bus ride over from Kowloon that stops at every luxury development in Hung Hom. I grow close to two girls, Alana and Charlene. We call ourselves the Mashimaro Club, named after the Korean white rabbit cartoon character. At recess, instead of reading books at the library on my own, we learn how to do cartwheels on the playground together. They talk about their cousins and childhood friends and siblings, and I fall silent.

One day at school, I show up with a small booklet, one of these commercialized diary booklets with question prompts about your hobbies and favorite movies. The booklet is printed with photos of white girls. *They're my friends outside of school,* I tell Alana and Charlene. *We grew up together and do sleepovers and braid each other's hair.* They look back at me, unconvinced by my blatant lie.

My extended family lives frugally, since my father did not extend the comforts of his wealth to them, and they too refuse to indulge my frivolous desires to fit in. At the coral-hued building my father was raised in and where I spend my after-school hours with my aunt, the hot water is erratic, the staircases are chipped, and the rat infestation persists even after we adopt a cat. After family dinner, I go home to our comfortable flat on Farm Road, where I soak in our bathtub while reading a book. In the showers after swimming class I hide myself and the cheap elastic band around my waist from the other girls, so they won't find out that my grandmother buys my underwear from the wet market.

But still, I visit highland castles and walk through the woods of New Zealand on the school's expensive educational overseas trips my father pays for. I take part in an Outward Bound training camp, ask for money to take guzheng classes so I can play in the orchestra, and tour with the choir to Singapore and Malaysia. Later, as an adult, it occurs to me that my misplaced self-pity means I truly am the *ungrateful little shit* my father accuses me of being.

But children do not know that microaggressions and bullying are not the same as structural oppression. I am too young to know what the rest of the world looks like. My vision is limited to the elaborate birthday parties my friends' parents throw for them at the 550,000-square-foot invitation-only Aberdeen Marina Club, which has its own private ice-skating rink. Stories about cruise holidays and hotel buffets at the Peninsula or the Four Seasons. While some children ostracize me in the early years, their parents are always generous. They drive over to pick me up when my father won't and take me to weekend lunches at the Festival Walk mall. I mention to a friend that I really want to check out this simulation game that everyone's playing, and on my birthday her parents gift me a copy of *The Sims* they purchased with their frequent flyer miles. Another friend's mother buys me a bra from Triumph, not because puberty had a noticeable effect on me but because she noticed the way I look when I pull over the wimpy pads. I oscillate between feeling bitter and undeserving, an outsider and part of the club.

I join the athletic team despite being a bad runner, because I am competitive and cannot resist even the possibility of winning anything. After much begging on my part, my aunt takes me to buy a pair of sports shoes, Reeboks with the logo in purple. On the track, Alec, in his beautiful Nikes, sizes me up and beckons the others over. *Look at those shoes, ew, who buys shoes in such a gross color, and Reeboks?* I don't say anything. I walk over to the starting line, and finish last of the pack.

In December, Katie and I wear red ribbons in our hair and take our place on the steps at a shopping mall in Hong Kong Island East. After the first few Christmas songs, the choir parts for us to walk to the front, where we each perform a solo verse of "Jingle Bells." We beam at the audience when the applause comes, and she waves at her parents. I look around for mine, even though I already know they aren't there.

Katie and I became sleepover friends in fifth grade, always me at hers, never the other way round. Like me, she's also a choir girl, and a guzheng girl in the Chinese orchestra. Before each rehearsal, we sit cross-legged on the floor behind the auditorium, wrapping white tape round our fingers to secure our guzheng picks. First we become competitors, then frenemies, then inseparable.

That summer, Katie and I lie next to each other in her room, our faces so close that I can see each individual colored square on her braces. Our skin tingles from sunburn: Earlier that day, her parents took the two of us to another exclusive country club, a relic of the colonial era reserved for the wealthy. We lounge by a private pool over little cups of Häagen-Dazs ice cream, feeling like models in teen magazines. Katie has round puppy eyes behind her metal-frame glasses, and her hair is always in a pair of French braids.

The next morning after the sleepover, her family's domestic worker weaves my hair into French braids just like Katie's. Her twin schnauzers linger in my arms and lick my face. Her father drives us to school and never complains about the traffic near the Aberdeen Tunnel. When I'm home, tossing in my familiar, less comfortable bed, I think about how much I want to steal her family: generous, gracious, unambiguous.

At the end of the school year, I stand in the school canteen with dozens of other families. Over the vats of spaghetti Bolognese, I can still catch a faint whiff of chlorine from the pool next door. It's the annual awards ceremony, and I've won some sort of academic prize. My grandmother is here, sweating through her thin, flowery blouse, and so is my aunt, with patches of dark moist stains on her peach polo shirt. Their faces are scarred from the acne that runs in the family, and their hair sticks out like the last tufts of grass on a barren field. All the other families are in pristine, fitted suits, like they'd walked straight out of an HSBC billboard ad. We came on Bus 107 from Kowloon to Aberdeen. The other students and parents had taken a cab or driven up the school's spiral car park.

My aunt and grandmother plant themselves onto the plastic chairs, exhausted from the journey across the harbor, then up the slope. They wait for me to join them, but I don't sit down. I know that if a teacher were to come over to congratulate me, or a classmate's family tried to make small talk, my grandmother would only be able to respond with the two English words she knows: *rainbow, castle*. I walk past them and sit with a classmate's family.

I don't know this classmate well, and I've never met her family, but they ask me polite questions and I answer all of them except *Where are your parents?* They aren't here; they've only been to one Christmas performance in six years. I glance back, something acrid welling in my throat. The two women who have shown up for me are sitting there frozen, lost amid the flurry of English conversations engulfing them.

That evening, we go to dinner with the rest of the family, at a seafood restaurant called Hang Fook Lau, the house of bliss. It's inside a neighborhood mall that smells like stale air-conditioning, and we come here for all of our celebrations: mid-autumn, Lunar New Year, birthdays. Prehistoric sea creatures swim around in tanks, and today the centerpiece of the rotating tray, surrounded by steamed razor clams and roast duck, is a cheesecake from the Opera Patisserie, my favorite bakery in To Kwa Wan. I know that it's light and fluffy, just the right amount of sourness, but I also know that it's HK$30, and now I'm thinking about the $300 luscious chocolate cake from Cova at my classmate's hotel party last week, and I feel my eyes leaking. For a moment, we sit in silence listening to the chatter of the diners around us, and then my aunt says, *It's starting to feel like nothing we do will be enough for you.*

When you can attend schools like these, even mediocre caterpillars emerge as monarchs. I graduate from primary school in 2005, placing third in class. In my final two years, I publish a short story in the youth section of the local English newspaper and compete in the Math Olympiad. My classmates will go to other international schools, but my father can't afford the school fees anymore. He writes letters to the principals of traditional girls' schools—a range of academically competitive public and private schools with different fees— including a school just up the road from where we live, asking if they'd take me. *Let me introduce as father of Karen, who is studying P6. I am writing the letter to your attention because of the issue to admission to the secondary schools in Hong Kong.* We don't hear back from any of them. We finally make plans for me to attend the same public school that he and my aunt attended three decades before me.

This school isn't fancy. There are no French lessons, no private pool, no gimmicky fashion shows of students prancing down a runway in national costumes made of recycled material. Our auditorium doesn't have plush red seats, only low wooden stools that make your back hurt even at the age of thirteen. The school's five stories surround a small playground that is sometimes a basketball court and also a mini football field. You can see the entire school no matter where you're standing at any given time. The canteen is too small to accommodate everyone in the school, so the senior students sit at the public playground on Oxford Road and buy 飯飯

of luncheon meat and chicken thighs doused in black pepper sauce from the snack shop for ten dollars, or walk down to Kowloon City. The most beautiful room in the building is the chapel, which will later be restored to include a stained-glass wall.

The school was established in 1961, in colonial Hong Kong. My aunt wore the exact same sailor dress uniform—a white dress with a blue oversized collar and a blue fabric belt—when she and my father studied under Helen Wong, the school's first principal, in the late 1960s and early '70s. Our school motto is *Non Nascor Mihi Solum* ("I was not born for myself alone") and the school song is "Jerusalem," the lyrics of which are based on a William Blake poem; my favorite line is *And was Jerusalem builded here / Among these dark Satanic Mills?* The school is run by the church, and painfully Christian—teachers warn in class that queer people will go to hell, and almost everyone graduates a virgin.

On Tuesdays and Fridays we stand in the school playground under the sun to say prayers and sing hymns. At the international school, we'd been trimming inches off our dresses since we were eleven. Here, the other girls and I are never allowed to take off our woolen sweaters because of how much our dresses reveal in the sweat, and we're always sweating. By the end of the assembly, at least one person would faint under the heat. The disciplinary teacher makes the girls dye their hair black even if it is naturally brown, and curls are forbidden. A few years after I graduate, the school will try to ban dating and will only back down after our alumni return to debate the issue with them in a forum. On weekends, after Bible study sessions at the church, my friends and I navigate the intoxicating labyrinth of mannequins at the Argyle Centre in Mong Kok, picking out punk tartan dresses and jeans that smell like bleach while clutching little transparent bags of cold noodles. I get my cartilage pierced for twenty bucks.

My public school has a predominantly English curriculum and is ranked Band 1 in Hong Kong's three-tier school system. Even within each tier, the level of English proficiency differs dramatically. Students in elite local private schools could pass as native speakers; others struggle to keep up conversations in the language, and couldn't care less that the government insists English is an "official language" in Hong Kong. At my school, Cantonese still reigns on campus, and English is almost never spoken outside of class. My classmates can understand classical Chinese texts with archaic words no longer in use, but their fluency in English is limited to *tectonic plates* or *self-strengthening movement* they learn in geography or history. English is no longer a key to my survival, but a snobbish anomaly. In economics class, a teacher looks straight at me and tells me, *You'll know once you're out in the real world that your English is nothing.*

We rotate between world history lessons on World War I that are taught in English, and Chinese history and culture lessons that trace the country's development from the earliest dynasties to present-day China. The curriculum tells me close to nothing about my own city's history except how Hong Kong was ceded to Britain after China's defeat in the First Opium War in 1842, but I've had to study the demise of the late Qing empire three times in two different languages. This is before liberal education reform, and Hong Kong is not considered significant enough in its own right to earn a place on the syllabus. I cannot name all, or even most, of Hong Kong's governors, but I can list China's dynastical periods in chronological order.

In secondary school, I figure out how to fit in much more quickly. On the first day of school, I meet three new friends, and they convince me to join the school dance team with them. I wrangle my hands into lotuses, wave a straw Japanese hat about in our routines. My new friends and I go to karaoke in Kowloon City. *Wait, so you don't know any of these songs? Stephy Tang and Alex Fong? Kary Ng? Janice Vidal?* No, I mumble. That night, I immediately fill my iPod with these songs, downloading them from the Chinese search engine Sogou. When they text me in Cantonese 口語, I learn to do the same. I make a blog on Xanga to keep up with my classmates' intimate, gossipy musings about life as a teenager: a mid-2000s web page with glittery text banners made with Ulead animator, and autoplay background music.

Like in most public schools, the students come from a range of class backgrounds. Some live in public housing, others in the low-level luxury flats in the upper-middle-class Kowloon Tong district. Even though my father's business is failing and we have not paid off our mortgage on our flat, we are still well off, smack in the middle between the kids on social welfare and the ones who get sent off to English boarding schools. During the summer break, my classmates and I take a trip to 東堤小築, a low-priced resort in Cheung Chau that's rumored to be haunted: In the early 2000s, a series of suicides by burning charcoal took place in the holiday homes. We rent out a small room near the sea, the girls taking turns sleeping on the only three beds available. We watch *The Ring,* and go for morning walks by the beach under a freshly boiled sun. For the next three days, everyone except me takes turns playing mahjong.

I grow close to Evelyn, who is still one of my best friends today. Evelyn has straight bangs, cute fanged teeth that stuck out before she got braces, and bottomless patience for my bullshit. When I suddenly dissociate, she waits for me to return. When my father screams at me at home, she listens to me cry for hours on the phone. We pass each other notes in class: *Takoyaki after school?* We raid the photo-sticker booths, which have filters that make our eyes pop and our hair silky. At Dragon Centre in Sham Shui Po, we go ice skating, and afterward we get terrible all-you-can-eat sushi for fifty bucks at the notorious establishment of Ming General, laughing so hard at the red bean warship rolls that the other diners throw us looks of annoyance.

In my first year, I rank bottom of a class of forty-two students in religious studies and Chinese. My classmates laugh at how bad my Chinese is, and I don't understand much of their slang. Teachers often thrust me into morning assemblies to read out school announcements in English, and soon, other students notice me and decide that I'm a show-off, a spoiled brat. These rumors make it back to me, but it doesn't bother me. I have friends, and no one excludes me from their after-school plans. The school has a bit of a reputation for being one that parents send their kids to when they want them to be honest, modest, and innocent to the point of naïveté. But everyone who has studied there will tell you that the school has always been one that is populated with kind people, good Christians. I make it through six years of school, unscathed.

My ex–international school classmates and I return to the primary school for a Christmas fair, where rich moms cook up steaming pots of authentic laksa. Katie and I lost touch quickly, but Alana and I are still friends. We sip on ice kacangs and gather at the tables of the gray canteen, where overactive children used to season our food with pool water dripping from their hair. We're fifteen now and puberty is a full-fledged beast. My English is rusty, so I stumble a little over my words. My ionic-straightened hair, they say, is a little bit MK, meaning it looks cheap like the Mong Kok street style. While I'm bingeing Taiwanese soap operas and TVB dramas, they're watching *The O.C.* and *Gossip Girl* and *Glee,* and so I try to keep up with these shows, too, imagine what it's like to have prom or go surfing after school. Some of them are already spending nights out at Lan Kwai Fong. My ex-classmates start calling me *local.*

At my public school, schooling is free, and outside of necessities such as books and lunches, we pay less than HK$1,000 a year to the school for printing fees and other miscellaneous expenses. International school fees for second-ary level are around HK$80,000 a year at the time, and some schools, officially or unofficially, even require parents to pay "debentures" and "bonds" of up to millions of dollars, a sum that may depreciate or not be reimbursed when the child leaves the school. My international school had computer rooms and state-of-the-art classroom equipment. My public school prints worksheets on cheap, brown paper instead of crisp A4 sheets, and the students on duty constantly cough from the chalk dust while cleaning up the blackboard.

I know that when they call me *local,* my ex-classmates don't intend it as a synonym for Hong Konger. They are making a classist jab at anyone who doesn't also study in an international school. Even though international and local school students coexist in the same city and hang out in the same streets and malls, they are separated by class, language, culture, sometimes race, and eventually politics. Many children in international schools have parents who will soon be posted elsewhere; Hong Kong is merely a transit stop and not a destination. The more curious breed of students are Hong Kongers who were born in Hong Kong to Hong Kong parents, have lived in Hong Kong all their lives, and have family that speak fluent Cantonese and are of ethnic Chinese origin—yet distinguish themselves from the locals as though they're not also part of the local Hong Kong community.

My ex-classmates tell me about plans to go to university in London, New York, California, Oxford, Australia. My family has made it clear to me that they can afford to send me only to a local university. After school I find a seat in the study rooms in the library above the Red Apple wet market in To Kwa Wan, the one that smells like chicken feathers, and memorize facts about World War I until the library staff kicks me out. My classmates and I cram our adolescence with memories of studying for the public exams, and we've never seen the inside of a bar. Still, a third of my class never makes it to university at all. None of my international school classmates ever have to worry about being unable to get a college degree: Even with poor grades, their pool of options is infinitely expanded by the fact that their parents can afford for them to go to any school in the world.

But for international school students who go on to study at local universities, fitting in might prove difficult. In a feature story by student publication *Varsity,* one international school graduate at Chinese University describes finding it difficult to understand Hong Kong university culture, being publicly humiliated by his mentor for his lack of knowledge of local politics, and "experiencing culture shock in his hometown." Another mentions struggling to understand what the local students are saying, and how "there was little discussion of Hong Kong news" at her international school and "more emphasis was placed on international or American news." The *locals* describe international school kids as 離地, meaning literally "to be levitating off the ground," with no grasp on reality.

When I'm sixteen, I start spending more time online than with my friends in school. I become obsessed with metal and hardcore and wade deep into the Hot Topic–wearing corners of teenage emo internet. I watch hours of videos by Asian American and Australian creators on YouTube. As queer culture takes off on Tumblr, I become involved in the early communities of performative internet allyship of the early 2010s. I post black-and-white photographs of signs that say "No child is born homophobic." In between the Kurt Cobain quotes and GIFs of wilting flowers, my Tumblr shows a blond woman holding a placard: "Society teaches 'Don't get raped' rather than 'Don't rape.' " It's standard teenage angst, but I love feeling morally superior.

My friends and I are brought up in traditional, conservative Chinese families who believe that only kids who end up becoming "gangsters" would have tattoos. We do not have the language or experience or education to discuss racism or white supremacy, which are topics that never come up among my peers. Religion is still too deeply ingrained in us for discussions on spectrums of gender identity and sexual orientations. I feel further away from secondary school and closer to the fellow adolescents I debate social issues with online, less of a Hong Konger and more a child of the internet.

As public exams approach, I begin timing my showers

and returning home only when the library is closed. I study Chinese history and literature, tread in the ancient Chinese texts that once terrified me. I like the reliability of academic performance, how I can use language proficiency as a gauge for how well I am fitting in. A retired teacher from another school gives me free monthly private lessons so I can take English literature as a self-study for my public exams. I score thirty out of thirty points and automatically qualify for the early admission program to a local university.

My teachers push me toward studying law, even though I lean toward journalism. They say it'd be a *waste,* as in, it's stupid to give up the opportunity for a nice middle-class life that's right before me. If my school had guidance counselors, I would have known to try for scholarships at universities in the United Kingdom or America. I won't know what a "liberal arts college" is until my early twenties. To the world I am in then, the University of Hong Kong is the holy grail. When I receive my acceptance for the law and literature program, it feels like the first day of the rest of my life.

I leave the secondary school at the end of the first year of my senior form, while the rest of my classmates study for the A-levels university entrance examination. On my seventeenth birthday, ten days before my last day in school, my classmates gift me a jar of hand-folded origami hearts. Evelyn doesn't understand fandoms, but she makes me a daily planner plastered with photographs of my favorite bands. Everyone writes sweet messages in my farewell book. I write a teary I'll-miss-you blog and post it to Facebook. I never felt like I fit in at the school. But I'm still friends with my old classmates today.

. . .

By the waterfront in Izmir, Turkey, I drink Raki shots with a group of young adults from ten different countries as the sun falls into the Aegean. The summer after my freshmen year in university, I stay in Turkey for six weeks for an exchange program to teach English to Turkish kids. It turns out to be glorified day care; none of us were trained to teach, and it is nearly impossible to teach kids with whom you share no common language. But in return for taking care of the kids while their parents are at work, the city council in Balçova pays for transport and lodging.

I share a room with a mainland Chinese girl. Within the first week, she lets me know that I am dumb for assuming no one in China knows about the Tiananmen Square massacre, and once we get that out of the way, we become close friends. The others in my program are from Hungary, Colombia, Indonesia, Slovakia, and the United States. We live in a three-story house, eating cig kofte wraps out on the porch fringed by weeds. We drink beers on the balcony while studying Turkish phrases with our Lonely Planet guidebooks and celebrate post-Ramazan with a feast of menemen and dolmas made by a Turkish family that sometimes came by to check on us. At the end of the program, we take a bus up to Istanbul. I sleep on a beanbag on the roof of a cheap hostel across from the Blue Mosque in Istanbul, and awake to the morning prayer call.

My housemates and I get along so well that we become unwitting poster children for the myth that cultural exchange brings peace. The organization that has sent us on this exchange was born out of the post-boomer savior mentality that we can "do something" for the world as long as privileged kids can afford trips to "less developed" countries and attend conferences. But at this impressionable age, before discourses on voluntourism become mainstream, it is exactly the sort of activism I was hoping for during my Tumblr days. At one of the organization's conferences in Hong Kong, I learn about the carbon footprint and meet environmentalists, and I decide to go pescatarian. In my second year of university, I become a committee member at the local chapter of the organization at my university.

This is what most of my university is like: being vaguely *international*, identifying with being a *third culture kid* because I feel closer to "Western" culture than I do to Hong Kong's. My international school education had distanced me from the city, and I failed to learn about the city's political and colonial history during my local school years; my university years followed this natural trajectory. I make friends with white and Asian diaspora exchange students with whom I'd go to Lan Kwai Fong or to Mr. Wong's, a notorious Mong Kok eatery that offers only to exchange students an all-you-can-eat food and beer deal for under a hundred bucks. I take a bus to Hanoi from Hong Kong through Nanning, chug a tower of beer at Khaosan Road in Bangkok, and sleep in hostels where couples fuck in the bunk underneath me. I caption photos with #wanderlust unironically, chatting up fellow backpackers and believing that they could serve as conduits through which I could understand more about a world of which I had seen so little.

At the two on-campus Starbucks I rotate between, I keep tabs on tech sites and start-ups, holding on to the millennial delusion that a good business idea or a new app could radically improve our world. Being loud online on issues like climate change and racial inequality lets me pretend I'm part of a global conversation, yet at enough distance for it to not affect my daily life. After a childhood of not fitting in, this participation and distance feels safe.

But sometimes, when I pass by the student union offices and see the booth for their latest political campaigns, I feel that gulf between me and my surroundings. By now I'm an adult, with the space and opportunity to explore Hong Kong; I can no longer blame indifference on the school environment I was placed in. My ignorance is starting to feel like a choice, and it makes me ashamed. Outside my university, a fifteen-year-old boy is organizing protests against a national education law that he says will introduce a brainwashing pro-China syllabus in schools. And even though I'm only fifteen minutes away, I don't go down to the government offices to see what happens, not even once.

# PART II

# 2003

For my ninth birthday I beg Buddha to trap me inside somewhere while the world dissolves outside my window, even though my aunt told me this isn't how the religion works. I romanticize the typhoons that blow apart the trees outside my flat, imagine the waves tearing open their mouths near the Praya then swallowing themselves back into the sea. My father tells me stories about how he was a typhoon watcher in his youth, getting as close as he could to the hissing waters. I want only to be safe under the covers with a Game Boy or a book, listening to the rain spill like a bag of marbles against the window, sure that nothing could touch me. I want to watch and not participate. A forced hiatus from reality. To say, *stop*, and be sure that everything else stopped with me.

School is suspended. The adults tell us there is an epidemic called SARS with a high mortality rate, but death feels abstract, the way everything does when you're a child: words on a vocabulary sheet to learn for the next quiz or sounds that loll out of an adult's mouth. Even before the suspension was announced, the school started adopting temperature sheets. We're supposed to stick a thermometer in our ear every day before school, and get our guardians to sign it, to prove that we aren't going into school while we're sick, as if this is something any kid would do. Most of us fake a number between thirty-six and thirty-seven degrees Celsius on the school bus in the morning, and sign it in a sloppy imitation of our parents' handwriting, often with their blessing.

In grade four, my classmates don't call me toilet queen anymore. I am, if not expressive, at least fluent in English, but still lonely. Now that I don't have school, I can take a break from the devastation of Monday mornings, when I'd find out about yet another party over the weekend I wasn't invited to. No more agonizing recess periods hiding out at the library while my classmates played a game of tag they called "girls catch boys." No more polite small talk with the school bus auntie, our chaperone figure, on the rides home; there is no one else to talk to, after the cool kids at the back banished me from their group. But for now, I can stop trying so hard to be seen.

For three months I make my way to my gran's place every morning, to hang out with my aunt and get away from my volatile father. I've been acclimatized to his absence all through childhood, but now he's at home too much. His office is in Telford Plaza in Kowloon Bay, a block away from the SARS-stricken Amoy Gardens, where over three hundred residents were infected after the disease spread through connecting sewage systems. I wear kid-sized pink face masks, poke elevator buttons with a tissue over my finger, take care not to touch anything as far as possible on the way, and then hike up the tong lau stairs, trying not to think about the rats that play hide-and-seek around the rubbish bins. I scrub my hands with soap and hot water once I arrive.

My aunt and I play Scrabble and cards, and when I lose I throw a fit and knock the board over or crumple up the cards. She mutters, *You certainly inherited this temper from your father.* We listen to political commentators Albert Cheng, or "Tai Pan," and Raymond Wong shout themselves hoarse on the radio, debating politics with such vigor that I'm almost jealous these two people have found something they care about so much. We put on *Letter to My First Love,* Christine Samson's album with the legendary deejay Uncle Ray. My aunt hums along to every song except "Anak," where Samson, who is a Hong Kong musician of Filipino descent, sings in Tagalog. My aunt tells me she once took singing lessons, could have been a singer, too, could have been many things, but in the end it was her brothers' education my gran chose to fund. We make mixtapes of folk songs: Simon and Garfunkel, Au Sui Keung. I read *The Princess Diaries* and Sweet Valley and Mary-Kate and Ashley books, wondering what it means to have strawberry blond hair like these white girls.

I don't know what SARS does, except that it involves the lungs. I don't know where it came from; grown-ups say that it's from the consumption of wild animals, maybe bats. But its origins matter less than how it spread to us. In February 2003, Liu Jianlun, a professor and respiratory specialist, traveled from Guangzhou to Hong Kong for a wedding banquet. He stayed in Room 911 at the Metropole Hotel in Kowloon, and soon checked himself into a hospital. He never made it to his nephew's wedding. Seven other people staying on the same floor at the hotel caught the respiratory disease; Liu was admitted to the ICU and died ten days later.

It was rumored that Liu had known what he'd caught, and why he was sick. What we do know is that China already had knowledge about the disease and did not promptly notify the World Health Organization; Hong Kong was in the dark until it was too late.

By the time SARS subsides, 299 people will have died in the city alone. Years later, I'll read about how traumatic the year was for Hong Kongers, but during those months all I can think about is how deceptively peaceful it feels, being away from my defeating school life. How I've become acquainted with the scent of my own breath from inside the mask, the thin strip of metal that rests gently on the bridge of my nose, the cool gel of the hand sanitizers that have been installed in malls, restaurants, and schools. My grandmother doesn't seem worried about it, even though she is perhaps most at risk out of everyone in the family, so I take it as a sign that I shouldn't be, either; it never occurs to me that she is faking it for my sake. I won't cry about SARS until it has all ended, when I see the 2004 film *The Miracle Box,* a fictionalized account of Dr. Joanna Tse Yuen Man, a woman we would later call "Hong Kong's daughter." Her husband, also a doctor, passed away from cancer before SARS began, and Tse volunteered to serve in the SARS ward. She died in May 2003, only thirty-five.

*SARS was a blur,* I'll say to a friend over a lunch of French toast in 2019, after the first wave of the Covid-19 pandemic has been temporarily contained in Hong Kong. *If I had been older back then, like I am now, I suppose it would have been a lot scarier.* My friend stabs the butter-drenched bread. *It was different for me,* they say. *My parents worked in the hospital, so every day was a lottery—whether they'd come home safe or sick.* I wanted the world to stop for me, but it was only because I thought nothing touched me. I thought about my childhood prayers for typhoons and school suspensions, how the world began and ended with my naïve desires to escape life. In my father's typhoon stories, he never once mentions that despite his childhood poverty, our family never had to live in a flat where the water would rise above our ankles, where he would break his skin picking up pieces of glass after the wind smashed the windows.

SARS is still wafting through the city when another tragedy strikes that year, one that my father would never get over: In April 2003, Leslie Cheung Kwok Wing dies by suicide.

I heard Leslie's voice long before I knew what he looked like. In the eighteen years that I lived with my father, he would play Leslie's songs on his bespoke home audio system with such a feverish dedication that still now, I could sing along to his songs《風繼續吹》and《無心睡眠》and《有誰共鳴》. To the diaspora, he was the star of Wong Kar Wai's films, playing a terrible lover or a rascal bird with no legs, destined to fly until he ran out of breath in death. Leslie Cheung was part of a cast of actors in the eighties and nineties film industry in Hong Kong—but no one, not the four male Cantopop stars dubbed the Four Heavenly Kings, or even his sometimes co-star Tony Leung, burned as bright as Leslie did, or was as beloved.

Leslie Cheung, nicknamed Gor Gor by Hong Kongers, was the youngest of ten children. He studied at Leeds, then joined the entertainment industry after placing second at an Asian music contest, singing "American Pie" in a cowboy outfit. His idols were Cantonese opera stars Pak Suet Sin and Yam Kim Fai, one of the earliest androgynous public figures in Hong Kong. Leslie was bisexual and flirted with gender conventions at a time when attitudes in Hong Kong toward queer folks were even more conservative; along with fellow megastars Roman Tam and Anita Mui, Leslie opened up a realm of possibilities for gender-fluid performances.

When I saw him on the screen for the first time, I became obsessed with the elegance with which he moved, his bad-boy good looks, dark eyes that betray sorrow. At home, my father had DVD and Blu-ray copies of every film that starred Leslie, including *Happy Together, Days of Being Wild,* and *Ashes of Time* by Wong Kar Wai, as well as *Rouge* and *Farewell My Concubine.* After Leslie falls from the twenty-fourth floor of the Mandarin Oriental hotel, my father puts his albums on repeat till three in the morning while gazing at a shot of Leslie in the 1987 martial arts–romance film *A Chinese Ghost Story* on the screen, forever frozen. Our living room becomes a Leslie shrine in the form of a dark room shrouded in ghostly television light and loud music.

My aunt, a devout Buddhist, has more practical concerns. She goes to a monastery in Hung Shui Kiu in Yuen Long, and every month I tag along, because I have no other week-end plans; an afternoon of being on my knees, chanting in-cantations, high on incense. At a vegetarian teahouse with slimy laminated menus and stale chili sauce, she and her friends discuss the next steps over pu'er and char siu made of soy. Brenda, my aunt's oldest friend, suggests putting together a 法事, a funeral ritual, to usher Leslie into the next stage of reincarnation. *Otherwise, he'll be stuck in hell for all of eternity, forced to relive his suicide over and over again.*

My favorite film of Leslie's, possibly my favorite film of all time, is *Farewell My Concubine,* which still hurts if I think about it too hard, even years after I first saw it. An epic that spans decades of Chinese history from the 1920s to just after the Cultural Revolution, it is told through the lives of two

Peking Opera stars, aching with frustrated desire and the fu-
tility of individual ambitions against the grand course of history. Cheung's character pines after his big-brother figure, a
love that can never be reciprocated. It is the only Chinese-
language film to win the Palme d'Or at Cannes, and Leslie
earned a best actor nomination.

In 1990, when he was thirty-three years old, Leslie briefly
moved to Vancouver. In 1997, he said, *I had believed that Canada was a heaven, and I only realized when I got there that it
wasn't; the real heaven is Hong Kong.* Even though he had fans
across the continent, Leslie still struggled to find out where
he belonged. Leslie, with his gender-neutral name, exquisite
feminine features, and tenderness and nobility, never fit in
with the mainstream Hong Kong society, much less the mold
of the entertainment business at the time.

As Hong Kong is still coming to terms with SARS, Leslie
passes away. He leaves behind a suicide note that reveals his
struggle with depression, and a heartbroken boyfriend, Mr.
Tong. Leslie's fans ignore the SARS travel warning in Hong
Kong and fly to the city from all over Asia to pay their respects; even today, on the anniversary of his death, they
gather outside the Mandarin Oriental every year for a vigil.

After April 1, 2003, Hong Kong was no longer the same.
The poet, critic, and lifelong fan Lok Fung calls it a new era:
Leslie Cheung became a totem of the city, a marker of time,
a cultural phenomenon. Because Leslie never truly left us:
He's on that old film poster at the spicy noodle joint in Tai
Hang; he's singing to your minibus driver when you're flying
across the harbor at three in the morning. He's in a Peking
Opera huadan costume in the last scene of *Farewell My Con-
cubine,* his headpiece glinting underneath the blue stage
lights. *I am by nature a boy, not a girl,* Leslie's character Xiao-

douzi says; his bejeweled hand slowly draws a sword and he falls, off camera, with a thud. And then here: Leslie and Anita Mui in *Rouge,* feeding each other a spoonful of opium in a suicide pact, with a grace that eludes my generation, beautiful yet already spectral. (Anita, too, would pass away just before the last day of 2003.) Leslie in a black see-through shirt and a white skirt, gliding across the stage with his hair in a bun, reprising his "American Pie" performance, three years before his death.

My father in a white undershirt, slumped over on the couch at three in the morning, his eyes closed, as Gor Gor's velvet tones echo through the living room: *The breeze is crisp / I ask the stars against the dark sky / In the stillness of the night / Is anyone here with me?*

In the midst of SARS, chief executive Tung Chee Hwa's wife, Betty, visits a housing estate at Ngau Tau Kok, wearing many layers of plastic and a shower cap. It is supposedly a gesture of goodwill, but she is quickly made into a meme, a symbol of how detached members of our ruling class are from the common people. *Remember remember remember wash your hands wash your hands wash your hands,* she says during the visit. We double down on boiling vinegar, which is said to ward off the respiratory disease.

In early 2003, the Hong Kong government proposed a national security bill that would punish sedition, treason, subversion, and secession. The stipulation for the legislation of such a law was written into the "constitutional document" that governs Hong Kong after the handover, the Basic Law.

Colloquially, this bill was known as "Article 23." But, six years later, it has yet to be legislated, because of fear among the people that it would spell the end of our freedoms. What is considered secession or subversion? The crimes cover a wide spectrum, from writing a piece that criticizes the Communist Party's rule to actively plotting an assassination. Where is the arbitrary line where something becomes illegal? That uncertainty is the fear.

After the handover in 1997, my father had secured Singapore passports for the four of us as my mother began her move there. My father did not trust the Communist Party, their history of silencing dissenters and murdering their own people during the Cultural Revolution and the Tiananmen Massacre; like most middle-class Hong Kongers, he wanted a second option for his family, a country they could flee to at the first sign of danger. I never found out why they decided on Singapore. When I asked, my father said something vague about how we'd never have to apply for visas if we ever wanted to visit the States, but to this day I'm the only one who's ever gone to America on holiday, exactly once. Singapore is compared so often to Hong Kong that it's become a joke: strong economy, latent authoritarianism.

My father's life, which revolved around his business and being cared for by my grandmother, was too entrenched here for him to seriously consider moving. We stayed in Hong Kong. But now, the law renews fears in my father. If the national security bill passes, it could radically alter life in Hong Kong as we know it.

On July 1, 2003, the sixth anniversary of the handover, after the flags are raised and "March of the Volunteers" is sung, half a million people take to the streets. They hold "Down with Tung Chee Hwa, No Article 23" signs, wearing visors that would soon go out of fashion. Filling the football pitches at Victoria Park in Causeway Bay, they march past the banks and mango dessert shops and Wedding Card Street, past the strip clubs and law courts, to the government offices in Central. A black banner reads: "PEOPLE POWER." The MTR stations are so packed that protesters can jump over turnstiles. The police stand by in green uniforms, watching the crowd intently. It would be the largest turnout at a demonstration since the handover, codifying marches and protests into the Hong Kong culture.

By September, the bill is withdrawn. There is no timetable for reintroducing it. After the march, Tung Chee Hwa says: *It's easy to leave; it takes much more courage to stay.* Within a short while, he resigns anyway.

My family reads multiple newspapers before noon, but insists that protesting is something you do when you have too much time on your hands: 班人食飽飯無野做. They remain confident that if the people are against it, the government could not possibly go through with it; confident that we would have the freedom to protest, that no one would be arrested or beaten for simply being there. The alternative is so much easier. We stay inside and romanticize the scenes outside our windows. We watch Leslie's films and listen to Anita's songs. We could listen to political debates blare from our speakers, and wait for the world to fix itself.

No one in my family takes me to any rallies or marches, and I am seventeen before I finally take myself to one. But for a decade, the *Apple Daily* front page of the 2003 protests would sit on top of the pile of my father's old audio magazines—a street swamped with little blobs of tiny human heads like flecks of paint on a canvas. When the Communist Party reintroduces the law in 2020, the balance has already tipped so far in their favor that protests cannot stop the crackdown. But still, I remember the half million people who bought me seventeen years of freedom and delayed the inevitable. They made it possible for me to grow up in an environment without fear. It would have been much easier to leave, but they stayed. They marched. And because of them, once upon a time, we were fearless.

# Twenty-two Roommates

有時候，當她住進一所房子，甚至沒有打算把隨身物件全數從皮箱中取出。「家是什麼？」年幼的她曾經這樣問母親。「一種永恆親密的關係。」
—— 韓麗珠，《回家》

In To Kwa Wan, the flat of my childhood has floor-to-ceiling windows that look out onto a slope lightly dressed with trees, across from a primary school whose morning bells start chiming during the blue hour of twilight. I tiptoe across the shiny wooden plank floors, careful not to provoke the wall of albums always on the verge of toppling over my small body. My grandmother sleeps soundly next to me on a pullout bed, oblivious to the loud music my father plays late into the night; my room's window faces inward into other apartment blocks, a grid of miniature human life in each. I don't go to sleep until the lights from all the other apartments are extinguished.

There is another flat just five minutes away where my aunt lives, in a walk-up tong lau that smells of incense and is cloaked in a dampness that never leaves its dark staircases. It is the ancestral apartment that has been with my family for five decades. I am here every day during the time after school till before bed, because it is where my father is not. In the dreams that I still have, I walk through the streets of the old To Kwa Wan neighborhood, past the rotten alleys and Bar Pacifics and low-rises, trying to find my way home.

Then there is another flat in Western District across the harbor, then another, and another, until I lose count. These are the spaces I inhabit after I move out at eighteen. I sleep on bunk beds and couches in flat shares and dorms run by unscrupulous landlords. Over the course of six years, I and a rotating cast of twenty-two roommates stay in tenement buildings near our university, old private housing blocks just behind a protest hotspot, cramped dorms next to an old man with a hacking cough.

*You're crazy,* my secondary school friends say when they show up at my door year after year to help me carry boxes. Young people in Hong Kong don't tend to move out, and if they do during their university years, they move back with their family when they start working. Flats are tiny and not rent-controlled. *You'll never save any money,* they tell me. But I know if I stayed with my family, I would soon kill some-one, probably myself. I was tired of my father's temper tan-trums and verbal abuse, of begging him to turn down the music at three in the morning so that I could sleep.

Two weeks after the first day of university, Kit's parents pull up to Farm Road and I pack books, summer dresses and winter coats, and a couple of CDs, into the trunk of their car. I'd met Kit at an ecology summer camp just a couple of months earlier, and we became fast friends, bonding over our mutual love for Tumblr fandoms and fan fiction. She is a year older than me and calls me *honey,* like one of those white

suburban moms I see on television. Kit lives in an idyllic village house in Sai Kung, but she wants independence, adventure. We find out we will both be attending the University
of Hong Kong in the fall. *Let's move in together, let's move in
together,* we say.

My grandmother stands at the entrance of our apartment
block, looking devastated. She thinks it's because she failed
to save me. *I'll be back every weekend to see you,* I promise. *I'll
be back to save you and move us both out of here once I graduate,*
but I don't say that part out loud. I watch her hunched body
grow even smaller as we drive away.

## FLAT No. 1

Kit and I find the ad for Flat No. 1 drooping from a notice
board at the only halal canteen at the University of Hong
Kong, behind tables of students singularly focused on thrust-
ing down biryani and five-inch pizzas drizzled with mint
sauce before their next lectures. "Roommate wanted in
Water Street flat, rent $2000 a month. Contact Gareth," with
a phone number attached. Kit and I have been visiting property agents and prowling the internet for ads of flat rentals we
could share with other students. This is the cheapest we've
yet found. We give Gareth a call, and schedule our visit for
later that day.

The flat is on the twelfth floor of a lime-colored building
at the intersection of Water and Second streets, one panting
slope away from the campus. Gareth is an engineering student, with a head of spiky hair streaked metallic brown, and
a heart-shaped mouth with cigarette breath. He seems surprised to see two of us—his ad said "Roommate wanted,"

singular. Kit, with her jagged bangs and skin tanned from hours of collecting biology samples under the sun, me pale and skinny and too much acne. When I converse in Cantonese my sentences are punctuated with English words, and Gareth is immediately suspicious: Everyone he's met who speaks this way is an asshole.

Technically someone's taken the spot he advertised for, he says—a girl named Eva responded a few days before us—and there are already two more guys living there, besides himself. But if we don't mind the space being cramped, he could consult with the others. We would have to try to fit six of us in the two bedrooms. With this many people splitting the rent, it'll be even cheaper, he says. We look around: The flat's a little over three hundred square feet. There are bunk beds in the two bedrooms, and Gareth says we can fit pullout beds under each bunk. The kitchen is a slim hallway that can barely accommodate two people, and I don't know how bathroom logistics would work for all six people who need to go to a 9:30 A.M. lecture. But we're desperate. Maybe we could make an adventure out of it.

The other boys are Lee, a foul-mouthed aspiring teacher, and Francis, who plays bass and wears only black. They watch Stephen Chow movies and football games till way past midnight, and chug a nightly diet of Tsingtaos and HK$60 bottles of wine. I learn how to stab a can of Campbell's soup with a knife straight down and slice through the sides in lieu of a can opener. Late at night with the lights turned off, Eva and I talk about our oppressive families. Kit and I console each other through unreciprocated crushes by watching rom-coms together. In winter I wrap myself in layers of blankets and read books for my literature degree in my lower bunk, trying to catch the little sunlight coming through the small window in our room. All of us forget our keys so often that soon we give up on locking our door altogether.

Those days, Water Street is sleepy: The restaurants in the area are rat bait, and there is one pub called Derby West. A couple of laundromats and real estate agencies, an old hair salon that gives me a terrible haircut, a dodgy game arcade, all leaning lopsided against each other on an extended slope. We raid the grocer downstairs for fresh vegetables and fruits that we then leave in the fridge and forget to eat until they've wilted and gone moldy. We briefly entertain the idea of adopting a cat after being enamored with one at Sam's Kitchen, a neighborhood diner we go to for home-cooked meals. We organize hot-pot dinners, precariously balancing the boiling broth on top of a bar-height table flaking with cheap plastic. Life in the flat is messy, but we learn to have fun, a bunch of kids role-playing adults.

During that first year, nothing fazes me. I manually collect clumps of dust and hair on all fours with Scotch tape. I smother makeup over my bad breakouts from the dirty pillowcases. When a mosquito buzzes in our ear at four in the morning, Francis comes in with an iPad. We turn the lights off and push the screen brightness up to max. *The mosquito will be attracted to the pad, and then when it lands there I can slap it with the iPad cover,* Francis says. We wait for half an hour, whispering in the dark. The mosquito never shows up and we go to bed, laughing.

Sometimes on the way home from the supermarket, my arms full of bags of canned soup and instant noodles, I feel a ridiculous happiness bubbling over, like I'm Richard Ashcroft walking down the street in "Bitter Sweet Symphony." I inhale the autumn air as hard as I can. I'm so far away from everything that could hurt me.

No one has any personal space, but we're still young enough for that to be okay. Our flat is just a place to store textbooks and sleep at night. The university is so spacious and available that it is essentially our real residence. We sit on the brown steps leading to the open plaza outside the library, surrounded by a lotus pond and white buildings blanketed with vines. We read on the benches of the Main Building, walk down the arched hallway and over the historic tiles that have been there since the writer Eileen Chang's time. In winter, I run up to campus in a hoodie and sandals to turn in my paper a minute before the deadline. We crash at the study commons so much that the crowded apartment never feels like a problem. It is just the way things are in this city.

Hong Kong has a "land problem." As the story goes, the landscape is too hilly, and there are too many of us. Our buildings are getting so tall that they plunge into the sky; almost eight thousand of them are over 115 feet high. Still, the average dwelling of a Hong Konger does not exceed two hundred square feet per capita. Nearly half of the city's flats cost HK$20,000 or above to rent. The government and the media tell us that all other problems in Hong Kong can be attributed to our land problem. Young people have no room to have sex because we have a land problem. Pink dolphins are disappearing from our waters because of land reclamation, which we're doing only because of our land problem. Villagers are being evicted from their ancestral lands because we need to build housing—that's also our "land problem."

Young professionals pile into microflats and co-living spaces. Entrepreneurs rent out space capsules, modeled after Japan's capsule hotel pods: an HK$5,100 "private" bed space in a room you share with ten others. My generation has given up hope of ever being able to purchase a flat. The worst of the city's living conditions are subdivided flats where the toilet bowl is adjacent to a "kitchen," and caged homes that are bed spaces made of and surrounded by barbed fences. International media even attributes Hong Kong's protests to land problems—headlines say we're frustrated from years of sleeping on bunk beds and windowless flats. "He spends half his $1,300 [over HK$10,000] monthly salary on rent. This is why he's fighting for a fairer Hong Kong," one headline says.

But it's not entirely accurate to call this a land problem. The issue isn't exactly that Hong Kong doesn't have enough land; it's that the city is controlled by tycoons. The government is the city's largest landowner as well as the sole supplier of land. It profits off selling land to property developers— a practice that began during the colonial era—which inflates the price of flats so that they remain out of reach to even middle-class families, turning the market into a speculation game for the rich elite. Now government revenue is so dependent on land-related income that the property market is too big to fail. In *Land and the Ruling Class in Hong Kong,* first published in 2005, the writer Alice Poon explains that Hong Kong's "free" and laissez-faire economy produced an anti-competition environment in which collusion between the government and the property cartel resulted in an oligarchy of developers. Hong Kong's richest and most powerful families—the "economic lords"—are property developers who have built business empires. "The reality of a draining public coffer forced the government to resign to the fact that its interests were aligned with those of the large developers, while the majority of Hong Kong people continued to suffer in a distorted social and economic structure," she writes.

The entangled relationship between the government, property owners, and public services haunts every aspect of Hong Kong life: our gas and electricity are supplied and controlled by corporate giants that were initially property developers. The government is also the largest shareholder of the public railway company, which makes half of its money from property development. When the government sells the rights to manage the neighborhood malls and wet markets near public housing estates to real estate fund Link REIT, rent prices immediately skyrocket and family-run shops disappear, replaced instead by chain stores that erase the local character. Under the legal framework established in 1997, while ordinary residents are deprived of the right to vote for the leader of our city, "property tycoons and their close associates" in banking and legal fields, as Poon notes, occupy seats on the small election committee that chooses the leader. (The inability of Hong Kong people to vote democratically for the leader of the city is what triggered the 2014 protests.) The government has long been known to be cozy with developers, sometimes even unethically and illegally so.

In the late 2000s, a new wave of left-leaning political activism ushered the term *land hegemony* into popular usage, and for a while it remained one of the rallying calls at protests. This was especially prominent among the "post-'80s" group of activists, young people born after 1980 who are "aware of the property oligarchy's monopolizing land and other economic resources and all the unfairness associated with it, and they are determined to fight back," Poon notes. Unlike previous generations, which were concerned with upward mobility and material wealth, these young activists cared about "anti-market fundamentalism, anti-materialism, pro-social justice, pro-humanity, pro-environment and pro-heritage conservation." By the late 2010s, the concept of land hegemony is so deeply ingrained that people don't even bother shouting it at protests anymore.

Public awareness is also continually raised through non-profit research organizations like the Liber Research Community, which often present data to debunk the government's narrative that it is left with no choice but to build artificial islands in our Lantau waters to increase land supply (as was laid out in the chief executive's policy plans in 2018), destroy parks with high ecological value, or take land from rural villages and farms. Even though the government has launched one massive development plan after another over the past two decades, the living conditions in Hong Kong have not improved. Through its work and research, the group hopes to "smash the myth that 'Hong Kong has a huge population on very scarce land'" and prove that "the land problem in Hong Kong is caused by uneven distribution instead of inadequate supply."

When I was in secondary school, my classmates spoke about how they would apply for public housing the minute they turn eighteen. Under the Home Ownership Scheme 居屋, the government sells housing units to the general public at a 30 to 40 percent discount rate; such flats are so scarce that when applications for these flats open, some Hong Kongers start lining up at three in the morning for a form, and just before the deadline there will always be some poor sap sprinting to the office like their life depended on it. It's widely referred to as 「抽居屋」—抽 roughly translated as "draw," as though it's a lottery or lucky draw. Including public rental housing, which is rented to low-income families at a subsidized rate, a total of 45 percent of Hong Kong residents currently live in public housing.

For the many waiting for the government to allocate them public housing, the only option may be subdivided flats—apartments that have been illegally divided into multiple residences, against land regulations. When fires break out in these densely populated rooms, they often result in fatalities. Places that are away from the city center offer bigger spaces for lower rents, but the commute costs time and money. Even young professionals and university graduates are unable to find places they can afford; I was twenty-five years old when I finally had my own room for the first time in my life. Everywhere we look in Hong Kong, we're confronted with the impossibilities of trying to make a home in a city where the game is rigged.

During the 2019 protests, an image of graffiti at the side of a road, originally a rap lyric by TXMIYAMA, goes viral: *7K for a house like a cell and you really think that we out here are scared of jail?*

## FLATS NO. 2 AND NO. 3

After a year in Flat No. 1, four of us from the original Water Street crew, including Kit and me, move into Flat No. 2—a high-rise on North Street in Kennedy Town with a view of the sea. We find new flatmates and stick to our three-people-a-bunk arrangement. Our building is five minutes away from the Praya, where students smoke and old men fish. Kennedy Town is on the western end of Hong Kong Island; the buildings gradually disappear to the west as the land turns the corner into the sea. The neighborhood is still quiet before the arrival of the train, and shop cats yawn and stretch on the tiled floors of old pharmacies. Like all of Hong Kong, the terrain changes suddenly; slopes emerge at the end of streets when you least expect them.

It had been years since I lived so close to the water. After class I climb onto the large sill of a window that looks like a rectangular hole in the wall. I stare out at the flickering buildings across the harbor or the nautical lights on the ships, watch the sea barely ripple like a very slow movie. I read and write poetry. Gareth leaves me risotto in Tupperware boxes to reheat when I return at three in the morning after a night of law school assignments and literature papers. We constantly run out of toilet paper, even though we live one minute from a supermarket. We go out to Sun Hing, a late-night yum cha place popular with students and kaifongs. The hot custard bun explodes in my mouth, oozing yellow. We crane our necks to try to catch a glimpse of Cantopop star Eason Chan, rumored to be a regular.

But then the green mesh and scaffolding goes up, and blocks everything outside our window, including the view of the water: They're renovating the exterior of our building. Gareth and Francis move out after graduation. I try for the university residential halls again, but am rejected. I was so sure that I'd finally make the halls this year that I gave up my spot at Flat No. 2, and by the time I receive my rejection, the others in my old flat have recruited new flatmates. I realize I have nowhere to go. Kit asks if I want to stay, but I'd have to take the sofa in the living room, since they've already found two new girls for our old bunk. I close my eyes and think about my father in a white undershirt against a musical backdrop of the Stone Roses and I say, *Yes, yes, I'll take the couch.*

In my second year at Flat No. 2, my bed is a bright cherry

sofa. There are seven of us in the four-hundred-square-foot space, three in the living room alone: Kit and another flatmate are both on the floor, sleeping on two bed mattresses at two different corners, no frames. My clothes are in a makeshift closet made of foldable black cloth that dangles from a railing. Turning in my sleep proves to be impossible: My back is against a wall, and I am always on the edge of falling off my couch. Every other night, the exchange student I have a bad crush on comes over and smokes weed from a homemade bong in my kitchen.

I come home to find a load of my laundry, still wet, dumped onto my sofa "bed" and soaking into my blanket, because someone needed to wash her own clothes. Another flatmate brings home guys late at night, and wakes everyone up with loud, high-pitched moans. The next morning she denies everything, and says with a straight face that we can't possibly have heard what we say we did, because she's still a virgin. When our lease is up, I am relieved to never have to see some of them ever again.

That summer, I crash with any friend who will take me. First I sleep on a sofa at my friend Lo's flat in Tsim Sha Tsui, where her cat sits on my face in the dead of the night. Then I'm on a mattress on the floor of another classmate's flat in Sai Ying Pun, watching a sky bruised with sunsets from the window, eating dinner out of Styrofoam boxes. My belongings are in two red-white-and-blue bags, stashed in a room at a public housing estate where an ex-flatmate is squatting. I feel like Greta Gerwig in *Frances Ha,* moving from one friend's place to another; undateable and not-a-real-person-yet, but without the cute suburban family to take me back in when I've run out of options.

And then, thank fuck, Flat No. 3: A university dorm up

Lung Wah Street in Kennedy Town finally gives me a bed for a month, because there are enough vacancies in the summer. It is the only time I stay in a university residence for the six years I am in school. I debated telling my dorm administrators about my father for a spot, and maybe there isn't much to tell anyway; he never once hit me. But school dorms operate like fraternities, and fellow students make the decisions for offering bed spaces. I am not rich enough for the elite halls, athletic enough to join a hall sports team, or pretty enough for the seniors who preyed on the freshmen girls. A fellow law student volunteering at the legal clinic later tells me that the university has refused to offer her permanent lodging even after she confessed to being physically abused by her mother at home. Instead, she moves from one dorm to another every semester because they continuously kick her out for not "contributing" enough to student life. She reapplies for a new dorm whenever that happens, explaining her story all over again.

By this third year, I'm exhausted from the endless choreography of packing up everything I own into bags, dragging my belongings up staircases or into elevators. *Surely moving back home can't be worse than this,* they say. The problem is, I'm not sure I know where home is anymore. Maybe it's the place where someone remembers to leave me a plate of cold risotto on the table.

When I first learned English in kindergarten, the teacher taught us ways to describe where we live. *My house has a kitchen, two bedrooms, and a living room,* she says. The worksheet she hands out orders: *Describe your house.* But I've never lived in a house, and at the time I don't think I've even seen one before. Still, we say *house* because that's the universally accepted standard for a residence. I continue to use it interchangeably with *home* until I am older and realize you can't pass off a tiny apartment in a tall building with a term as grandiose as *house.*

When my friends and I text we have our own language, a mixture of Cantonese and English and internet lingo and typos and everything else. *I am homed,* a friend tells me after a night out, to let me know they've gotten back safe. *Homed.* As if home is standing at the door begging you to come back indoors as rain runs down the bridge of your nose. And just like that you're back again, letting the four walls cage you in, like you've returned against your will but you couldn't quite help yourself.

To have a place you not only need not run away from, but can feel secure in—no leaky toilets, no abusive family members, no unstable political situation—some of us go through our lives without ever knowing what this feels like. A home is the only space that aspires to be a constant. But a home is also a space that always represents everything we can be, and because of this, *the perfect home* is an insatiable thirst. Buoyed by a façade of stability, you start accumulating things. The strategically placed bookshelf in your study behind you during online meetings as a nod to your intellect. The scented candles and artwork on the wall that guests compliment you on at dinner parties. A portrait of a smiling family casually sitting on top of the piano, to flaunt domestic bliss. The instruments and amps scattered across a carpeted floor, a cabinet full of jazz records. You want to leave your past behind, a decade of putting roses in a beer can in lieu of a vase. You want an ever-expanding place that deserves these things. But what if you live in a city where there was never any space for this to begin with, where permanence can never be promised?

Among Hong Kong's most recognizable façades is Choi Hung Estate 彩虹邨 in Kowloon, one of the many heavily subsidized public housing rental residences known as 公屋. *Choi hung* means "rainbow" in Cantonese, and the exteriors of the building blocks are painted in various shades of pastels. Every day the walls draw flocks of photographers and tourists, setting up tripods at the estate's basketball court for a shot that would rack up the Instagram likes.

"There was a Korean TV show that brought some pop stars over to the basketball court, and they were shocked and disappointed when they actually got there," says Jimmy Ho. "You have to edit your photo and turn up the contrast to a hundred in order to see a rainbow. . . . In reality the colors are all grayed."

Jimmy Ho is twenty-eight years old, and has lived in Choi Hung Estate all his life. We were secondary school classmates, and I've known him since we were twelve. He studied journalism at Hong Kong Shue Yan University, and now works at the Hospital Authority. One afternoon when we were teenagers, the two of us and some classmates bought chips and an HK$20 CD of the 2007 horror-comedy film *Teeth* from a supermarket in Choi Hung, and watched the movie at Jimmy's flat. In class, Jimmy brought up the fact that he lived at Choi Hung without any prompting so much that it became a running joke. It was an unofficial landmark in Hong Kong, and he wanted everyone to know he lived there.

Jimmy went to a primary school five minutes away from his building, and spent mid-autumn festivals celebrating with his neighbors on the basketball court, wielding lanterns and lighting candles. To him, Choi Hung is a self-contained fortress, impenetrable even when neighboring districts were tear-gassed in 2019, with shops that cater to every need. The old Shanghainese barber shop in the estate has stood for over twenty years, and Diamond Café has operated since the 1970s. There are manga and DVD rental shops, a liquor store, and convenience stores. It's also well connected via the train line, and the Choi Hung subway station is named after the estate itself. Jimmy says it feels like home as soon as he steps off the train. "There's no place better than here," he says.

Jimmy's father was a television repairman who came to Hong Kong from Guangzhou, and has lived in Choi Hung Estate since. He arrived in Hong Kong with just HK$50 in his pocket, and still managed to raise his family. Public housing gave them a roof over their heads; purchasing a flat was never a priority. Jimmy himself is aware of Hong Kong's fetishization of owning property as the ultimate middle-class dream, but isn't particularly interested in playing the game. "Societal opinion used to be 'I don't want people to know I live in public housing,'" he says, but now people would rather pay low rents and use the money they save on holidays.

The average waiting time for public rental housing is over five years, and the monthly income for a single-person household—meaning applicants without spouses or other elderly family members—is set at HK$12,940. Many working-class jobs, from bus driving to selling bubble milk tea, pay over this amount. To qualify for public housing, applicants are forced to lie, consider unemployment, or take day jobs. Once you're allocated housing, the government will not check your income levels for ten years, and following that, every two years. Jimmy's family pays around HK$3,400 a month, and is subjected to income checks via a self-declaration form. "You can ask your boss to not pay you these few months, or pay you by cash. Or you can quit your job and study, so you won't have an income. So many people do this, because there's no other way," Jimmy says. "It's about how 'clean' you are on paper when you see the government officer."

Jimmy still shares a bunk bed with his brother, but says he probably won't consider leaving until he has to start a family of his own. He has witnessed my moves throughout the past decade, helped me pile my belongings into boxes and take them from one small room to another, and he does not envy me. His family's two-bedroom flat has low ceilings and the walls are stained; there are no decorations save a red-gold fai chun on the gray door. But there is a small balcony from which he's seen fireworks, and Jimmy says he can't imagine living in a flat without one. "You can sit there to enjoy the sun or hang your clothes. That's something you wouldn't have in many private flats."

Choi Hung was built in the 1960s, and has since then became the "model" public housing estate in Hong Kong; its award-winning design was by Palmer and Turner, the city's oldest architectural firm. Choi Hung was such a source of pride for the Hong Kong government that when Richard Nixon was in Hong Kong in 1964, he visited the estate and played badminton with its residents; Princess Margaret also toured Choi Hung in 1966. Until ten years ago, there was no elevator; even grandmothers would have to climb the steps to reach their apartments. Its population is now aging, and in recent years more South Asian families have moved in, Jimmy says.

Public housing's connotation with low-income populations and the working class is at least in part influenced by its
portrayal in popular media, appearing in films in dim lighting, depicted as stifling spaces. *Weeds on Fire* (2016), a movie
about the first baseball team from Hong Kong to win a
league, centers around the story of Lung, who lives in the
Wo Che Estate in Shatin, a housing block formation arranged in a 井 shape, the Chinese character of a well. In one
scene, Lung's mother rides his father expressionlessly in their
public housing estate flat with Lung in the next room, and
he remarks in a voiceover: "No secret can be hidden when
you live in public housing." *Port of Call* (2015) features a
young sex worker whose family are new immigrants from
mainland China living in public housing; seeking a better
life, she begins earning money through compensated dating
and is eventually brutally murdered.

"Some people like to emphasize they climbed upward
from a place like Choi Hung Estate," Jimmy says. But in a
way, he says, growing up in public housing has taken the
pressure off him, because any move would be a positive one.
The dream is somewhere with a view of Hong Kong, where
the walls aren't so thin that he'd hear his neighbors' fights, or
Taikoo Shing, a middle-class private housing estate on Hong
Kong Island, though as he says this he's laughing a little, like
he doesn't think it is possible. In a sense, public housing has
come to represent a quintessential Hong Kong-ness, a symbol of the spirit that there is nowhere to go but up.

## FLATS NO. 4 AND NO. 5

Flat No. 4 is an HK$3,800 bunk bed space in a ninety-square-
foot room on Sands Street in Kennedy Town. I find it on a

website while I am on exchange in Glasgow and transfer the deposit without ever having seen the space, because I want to make sure I have a place to live when I'm back. The website promises the "hippest off-campus student housing that is fully furnished, absolutely convenient and affordable for students." Translation: It's a renovated tenement building run by an unscrupulous businessman who realized that he could easily take advantage of University of Hong Kong students. The landlord charges us a couple of hundred dollars each time to open our room door if we lock ourselves out.

A weekly cleaning is included in the price, and the furniture, if rudimentary, is in good condition. For some reason, there is a pop art print of Audrey Hepburn peering down at us from the wall. But there is no common area except for a roof deck shared by about thirty other tenants, so my new flatmates and I sit on the floor of the hallway when we want to hang. When we make dinner on an electric stovetop at the end of the corridor (the "kitchen") we open the front door to avoid fogging up everyone's rooms with cooking fumes. The toilet is so small that when I sit down to pee, the tip of my nose hits the door.

During these months after my return from Glasgow, depression fogs up my brain, so I don't do much except sleep or crawl to my friend Ibrahim's room to watch *Game of Thrones*. We drink so much Blue Ice beer that cans are stacked up into a tidy pyramid in the corner of his single room. This is when my mental health hits its lowest point, in the aftermath of a traumatizing breakup. I am on so many antidepressants that everyone feels like an apparition. I spend most days on my bunk bed. I end up in the psychiatric ward and take a leave of absence from law school. Ibrahim sets my suicide note on fire and makes me watch the wisps wither in the sink.

I stay at the flat for six months until Kit gets tired of my sadness and tells me she'll find us a place to move into. She goes to a property agency and signs a lease for an apartment at Kwan Yick Building at Des Voeux Road West, just across the road from Flat No. 1. She immediately befriends the property agents, two middle-aged women, and within a week she's secured all the secondhand furniture for the place and set up our internet. The road is open and wide, horizontally divided by a tram line and flanked by old apartment buildings with water-stained exteriors. One evening in Flat No. 5, as Kit's making illustrations of short-legged toads and mongooses on a drawing pad for her wildlife art Instagram, I pop the question. *Hey, Kit, you want to be my emergency contact?*

*Okay,* she says. She doesn't even look up or ask what it means. It doesn't really mean anything: If I am hospitalized again, it is still only my immediate family who will be allowed to sign me out. I can put down her name when I buy plane tickets; they'd probably call her if anything happens, but legally there is nothing she can do. Still, when she says yes, some unmoored part of me stops drifting. I've waited for this moment all my life: to have someone who promises to show up.

At Flat No. 5, Kit and I do something ridiculous, more ridiculous than sleeping on a couch in the living room: We get a dog. We pick Boonboon up from a foster home in Yuen Long, a baby mongrel born eight months ago in the hills of Lai Chi Wo, a Hakka village close to the border with Shenzhen. At that point Kit and I have assumed we'll be liv-

ing together forever. We have a color-coded dog walk schedule that determines who takes her out to the pier in the
morning and evening, but we never sign a prenup to figure
out who would get custody later. We give her everything she
wants: steaks on her birthday, hikes to the peak, an advent
calendar filled with doggy treats. In exchange, she turns the
place into a home—a place where you're always greeted at
the door by one that never fails to love you.

The flat is the largest we've lived in yet, but the living
room has only one small window that faces inward to the
other blocks in the building; natural light eludes us. Boon
sleeps in the bedroom Kit and I share—we're still bunking to
save money, and sometimes our boyfriends stay over. In the
intimacy of a seventy-square-foot room, the five of us take in
and recycle each other's breath. In the morning the sliding
*whoosh* of the trams slips its way into our dreams. We're only
a block away from the China Liaison Office, and after protests journalist friends come up to the flat to take a shower. I
am in recovery from depression, drinking at least a liter of
beer every night in a hole underneath the kitchen mantel.

In just half a decade, I've had twenty-two flatmates. Some
are still my good friends today, our bonds forged under the
forced closeness of shared flats. But I haven't had the space to
be by myself in almost a decade; I can't read two pages of a
book without being interrupted by a flatmate. I'm distant
from my parents. In 2016, I go back to law school because I
want to finish what I started, but I am miserable and have to
take out loans to pay the school fees. I have no savings and
work multiple freelance jobs to afford rent. Every evening, I
reach for the glistening can of beer and curl up there in that
tiny square tile on the floor for hours every night with earphones on, adding footnotes to my papers and thinking,

*Someday I'd like to not be a fuck-up anymore.* I don't always go to class, but at least I never miss a dog walk.

I am one year away from graduation, one year away from my fantasy of moving my grandmother into a flat where natural light would touch every corner. But that's not what happens, of course. Midway through my final year, she passes away.

Lamma is an outlying island southeast of Hong Kong Island, a twenty-five-minute ferry ride from Central Pier. A few months after my grandmother dies, I begin a tradition of escaping to Lamma every other weekend to jam and record music, to write, or to find solace from the claustrophobic city.

Alight at Yung Shue Wan, Lamma's main center of activity, and you'll find a long strip of pier where young people and retired men dangle their feet above the water, chugging beer and cursing heartily. Children walk into the Bookworm Café barefoot, leaving a small trail of muddied footprints behind them. Residents that look like they came straight out of Woodstock sell bracelets and vintage clothing on pieces of tie-dyed cloth draped across the street. *I just did ecstasy last night at a rave on the beach,* a friend says to me, yawning. In recent years more expats have moved onto the island, drawn by its airy spaces and affordable rents. But grocers still sell necessities and fruits for reasonable prices, and old mom-and-pops coexist peacefully with record stores and shops that specialize in tofu cheesecake. English is spoken everywhere on the island, but there are also villages guarded by rabid dogs that froth at the mouth, where old men with vested rural interests eye you suspiciously if you wander in too far.

In summer the island is swampy, creeping with bright insects that ooze and buzz. But you're always only ten minutes away from the beach.

In June 2020, I visited Taiwanese journalist Liu Hsiuwen's flat on Lamma Island with a couple of friends to celebrate the publication of *Aftershock,* a book of personal writing we contributed to about the anti-extradition bill protests. Hsiuwen, wearing a white T-shirt and jeans, has boyish short hair and eyes that give her an expression of earnestness. Her place is the ground floor of a village house about ten minutes from the pier, bright and spacious with plenty of houseplants and books.

Hsiuwen, who is twenty-six, grew up without a permanent home address in Taiwan, shuttling between different residences in Taichung and Miaoli after her parents' separation. When she was in secondary school, she found an advertisement for Hong Kong universities in a magazine. At the time, she didn't know much about what life was like across the straits—her only reference points were Wong Kar Wai movies and Eason Chan's songs. Nevertheless, she applied to and was accepted by the prestigious journalism program at Chinese University of Hong Kong. She didn't know if she wanted to be a journalist then, she says. She just wanted to write.

She arrived in 2012, the year student activist Joshua Wong initiated a series of protests against a controversial policy to introduce national education in Hong Kong's schools. The government ends up withdrawing its plans, a rare win for Hong Kong. But Hsiuwen struggled to keep up with protests and press conferences. "I didn't know anything, and I couldn't speak Cantonese." She speaks it fluently now, with a slight accent. In 2019, Hsiuwen cowrote a piece titled

"Where I Sleep," which opens with ten couples waiting patiently at an hourly hotel in Jordan for a room to have sex in. The idea to do a feature about housing came to her when she was living in Sham Shui Po, and the washing machine in her rental broke down. She started going to a self-service laundromat in her neighborhood, and realized that the proliferation of the businesses had to do with how most Hong Kongers do not live in apartments large enough to accommodate a washing machine.

The article is a deep dive into Hong Kong's housing policies, going into phenomena such as mini-storage spaces and nano flats. In the early 1970s, the piece notes, Hong Kong began to transition away from a manufacturing-centered economy, and the city's economic development became contingent upon the property market. That is why the government has to ensure property prices stay at a certain level, and perpetuate the land shortage mirage to benefit developers. The result is that many apartments in Hong Kong are vacant; apartments weren't for housing a family, but investment and speculation. "A government's housing policy is a good indicator of how it treats its people," Hsiuwen later tells me. In a blog that she wrote after the feature, she concludes that the whole city is one big capitalist playground, and everyone is an accomplice—in order to survive, those who are oppressed are forced to seek out ways to oppress others, she writes.

After Hsiuwen left university, she started flat-hunting in Hong Kong, but her options were limited: She was broke. Over the next few years, she moved into one nightmarish flat after another. She slept on a rolled-up bed in a living room in Yuen Long, then an apartment near Sham Shui Po on the fifth floor where the window faced the street, with exhaust fumes wafting in; her roommates were slobs and their bathroom was "dirtier than a public toilet," she recalled.

She started developing eczema and a series of other health problems at the flat. Water burst out of the toilet, seeping into the flat below. She stayed there for two years, then squatted at a public housing apartment that the uncle of a friend illegally sublet to her, against public housing regulations. "It was too many years of always being on the move. I was prepared to leave anytime; if you kicked me out the next day, I would just take my belongings and luggage," she says of that time. "I never bought anything, even books. I didn't feel like I had a life, just floating around not knowing what I was doing."

She made the move to Lamma in 2019, and now lives with an ex-colleague in a seven-hundred-square-foot apartment roomy enough for a bookshelf, with no traffic pollution or roommates she has to tidy up after. She pays HK$6,000 for her share. "Once I got here, I felt more settled," she says. She's lived on the island for over a year now. For years she resisted buying living essentials, in case she had to move at a moment's notice. Now she has an electric rice cooker, a coffee machine, a television. In the morning, she makes a cup of coffee and sits outside to write, not quite believing her luck. "Just thinking about moving again makes me shudder."

It's a couple of weeks after that contributors' gathering, and we're walking from the main street back to hers. I mentally take note of the couples clutching craft beers in plastic cups, the dogs wandering around freely, worn turquoise railings among footpaths surrounded by many shades of green. I've lived in Hong Kong all my life and yet I've never known what it's like to gaze out my windows and not see buildings towering over me, or the night sky without light pollution.

I could see why Lamma was the first place where Hsiuwen felt she could retreat from the world after a long shitty day, a place close to what home was supposed to be.

Hsiuwen has been in Hong Kong for almost ten years now. She isn't the same person who could not keep up with press conferences anymore. She won a Pulitzer Center fellowship and is currently working on a series of stories about trauma and social movements in Hong Kong. Her family is in Taiwan, but her life and all her friends—mostly other journalists—are in Hong Kong. When they are depressed from covering the news, they escape to her place on Lamma; they lounge on the beach and drink until it is time for the last ferry back to the city. "You never know what's going to happen tomorrow," Hsiuwen says.

When Hsiuwen last returned to Taiwan, her friends from school all had stable jobs and were starting to buy property and think about marriage. She felt like she was living a different life, covering Hong Kong news and moving all the time. Everyone there asked her why she hasn't moved back, given that the political situation had deteriorated so much that Hong Kongers were fleeing to Taiwan. She does not have an answer herself. It is not only out of something as grandiose as a duty to cover these turbulent times: The longer she works as a reporter, the closer she feels to Hong Kong—and the harder it is to leave. She isn't sure where home is, or even what the concept of home means. She and her Taiwanese and Chinese friends often discuss whether they can consider themselves Hong Kongers, and whether they would be accepted as such if they called themselves one.

"I truly want a place to call home, a place I can always go back to and feel safe at. But this doesn't feel possible, at a moment like this. This idea that there's a place that is 'forever' and 'unchanging'—I don't think I can find it. It's especially impossible in Hong Kong, given all the uncertainties."

I've never met a millennial who lives in a major city and who doesn't have some housing-related horror stories, stories that we trade over coffee like we're jokingly trying to one-up each other. *One time my flatmate got pregnant a month after she moved in and soon she and her newborn child and somehow also her mother took over the flat, even though I technically held the lease, and I ended up crashing with friends for a month,* I tell them. My friend Wilfred says that he slept with noise-canceling headphones and white noise every night when he lived in a place in Chinatown that was right above a bar. Another friend once had a landlord take away her staircase: *We just woke up one day and it was like, gone.* Rising rents, hell apartments, shoebox spaces: It is all part of the contemporary experience of living in cities. But in Hong Kong, there are different ways of being vulnerable outside of shuttling from flat to flat. You can be evicted even when you and your family have lived on the same piece of land for decades.

Wang Chau consists of three villages not far away from the urban areas in Yuen Long, a new town in the northwest of the New Territories. The villagers live a life unfathomable to most who grow up in urban parts of Hong Kong: gazing at stars to the croak of toads, farming their family's land, and rebuilding their houses by hand when they are torn down by typhoons. They share a bond with animals and never lock their doors. But when the government wants to reclaim their property for housing projects, their rights are not guaranteed. For years, villagers of Wang Chau have been fighting to remain on the land, the only home they know.

Wang Chau villagers are non-indigenous, meaning they have no privileges or protections when facing eviction. To this day, under what is known as the "small-house" policy, male descendants of indigenous villagers are entitled to land where they can build a three-story house subject to certain architectural restrictions. Holders of this right to build a house on precious land in Hong Kong often illegally sell them to property developers without permission, and the beneficiaries have been known to deploy triads (Chinese crime mobs) to silence those who put up a fight against the archaic policy. Non-indigenous villagers have no such rights, even if they have grown up, gotten married, and lived their whole lives in a village. The difference between whether a villager is indigenous or not depends only on whether they are members of the Chinese families that have been in recognized villages in the New Territories since 1898, under a policy adopted in the 1970s. There is also no ethnic difference between indigenous villagers and the rest of Hong Kongers, and neither were they more colonized than the rest of the Chinese population; the division was a purely arbitrary move by the British government to appease the powerful rural forces in these villages.

In 2017, villagers in Wang Chau wrote a series of letters addressed to Hong Kong's leader, Carrie Lam. A seventy-six-year-old named Mr. Wong wrote that his parents came to Yuen Long while escaping Japanese soldiers during the war, and moved to the village when they fell on hard times. They built their own house, dug a well, and reared pigs and ducks; they lived a quiet, self-sustainable life. They just wanted to spend their remaining years on earth in peace. They pleaded with the leader, asking her to reconsider tearing down the village; the government was planning to take the land and build tall public housing towers. Despite the villagers' efforts, the government moved forward with the proposal.

Three years later, my partner and I take a trip to Wang Chau, where villagers and land activists are hosting a summer festival to celebrate the jackfruit harvest, with music by Wong Hin Yan and Teenage Riot, a performance by the artist Sanmu, and a tour of the area. The jackfruit festival has been put together by activists to raise awareness of the government's plans to evict Wang Chau's villagers, and this would be the last event. Demolition of the village would begin that following week.

The jackfruit festival is at once jovial and somber. The sun has turned up the saturation on everything it touches, coating the bushes and tents in a golden light. There are tiny aquatic plants sitting in cups that people can take home. We queue up for a jackfruit tasting, the trees of which are found on Wang Chau land. Jackfruits have a hard casing that resembles a durian's with less aggressive spikes; when you crack it open you see small slivers of tangy, yellow flesh. Mrs. Auyeung is sitting on a makeshift stage, in a green T-shirt that says "No eviction, no demolition, protect our home." She tells the audience how her family has lived in the village for four generations. The tall housing blocks in the nearby Long Ping Station jut into a corner of the sky.

"We're being scammed, that's what's happening," one villager says later during an interview with the media. "I'm so damn angry." She is in tears. Another says, "We can't afford to buy a flat. A three-hundred-square-foot flat is around five million."

Villagers who have faced such fates include residents of Choi Yuen Village, which was demolished for a Hong Kong–China high-speed rail; three northeast New Territories villages that were the subject of protests in 2014; and now, Wang Chau. The activism surrounding Choi Yuen Village in 2008 was instrumental in prompting Hong Kongers to seriously consider for the first time the meaning of the right to home, and the right for rural life to exist alongside the bustling cityscapes of Hong Kong.

In the case of Choi Yuen, the government moved the entire village elsewhere, to a new piece of land in Hong Kong where villagers could rebuild their homes. Wang Chau is a different story. The villagers are asking only for fair compensation, and to be relocated to a piece of land. The government tells the villagers they could apply for public housing, but most of them are retirees and do not meet the means test. The compensation they receive is well below market rate for the property. In Hong Kong's quest for "development," the affected communities and residents always end up becoming sacrificial lambs. Their land is not their own, even when it is the only land they have known.

Unfurled across the stage at the jackfruit festival was a large scroll made of a patchwork quilt, sewn with the words: 何處是吾家, "Where is my home?"

## FLAT No. 6

Flat No. 6 is a cul-de-sac in Po Hing Fong, Sheung Wan. The surrounding Tai Ping Shan Street was the worst-hit area during the 1894 plague and subsequently demolished and rebuilt. The first time I pull up to my street for a flat visit, the taxi driver tells me that he has always loved Tai Ping Shan. *My wife wouldn't let us move here, though. She doesn't like the coffin shops!* I feel a wave of recognition: I'd been there as a teenager, when my school made us walk the "Sun Yat-sen

Historical Trail," a series of checkpoints that details the history of Sun, the Chinese revolutionary father. The street was the site of a reception center of Tong Meng Hui, the anti-Qing group.

Po Hing Fong is a secluded street in an otherwise busy neighborhood, surrounded by steps and historical buildings. I'm paying HK$6,000 for my share of the rent, a steal for a gentrified street that's only a five-minute walk away from the art library I've been working at for three years. My apartment faces a stoic banyan tree, with draping aerial roots, that guards me from storms and draws morning birds that chatter and flutter. I'm on the fourth floor, and every sound is echoed and magnified. French and American expats partying down on the balcony at one A.M.; parents sending their children off to the primary school down the road while I'm still in bed; teenagers who go *Wooooh!* whenever they score a goal at the courts downstairs; the rubbish truck that pulls into the street at two A.M.

Down the road is Mount Zero Books, a tiny, homely bookshop that stocks local authors and art books, and hosts mini-concerts and readings. On social media, I mention in passing that I was looking for Lee Chi Leung's book. *I have something for you!* the bookstore owner tells me in a message. When I'm at the bookshop, the shopkeeper hands me the book. *This is for you. No, no, don't pay—it's a gift!* The book comes with a note that tells me to gaa yau.

Another downhill slope, and we're back in the main streets of Sheung Wan, the clanking of workers unloading crates of goods from trucks on narrow streets as sweat grazes their cheeks. Blankets and Chinese sausages lie under the sun on lazier streets. The alleys reek of dried fish, bitter herbs, and cooking smoke that sprays out in bursts.

In the summer of 2019, after my flatmate moves out, I can't afford this three-hundred-square-foot place on my own anymore. I Airbnb out the spare room, and during lunch breaks I run home from work to change the sheets for my next visitors, and then dash back to the office. One of the guests gives me bedbugs. An exterminator costs too much, so my partner buys a steam cleaner and for a week we blast every corner of our bed and carpet with hot air, tearing open seams to check for eggs.

In the meantime, I interview flatmates. I let them inspect and pass judgment on every nook and cranny: the water-proof floor stickers I ordered from Taobao and painstakingly cut, measured, and pasted strip by strip onto my bathroom floor to hide the embarrassing decade-old water stains; the single hotplate on a block of cement protruding out of my kitchen wall I described as a mantel; the floral curtains that haven't been washed in over a year. My empty wine bottles stashed into a corner of a room, my antidepressants safely tucked away, my favorite albums on prominent display on the shelf.

But none of them want to live with me in this flat. *Too small,* they say. *Toilet too old. Air-con too loud. Too far from the train station.* After they leave, I sink onto the carpet in silence, looking at the walls my partner and I spent hours repainting, wondering what the problem is. The flat's the only thing I have and is good enough for me, but it isn't enough for anyone else.

To this day, I've never fully kicked the habit of scrolling through flat rental listings on Facebook groups. I am always looking for the next place to move to. Recently I found an entry on the HONG KONG RENT group that says "[Mid-sized Room] for 5,000 HKD monthly or glamping in the living room for 3,000 HKD monthly." Posted with this are blurry photos of a silver tent surrounded by fairy lights, pitched on a living room floor. During the pandemic, *The Wall Street Journal* interviews a white family working from home in their 1,100-square-foot flat in Hong Kong, described in the subtitle as a "small apartment." The father is sitting with his laptop on their balcony, taking work calls and answering emails, as their three kids study at home during the school suspension. Hong Kong Twitter was amused: *They think this is bad?*

Here is how you can document twenty-two flatmates and six residences in five years instead: Count the frequencies of orgasms from the sounds seeping from under the door. Keep spreadsheets of bus routes, door codes, names of the security guards. Stock up on paint to fill the gaps left by Blu-Tacked photographs. Put the number of the moving company on speed dial. Tape love notes to future tenants to the ceiling. Take Polaroids of each ash-stained smoking corner. Then you can move on, again.

Sometimes when I walk past the real estate agencies that are on every street in every neighborhood in Hong Kong, I stop and read all the property ads on the window fronts, enthralled. I imagine the flats I could have lived in if I'd just sucked it up and become a lawyer after graduation, instead of working in media and nonprofits. Studios with a terrace large enough for barbeques and yoga; private blocks with gyms and swimming pools; lavish apartments in the Mid-Levels that are accessible only if you have a car. Everyone in my generation is obsessed with owning a flat, even though it's impossible. We organize our entire lives around mortgage payments, if we have parents to help us get that far in the first place. Having a flat is the definition of having "made it." The Lion Rock spirit in the 1970s told us that if we put our heads down and worked hard we'd persevere and succeed, and my generation continues to cling to this lie even as capitalism and government collusion with the economic lords wring us dry.

I've been told by property agents and boomers and rich kids that renting is stupid, because you're giving money to someone else, whereas if you save for a down payment up-front and put *just a little more* than the monthly rent you're already paying into the mortgage, you're basically paying rent to yourself. I understand how this works in principle; I just don't know where that down payment or that *little more* would come from. Since graduation, I've been earning monthly salaries between HK$12,000 and $24,000. I'm still paying off my student loans for my law degree. But my finances are a result of the career paths I chose to take, so I suppose it's pretty much my fault.

A 395-square-foot two-bedroom apartment in the thirty-year-old middle-class private estate of City One Shatin, for instance, is going for HK$5.3 million. The agent on duty tells me that down payments in Hong Kong are a minimum of 10 percent, so that is HK$530,000 I do not have. On top of that there's also stamp duties and agency fees totaling to HK$752,000. Monthly mortgage payments for the apartment are listed as HK$19,790 a month, which is almost the entirety of my salary. If I don't eat or take transport or breathe or exist, and put all of my income into repaying the mortgage, it'd still take me twenty years to officially own the flat.

When my partner and I first started dating, we had a fight about buying property in Hong Kong. I want to own a flat one day, I said. He told me that it didn't make any sense to spend so much money and break our backs just to have a roof over our heads. *You don't know what it's like to have to move every year,* I yelled. *You have a nice room at your parents' and you never have to worry about anything.*

As I pull away from the window now, I know he was right. Our argument was stupidly hypothetical. I could never afford it. We may not even be in Hong Kong in a decade's time, given the political situation. My mistake had been to believe this was something I could logically plan for. But our land does not belong to us, and neither do our futures.

I wish I could tell you that the real estate market has finally wavered in Hong Kong and that I am now able to afford a flat on my own, but the truth is that even in the wake of social unrest in 2019 and the pandemic a year later, the rents never dipped to reasonable levels. I am nowhere close to owning property, and I don't know if I'll ever be able to live in a place for more than five years.

What happened is that I fell in love with a boy from a nice middle-class family and we got engaged after four years together. My partner moved into Flat No. 6 with me, where we still live. After my partner and I got married, an exhausting, overly drawn-out chapter in my life closed. I may never have a permanent home, but I found a permanent flatmate to shoulder the rent with. I was rooting for a feminist, fuck-capitalism spin on the ending, but I never found one.

I'll never know what it means to have a mortgage or a sense of security in a city of impermanence. But maybe home is just how it feels on a rainy day. Like this: It's drizzling outside. A jazz record is humming. The birds are tucked away in the heart of the tree, and the mist has smudged the corners of the redbrick building visible from my window. I'm reading on the couch with you, our legs stacked on top of each other's underneath a blanket. Tomorrow, we will bicker about why the dishes are still in the sink, undone, and whose turn it is to buy toilet paper. You will groan when I bring a few more books home, tell me that the plank drilled onto the wall will collapse under the weight of these volumes. The flat is so small that we are constantly knocking over things, bumping into corners. But here—this is the only place I want to be, homed, with you.

# 2014

I'm twenty, going on twenty-one. My teenage skin has cleared up and I feel reborn, so I go a bit overboard. The boy I was crushing on has returned to UC Santa Cruz after his exchange semester in Hong Kong, just in time for some 420 festival involving kids passing around a giant joint in a forest with their school mascot, a slug. To get over him, I pick up cheap tickets to Bali for the semester break, where I party with two English girls I meet on the trip. The next day, I throw up on a junk before signing a release of liability form for scuba-diving without a license.

**Back** in Hong Kong, my friend Adi and I go out to the **drinking** neighborhood of SoHo and put cocktails on her father's credit card. We wear near-identical red dresses to a dinner party. I tell her about the musician who makes me dal, watches Wes Anderson films with me, fucks me, then lectures me about my immaturity till I am in tears. Adi bakes me a lemon cake with vanilla icing for my birthday and sends me "poems." We get wistful at midnight. *im more and more sure that being sad is what makes me happy btw,* she says to me on Snapchat.

The carefree university life that felt so liberating in those first two years is fast getting old. I'm sleeping on the couch still, and Kit has just started dating her boyfriend, so I don't see much of her anymore. I'm crying every other day, but I don't know why yet. Sometimes I dream about leaving, moving to another city and becoming a writer. But this period, the early to mid-2010s, would be the last time undergraduate students experience any sort of carefree life at all, before university campuses become collateral damage or even the first frontier of the political battles happening in the rest of Hong Kong.

In school, my classmates debate about politics on our WhatsApp chats, or over lunch when the television is showing the news—the latest legal decisions, minor scandals involving politicians, or how much they hate the Democratic Party. I don't take part in any of this. I go to the annual June 4 candlelight vigils but read the news on a need-to-know basis. I vote in the district and legislature elections, and I know whom to vote for. I take a journalism class at university, but the students and even the lecturers don't pay much attention to what is happening in Hong Kong: The international media doesn't really care about us yet. I can't tell you much about local party politics, but a year ago I followed the reelection of Barack Obama with a fevered obsession, refreshing the vote count page every three seconds on my laptop during a lecture. I'm not consciously trying to be a spectator to the rest of Hong Kong; my growing pains and I just exist in a parallel universe from my surroundings.

But something shifts in me. Maybe it's because my ex–constitutional law professor, Benny Tai, is putting together a campaign called "Occupy Central with Love and Peace," a proposed movement to force the government to confront the question of our promised democracy, and I'm curious enough to care. Tai, along with Reverend Chu Yiu Ming and Professor Chan Kin Man, are envisioning a peaceful civil disobedience movement in late 2014 to demand universal suffrage in Hong Kong. Maybe I am simply tired of my shame over feeling alienated from my city, my life of privileged detachment despite the fact that I've never lived anywhere else and have no other place I call home.

When Hong Kong was handed over to China, Beijing and London signed an agreement known as the Sino-British Joint Declaration, laying the groundwork for the one country, two systems model to guarantee the city's way of life. In our Basic Law, the legal document that governs the city and came into effect in 1997, it is stated that the chief executive of Hong Kong "shall be selected by election or through consultations held locally," with the "ultimate aim" being "universal suffrage upon nomination by a broadly representative nominating committee in accordance with democratic procedures." The short version is this: Hong Kong's supposed to be a democracy at some point.

But by the 2010s, universal suffrage still has not materialized. The people grow impatient. It has been twenty years, and we still don't get to choose our leader. We vote only in district council elections, which are advisory committees with no real political power, and legislative elections, where the election system is designed to favor pro-Beijing politicians. Beijing starts dropping hints that any potential candidate for a post would have to be patriotic to the country—in other words, their true master would not be the people, but the Communist Party.

It is June 2014, and my Canadian friend Tom is in town. Tom had stayed with Kit and me the summer earlier, and we spent rainy days watching *The Fountain* and *The Princess Bride* before he returned to Canada. Tom, Kit, and I head to Derby West on Water Street, which before it closed was one of the only drinking holes in the district. We chat about my summer job organizing gigs and writing reviews at a local music site, reminisce about the time we jumped off a cliff in Sai Kung. I ask him if he's managed to keep practicing Cantonese in Vancouver.

Earlier that month, the Chinese government released a "white paper" claiming "comprehensive jurisdiction" over Hong Kong, and reminding us that we don't actually have full autonomy. Benny Tai's Occupy Central campaign has put together an online referendum, asking Hong Kongers to choose how they'd want to elect our leader in the 2017 elections: More than 787,000 people say they hope to elect the leader through direct election. The people want the candidate to be nominated by the people, with no additional screening conditions such as that they must "love Beijing." State media has a field day, calling it a "farce."

Kit and Tom are talking over Hoegaardens, but I'm distracted by the television behind them that usually airs football matches. Right now it's tuned to TVB; the evening news cuts to footage of scenes in the Legislative Council. I haven't been following the protests against the plans to develop the land in the northeast New Territories, but I know that the government is trying to evict villagers and build housing flats in the more rural areas. The pro-democracy camp says villagers weren't properly consulted, the villagers say they don't want to be evicted from their homes, and activists say Hong Kong should recognize that non-urban lifestyles have a right to exist, too. Ng Leung Sing, the pro-government committee chair presiding over the meeting, forces a vote on the preliminary funding of the plans while the Democrats, who have been filibustering for days, are out of their seats. I suddenly notice that I'm standing up, staring at the television, teeth clenched. Where is the procedural justice that my law professors assure me we have in Hong Kong?

In a year's time, when I become a journalist, I will obsess over the individual moments of political enlightenment that belong to the activists that came so many more years before me. Some of them were chaining themselves to the Queen's Pier to prevent it from being torn down when I was still in secondary school, having class discussions about the historical sites that are considered Hong Kongers' "collective memories." The year I took my public exams, protesters pressed their heads to the ground in a prostrating walk to stop the government from demolishing the Choi Yuen Village to make way for a high-speed rail to mainland China no one asked for. I interview them for the feature stories I write, to trace those parts of the history I remember only from flickers on the television evening news, trying to understand. What was the moment that converted them from a bystander to a protester? When did they just *know* that they couldn't sit back and watch anymore?

A week after that night in 2014 at the pub with Tom and Kit, for the first time, I go to the annual July 1 march, commemorating the handover. I stand in the rain for hours with an umbrella, trapped at Victoria Park because of how slowly the crowd is moving—it is the biggest turnout in a decade. There is no "Glory to Hong Kong" for us to sing then, and so we fall back to the only songs we all know by heart: Beyond's 《海闊天空》, which was released in the 1990s. There are half-hearted choruses of "Do You Hear the People Sing?" from *Les Misérables,* which has been adopted as the unofficial anthem of the Occupy Central campaign. Soon I am drenched, trying to locate my ex-flatmate Francis, who is easy to spot because he's the tallest person I know, and his long, wavy hair is bobbing up and down in a sea of faces. My legs are giving out, thanks to my deformed hip; in the following years this pain would become familiar, synonymous with protests. After the march, Francis and I find seats at the Japanese chain eatery Yoshinoya and order individual hot pots. We leave Central before the sit-in, before the police arrest five hundred demonstrators.

In August, I leave for my exchange semester in Glasgow, Scotland. At the airport, I eat fried chicken and weep. I say goodbye to Adi, and to my then-boyfriend. We'd met at a writers' gathering, and would go on to have a turbulent, terrible relationship that was long-distance for half of its duration. I say goodbye to Hong Kong, the first and only time I'd leave the city for more than three months. It would just be a semester: It'd be over before I knew it.

On the last day of August, China issues a decision for the election of the chief executive in 2017. Everyone gets to vote, but the candidates must be nominated by more than half of a committee populated with pro-China business elites. The candidate must "love the country and love Hong Kong." Beijing pretends to discharge its constitutional duty by rigging the game. What they're saying is: We're letting all of you vote, but we get to decide who goes on the ballot. People are pissed. Benny Tai says, "Hong Kong is now entering a new era—a new era of resistance." He wants to force China's hand by organizing this occupation.

I am in Paris. My writer boyfriend and I write excruciating letters to each other every two days. I tell him about the reeking subway stations, the stained-glass windows and gargoyles of Notre-Dame, the rusting clusters of love locks along the bridge, the poetry section at Shakespeare and Company. Early in the morning, outside the Louvre, I suddenly feel lightheaded and breathless, panic climbing up my throat. I duck into a Starbucks for its familiarity in a strange land, even though I'm finally in a city of many coffee shops. I travel to London on the Eurostar, and from there I take a £20 National Express bus to Glasgow, and snap photographs of ducks in a pond with caramel shortbread in my coat pocket.

Four weeks later, the Umbrella Movement begins.

University student unions and the Joshua Wong–led Scholarism group initiate class boycotts in protest of the new election rules. They sit outside of government offices for days and then try to retake a public protest space that's been closed off. The official occupation organizers, riding on the momentum of the student protests, decide to abandon their scheduled commencement date of October 1. At around half past one in the morning on September 27, Benny Tai yells: *Occupy Central officially commences!* He says it over and over again, with a small dazed smile, like he can't quite believe it himself.

The first canister is fired at 5:57 P.M. on September 28, 2014. Orange warning flags raised: "Disperse, or we fire." My friends in Hong Kong are tear-gassed as I sit in Scottish pubs, sipping Tennent's. I put on live feeds in the library and eat vegetarian haggis while watching protesters break out the iconic umbrellas—they protect them from rain and crowd-dispersal weapons. The occupation, known as Occupy Central, earns another name: the Umbrella Movement. The tear gas is what draws out a much larger crowd of people than the organizers intended—first-time protesters, other students, formerly apolitical Hong Kongers, on-the-fence keyboard warriors, all incensed that the police are using such heavy-handed weapons for a peaceful protest. The streets of the business district on Hong Kong Island are flooded with people, and soon protesters drag tents out and build a mini-protest village right there on the roads. Hong Kong is used to its regular protest-march calendar, where there are few escalations and everyone then goes back to work as usual, but this is different. It will become the first major occupation in Hong Kong's history, and last for seventy-nine days, at times peaking at a hundred thousand protesters in the occupation zones on the streets.

The Hong Kong chief executive, Leung Chun Ying, holds a press conference, calling the movement "illegal" and "coercive." In Admiralty, just a few neighborhoods down from Western District, the dark asphalt roads are now dotted with bright colors—yellow umbrellas, navy tents, magenta booths. Glasgow's buildings are gray, brown, beige, muffled by fog. *Where are all the fireplaces?* I wonder. My exchange student friends from Italy and Spain visit the solidarity booth at the Glasgow University campus where volunteers hand out yellow ribbons, and afterward we have Italian food at Tony Macaroni, looking out onto the quiet streets of Scotland.

On a weekend, I visit the Lennon Wall in Prague and pose in front of a giant graffiti that says *Hong Kong / Prague supports you.* Thousands of miles away, in Hong Kong, my ex-flatmates sleep in the tents in Admiralty, on a mat laid across the hard pavement, and go to work the next day without a change of clothes. I write shit poems about the pastel-colored town of Kutná Hora and the grave of James Joyce's parents, taking selfies with Oscar Wilde's bust. A social worker is beaten up in a dark corner in Admiralty by seven cops. Student activist Lester Shum says, *We're the generation chosen by the times*.

At Halloween I wear a cheongsam and slit my throat with fake blood. I smoke a joint outside the hall, and later that night I puke into a sink. My dorm mates bake me sticky toffee pudding and let me watch *The Prince of Egypt* in their room when I'm homesick. My Hong Kong friends and mainland Chinese friends argue in messaging groups. *It's useless to show the party the anger,* says the mainland student. The Hong Konger says, *Given that Hong Kong is already game over* 玩完 *even whether or not Occupy Central happens, I'd rather fight (though it probably won't do anything) than sit at home and pretend that everything will be fine. You won't treat Hong Kong as your home anyway.*

I call friends who are at the occupation, demanding to know if they're all right. I Skype friends on exchange in other countries, to commiserate together. Parties and fights break out at the Mong Kok occupation site. I'm at a gig, somewhere, chanting, *Here we, here we, here we fucking go!* with other Glaswegians. I eat mince pies and go ice-skating at the city center near the Christmas market, the first time I ever see an outdoor rink. The camps and street booths and banners are cleared away by trucks. I tweet: *I miss what I never experienced* and a Smashing Pumpkins lyric, *The street heats the urgency of now; As you see there's no one around.*

When I return to Hong Kong in late December 2014, the tents at the protest site have all just been cleared.

In the span of one year, so much would end: my relationship, the exchange semester, the occupation movement. History was made, and I was not here. I spend the next five years overcompensating by showing up to every protest I can manage. The tape in my head replays the same phrase over and over: *I will never miss a thing ever again. I will never leave this city, even when it no longer exists. Never never never.*

Hong Kong doesn't remember that I didn't fight for it, because it didn't need me. It was I who needed Hong Kong. Far, far away from home, I didn't know who I was anymore. *Home is where your credit is good at the corner store,* Suketu Mehta says in *Maximum City.* My corner store in Glasgow is a Sainsbury's self-checkout counter. When I pass through customs at the Glasgow Airport, the immigration officer looks at my visa and passport, then at me. *You from Hong Kong?* Yes, I'm a Hong Konger, I say. I may not deserve this identity yet—but I don't know how to be anything else.

# Through the Fog

You have no right to be depressed
You haven't tried hard enough to like it
Haven't seen enough of this world yet
But it hurts, it hurts, it hurts, it hurts

—WILL TOLEDO (CAR SEAT HEADREST),
"FILL IN THE BLANK"

I don't remember much about those four months away from Hong Kong except in flashes—news footage of the occupation, scenes from my exchange semester that are out of time, existing alongside gaps in the narrative that cannot be recovered. My memories are foggy because this period, when my friends are protesting on the streets in Hong Kong and I'm drinking pints to keep myself warm, is when my mental health begins to fail.

It is fall of 2014. I'm crying everywhere: at a graveyard in Dublin; on the steps in a hostel in York as backpackers trip over me; in my room at the West End in Glasgow as my roommate watches *Doctor Who*. I take a bus down to London to see my writer boyfriend, who has flown over to visit me from Hong Kong. He drags me to comic book stores in Camden and I sling headphones across his dark curls at Rough Trade Records. We trek across Hampstead Heath and fall asleep that night dreaming of moors, where the moss swallows the rocks whole and the last of the autumn leaves drip from the dry branches. After we say our goodbyes, I cry on the eight-hour bus ride back. In my dorm room, I call a suicide hotline and when I can't understand what the operator is saying through her thick Glaswegian accent, I break down and hang up. *I'm homesick and I can't find the sun, but I'll be better when I'm back,* I tell myself.

But I don't get better in Hong Kong. When I return in December 2014, I cry at the Western District pier while dogs race around me, in the alcohol aisle at Marks and Spencer while doing Christmas shopping, at family dinner over my father's scowls. I grew up with parents who implied that depression indicated personal weakness, friends who said *maybe you just* think *you have depression.* When I was acting "crazy" as a kid, my father made jokes about Castle Peak Hospital, the psychiatric facility that opened in 1961 that has become synonymous with mental health. I've always used the word *depressed* liberally, but *depression* sounded foreign. My boyfriend suggests that I get professional help.

The university clinic hands me a list of external psychiatrists: names, addresses, phone numbers. I call the numbers that have an asterisk marked in pencil—*recommended*—but the receptionists are vague and say there's a range of fees. They don't tell me what that range is. I give up after a couple of tries. Instead I message a relative who has been on antidepressants for the past half-decade and ask if she knows somebody. She sends me a shaky photograph over WhatsApp of a business card with a number for Dr. Leo. *Four hundred dollars for consultation, another couple of hundred for medication,* the nurse tells me over the phone.

I push the glass doors to a crowded clinic in a commercial building in Mong Kok, on a stuffy street packed with horse-racing betting centers and jewelry stores with gaudy diamond rings. At the clinic, I spot a wavy-haired boy who looks like he's in my comparative literature class, and I look down immediately. I'm not sure what to do with my hands, which are leaking with sweat. The nurse asks for my personal details and tells me to fill in the Beck Depression Inventory questionnaire, which I've already taken on three former occasions and scored *borderline clinical depression* every time. I circle: *I have to push myself very hard to do anything. I get tired from doing almost anything. I have thoughts of killing myself, but I would not carry them out.*

Dr. Leo is in a white dress shirt and rimless glasses. *I just don't know why I keep having these crying spells. It feels like there's this huge folding screen between the world and me. I'm so restless I can't even read. I went to a gig the other day where my favorite band was playing, and I didn't even feel anything.* The rest of him fades into a misty pulp as I reach for a box of tissues. I've been here for only three minutes and he looks bored already.

Dr. Leo tells me he will prescribe me some medication. Then he's already shooing me out. His parting words to me: "努力讀書孝順父母"—"Study hard and be good to your parents."

The meds don't make me better. All they do is knock me out and erect murky walls in my head. Sometimes I feel like I'm a hologram. Instead of crying, I sleep all the time. In the hours that I'm awake, I mourn my unproductivity. I'm in the fourth year of my law and literature degree, and I'm falling asleep in classes or missing them altogether. If this continues, I'll fail out of school. In my photographs from this time, my eyelids are drooping, clawing their way toward the ground. I wake up drenched, my bed stained with cold sweat from the side effects. The condition trails me around like a cold, bleary poltergeist I can't shake.

*It's not working,* I tell my writer boyfriend. Our relationship is toxic, but neither of us wants to admit it. We are perfect victims for abusive dynamics, having been raised to believe that nobody loves us. We take turns playing abuser and abused. We make plans and he cancels at the last minute. He tells me that sometimes when he's manic, he says things he doesn't mean. I sit on a staircase somewhere and pull out my keys, then dig trenches into my arms. We make up and schedule plans for the weekend. We geek out at the Space Museum and watch immersive movies at the Omnimax overhead theater and eat Korean fusion food and walk back to his place hand in hand. Then I get upset at him about something. He tells me it's irrational for me to feel hurt, and I should know better than to get upset because that could trigger an episode in him.

At Ocean Park, next to enclosures with sleeping pandas and flapping penguins, he tells me he wants some alone time that evening, and I refuse to speak to him, crying and wearing him down until he relents. I don't know if it's that we're shitty people or that our mental health has made us shitty partners or that there just isn't room for two mental health diagnoses in this relationship. But it feels like we're standing in the dark on an armchair with wheels, constantly expecting to fall, hoping that someone catches us.

I'm desperate to cure my depression, because I want to

save what we have. We're at the apartment he shares with his brother, an expensive loft perched on a hill and overlooking the sea. The marble of the floor is so cold. My boyfriend gives me the number of his psychiatrist. An hour-long cognitive behavioral therapy session with an old man with kind eyes, at a building in Central opposite banks and offices. He hands me 150 mg of something called a cannonball, which will jolt me awake, and 45 mg of mirtazapine, an antidepressant. The bill is HK$2,000 every two weeks. My boyfriend has old family money; I'm still a student trying to become financially independent from my father. *This will just be for a couple of weeks—I won't have to keep seeing this doctor,* I think. I do get better, for a bit. Then my boyfriend and I break up.

I can tell this story only in these broadest of strokes. I cannot write about my depression and leave this out, but I know that I am a selfish writer, and selfish writers write sentences into people's mouths, smooth out creases in our history. I never ask for permission to strip myself bare before the world while unclothing the people I love or have loved. This is all I can say: In the short eight months we are together, we flail about in the dark room, arms outstretched, but we keep missing each other.

*So, here's what you need to do after I die,* I tell my friend Joe at the pier one evening, a few days after the breakup. We're at the western end of Hong Kong Island, watching the water lap against the coral tiles on the sloping concrete slab. *I'm going to write dozens of letters and you'll mail them on my behalf to my grandmother, to convince her I'm still alive.* He groans. We chug another Tsingtao.

I'm only twenty-one years old. I can't get the image of

swallowing all my antidepressants in one go out of my head. The days stretch on endlessly, like someone has broken all the clocks in the world and time altogether. I message an artist, Matthew, who is patient with me and tells me I could head to the government's mental health community center, although I should probably go to the emergency room if I need urgent help. I call my psychiatrist, the one I'm still sharing with my ex. It goes to his pager, and I ask the operator for the fifth time that weekend if she's sure he received my message. When I get hold of him for a session, I'm so paranoid I'll bump into my writer boyfriend that I forget why I'm there.

Two weeks later, my friend takes me to the public hospital in my district. I've exhausted all other options. I sit in the waiting room at the hospital for four hours, sobbing and hiccupping, before a doctor finally comes and hands me a form of voluntary admission into the psychiatric ward. Because I haven't gotten very far with my suicidal ideation, I'm still allowed a thin veneer of autonomy. The hospital I'm at is full, so they transfer me to another, one with more serious patients, although I don't know this at the time. I just nod and sit on the stretcher as they transfer me in an ambulance.

The air is damp with soft moans, the room dark and sterile like the inside of a vacuum flask. The patient next to me is convulsing, and within minutes she's strapped in a straitjacket, filling the musty room with uneven screams. Everyone is wearing hospital gowns, which are in a lifeless tartan. The two girls close to my age are a thin bespectacled teenager (anorexia), and a wheelchair-bound twenty-something with long hair that looks like it wants to braid itself into the vehicle (failed suicide attempt).

*This is my third time in hospital,* the girl in glasses says.

*Though my first at Eastern Hospital. I was previously at Queen Mary.* I ask them if they know how long people with suicidal ideation usually have to stay for. *Days, weeks, months, no one knows for sure,* she says.

The dim ward is partitioned into three sections, each with around ten beds. A nurse asks me to remove all my jewelry, even string-knit friendship bracelets I can't swallow or stab myself with. Visiting hours are between three and five P.M., and other than that I'm not allowed guests. There are strict rules for using the communal phone, from the number of times you are allowed to make a call every day to the duration of each. I tear out a piece of paper and quickly scribble down a list of numbers of all my close friends before my iPhone is taken from me. I call my friend Lam. *Maybe the quiet will do you good, baby,* she says. Lo cabs over at midnight to drop off some necessities as well as my Kindle, but that, too, is confiscated by the nurse. *Don't say I didn't warn you—the more inconsolable you behave, the longer you'll be here for,* the nurse taunts.

In the morning we take our first round of medication under the watchful eyes of the medical staff. Then the patients queue up to shower in the one shared toilet in the facility, also supervised by the nurses. From between the poorly drawn shower curtains, I can see the bodies—expanding and drooping and wilting from lack of care. I make a call to the law faculty of my school. *I'm at the psychiatric ward at Eastern Hospital—I won't be able to hand in my administrative law essay today, I'm so sorry,* I tell the staff. *Um, we'll need evidence of that in writing; otherwise we'll have to fail you,* she says. I hang up.

The daily schedule has a color block marked with activity time: handicrafts, mood management workshops, and a stroll outdoors twice a week, the only time there would be fresh air. A depressed university student or a schizophrenic middle-aged woman or a bulimic teenager or a bipolar grandmother get the same treatment, only with varying medication. At some point during the day I'm ushered into a room to listen to a PowerPoint presentation about the different types of emotions. I'm away from my friends and there are no distractions to fill the void in my head. I had imagined a mental health recovery space with comfortable rooms, open grounds, and wide windows, not an ill-lit ward with mumbling patients. It feels like I'm being punished, but for what I'm not sure.

When the hospital's psychiatrist meets me for the first time, I'm calm and composed. My eyes are still puffy but I've held it in. *You don't understand,* I say. *I have to get back out soon—it's my law exams, and if I fail I'm not going to graduate. I've just had a bad breakup and I didn't know what I was thinking. It's really important that I do all my assignments. I have two internships lined up this summer.* I'm lucid, normal, responsible. I give a fuck enough about my life and my future to worry about assignments. I'm here for depression, but I'm not *that* depressed. The doctor peers at me, then tells the nurse to summon my emergency contact—my father. She ignores me when I tell her I'm not close to my family. *It's protocol, I'm sorry.*

My father arrives in a plaid shirt and black trousers. He and the doctor speak in a cubicle for an hour. When he emerges, he doesn't say much to me. *The doctor says you can go and she'll refer you to an outpatient clinic with the public hospital,* he says. *I have to leave for an appointment.* He disappears around the corner, leaving me to make my way home on my own. I call Evelyn and Kit, and they're here within an hour. I change into fresh clothes and am pulled into an awkward hug. It's midafternoon, and the sunlight is stumbling through the windows on the train, from Chai Wan to Heng Fa Chuen and then all the way back to Western District. I've momentarily regained my freedom, either because I'm an excellent liar, or the system is very broken. Kit takes me to Ka Kee and we eat clay pot vegetables and braised tofu. She invites me to stay with her family later that month, as if daring me to stay alive till then.

On the rare trips my family and I took to amusement parks when I was a child, on packaged tours overseas where they had little choice over the itinerary, I would beg to go onto the rides. My father had a bad heart, my mother acrophobia, and my brother was just not interested. *Scaredy-cats,* I thought. At Universal Studios Japan, I asked a young Hong Kong couple to accompany me, since I wasn't allowed to be on a ride by myself unsupervised. I was eleven; I'd return to my family later, triumphant and barely winded. My father often uses this anecdote, my brother says, as an illustration that I was 大膽. It was one of the only praises I'd ever receive from him, secondhand or not, but when I finally learn about this I am more pissed than pleased. If I knew all it would take is this, I would have gone onto all the roller coasters in the continent and made sure he was watching.

The most terrifying part of a roller coaster isn't the drop. It's the slow ascent up the steep tracks, when the train goes *clang-clang-clang-clang-clang.* Roller coaster architects know this, too, because the uphill climb feels like it deliberately lasts too long; at this stage you're too committed to be able to quit, and you just want it over and done with. During that split second before the drop, there is a moment when time suddenly stretches out and your stomach drops like you've missed a step somewhere and you're worried this is maybe how death feels. Then the descent comes, and it's over before you know it. Right away you want to line up and do it again. You forget how anxious you were. If you survived it once, surely you could do it again.

Another two weeks pass, and I'm sitting on a ledge at the top of my building when the cops come. *I'd rather die than go back to that psychiatric ward!* I screech at the sky-blue uniforms. Flashbacks to scenes in a TVB television drama from my teenage years, where professional mediators negotiate with suicidal persons on a roof and persuade them to come down. While I'm distracted, a friend pulls me off. The paramedics get a hold of me and bind me onto a stretcher.

I'm back in the waiting room at Queen Mary Hospital. This time, the wait is even longer: seven hours. The first doctor tells me they'll have to admit me, because this is my second attempt and I have a prior hospital record. I'm not going back in. *I was just drunk,* I explain. *Maybe it's the combination of alcohol and meds; I'm fine I swear. I'm turning twenty-two next week. Please just let me celebrate it properly.* Joe and another friend are in the corner of the curtain-partitioned "room." *We'll watch over her twenty-four seven, we promise.*

But the doctor doesn't budge. *If you don't sign a voluntary admission form, we'll get doctors to sign it and you'll be involuntarily admitted. It'll be even harder for you to leave then.* I later learn that they believe patients are, at this stage, controlled by their illness, and cannot make a decision for themselves; doctors then have to step in with involuntary admission to protect their right to life. My aunt shows up; the hospital's called my family again. *Tell them I'll be fine, tell them I don't need to be hospitalized,* I say. *I'll do no such thing,* she says, *unless you promise never to drink and smoke ever again.* I realize I need a new emergency contact.

At seven or eight in the morning, the hospital shift ends and the staff changes over. The scary doctor is gone. Instead it's a new doctor who looks like he has no time for this. *We'll take care of her,* my friends say again. And then we're out the hospital doors.

*Can you fucking believe this?* Despite myself, I let out a little cheer, as if I hadn't just tried to kill myself twelve hours ago. It's like a jury's just pronounced me not guilty and I narrowly avoided jail. We pass out at my friend's subdivided flat and when I wake up, I take them to an all-you-can-eat steakhouse on Wyndham Street in Central.


Two months after the suicidal episode, I go on a short weekend trip to Taipei to see my friend Tom. We eat egg pancakes and stir-fry in small breakfast places or open-air night markets far from the tourist crowds. We take a train to the beach, where I swim under the sun and pee in the water. Later that month, Francis and I go to a music festival at a village in Pat Heung; we fall asleep to the music of the Taiwanese band 晨曦光廊, our tents sinking deep into the muddy fields damp with August rain.

I stay over at friends' often, let them baby me and make me dinner: steamed pomfrets, honey-braised pork ribs, lemon chicken. I work at a refugee law firm that summer, and sometimes when I feel the onset of an episode, I sneak out to smoke a cigarette in grimy alleys. But the haze in my head is thinning. Perhaps my body has finally adjusted to the right level of medication, or summer has simply arrived.

I thought my depression diagnosis would give me some clarity. I know what the beast looks like, its quirks and habits, the shape of its shadow. All I have to do is cage it up and keep it from pouncing onto unassuming strangers. But I still don't know where it came from, so I keep retracing my steps to find out what I've done wrong. Maybe it's seasonal depression—ground zero was the dim streets of Glasgow, its gravestone-gray winters and the city's refusal to adopt the December sun. Maybe it's the hormones from the birth control pills I started taking; I spent hours on medical forums and blogs, sniffing out clues from the bodies of women facing a similar predicament. Maybe it's hereditary: My aunt was suicidal in her twenties, and in my youth my grandmother once threatened to hurl herself off the five stories of our tong lau, never mind the metal window frames. My now ex–writer boyfriend had the most absurd theory: Maybe I somehow absorbed his mental health condition out of empathy.

Once my serotonin levels return to normal, and my days are no longer dictated by the whims of my mood, I am determined to do everything right this time. I would never go back on the pill. I would never live anywhere above a certain latitude, where my seasonal affective disorder could come back. I would be properly medicated. I would control my art consumption carefully, constantly on the lookout for anything that could tip me over. I can't undo my childhood, but I could learn to block it out and limit my contact with my family. I would be careful about who I loved. I would never leave my friends, who would be there to make the days easier even if they could not rescue me from myself. I could stop being empathetic. I would excel at not being 大膽. Maybe then, I would never be depressed again.

Mental health experts speak of the desire to commit suicide as impulse, an impulse that you can learn to delay. But sometimes suicide feels less like what you do than something that happens to you. On the roof, I ask someone to text my writer boyfriend; I want him to know. In therapy later, I'd learn that suicidal threats can be motivated by pure emotional blackmail or abuse, which is in line with the dynamics of our relationship. But I cannot ascertain the purity of the motives of my twenty-one-year-old self; I know that I also wanted to die.

After the suicidal episodes, I find it impossible to make plans beyond three months, because I am never sure how long I will live. My life becomes a permanent state of limbo. A year later, I have a relapse, and I take it hard. My grandmother passes away and I am working so much to pay for rent and school that I can't stop to grieve the woman who raised me. My precariously held-together life falls apart. *I did everything right,* I tell the person who is now my partner, crying on the floor of the bathroom. *I thought that meant the depression wouldn't come back.* I'm stuck in a perpetual loop of that one second before the drop, when my body has shut down and the dread is all-consuming. I don't remember that I can open my eyes at this moment and look at the world around me. I don't remember that there exists an exhilarating ride after the dreaded ascent, that there is an after, a future.

.  .  .

*Mad World* is a 2016 Hong Kong film that centers around a man with manic depression, set mostly in the claustrophic subdivided flat the protagonist Tung shares with his formerly estranged father. Tung has just been released from the Castle Peak Hospital—he was involuntarily admitted over an incident that resulted in the death of his emotionally abusive mother. *Mad World* weaves in commentary on the state of Hong Kong's mental health system with larger economic problems such as the impossibility of affordable housing and social pressures surrounding status and marriage. At his friend's wedding, Tung yells at the guests for their incessant chatter about the size of the ring and the price of the wine. *They're getting married. Can you respect that rather than talking about money money money?* The groom later leaps to his death after being affected by mass layoffs at an investment bank where he works as regional manager; the news starkly announces that this is the third suicide in Central in a month.

But Tung's erratic self-confidence is even more crushing to watch than his gloom. Tung believes that his ex-fiancé will return to him, even after he left her with a mountain of debt for buying stock warrants. She resents him for shattering her dream of "getting married at the age of twenty-nine, having the first kid at thirty"—a plan that never allowed for setbacks or falling behind schedule, because that is how everyone survives in Hong Kong. Now she's left to pay their mortgage while he sleeps on a bunk bed with his father in a tiny room. At the psychiatrist, the doctor shoos Tung out once he says he is not suicidal. The film ends with Tung and his father agreeing to move out of the subdivided unit, after their neighbors protest and call Tung crazy.

On the roof of the building, Tung's neighbor, a young

boy, asks him: *How come all our plants died?* Tung says, *Maybe this isn't the best environment for them.*

In the mid-2010s in Hong Kong, we were waking up to, on average, one new case of student suicide every ten days. The Centre for Suicide Prevention and Research at the University of Hong Kong also found that the suicide rate among full-time students between the ages of fifteen and twenty-four jumped by 76 percent between 2012 and 2016. Mental health experts and the media generally refer to "learning stress" as a cause of suicide, in a competitive city where "those who can't enter universities would be regarded as 'losers' "—but it's a gross simplification for a narrative, a desire to attribute reason where there may sometimes just be none. At the time, I was working in a newsroom, learning how to cover this issue responsibly beyond slapping a suicide hotline number beneath each piece, careful not to encourage any copycat suicides. I didn't want to speculate on what went through students' minds when they ended their lives, but it also didn't seem unfair to believe that if they'd had a better support system at home or at school, the tragedies may have been averted.

In October 2017, the social welfare sector lawmaker Shiu Ka Chun addresses Hong Kong chief executive Carrie Lam during a question-and-answer session on her policy address. "This morning at 7:55 A.M., a ten-year-old student jumped off a building in Tai Po and is currently receiving emergency treatment. It's unclear if they'll survive," he says. There's been over seventy student suicides in two years, from graduate students to primary school students; he holds up a sign with a list of the names of the deceased. These aren't just numerical statistics, but individual lives—yet all the chief executive cares about is economic development, building infrastructure to benefit businesses with vested interests, he says. "It's all about money. How much is a human life worth to you?"

"No need for such emotional language," Carrie Lam says.

The following year, I attend a media-only closed-door gathering with the city's former justice minister, Wong Yan Lung. Wong was one of the rare government officials still relatively beloved, due to his reputation for being honest and righteous, and his rags-to-riches story—he grew up in public housing, and his father was an ice cream vendor. Wong was appointed by the chief executive to head a task force that would look at mental health policies in Hong Kong, including establishing "more integral and comprehensive approaches to tackle multi-faceted mental health issues in Hong Kong." A swarm of journalists including myself pack into a restaurant near Tamar Park just behind the Legislative Council. Wong Yan Lung arrives in a suit and a plum-colored tie, his hair salt-and-pepper. He tells us that he doesn't have an announcement to make at this press gathering; he is just hoping to get to know us, and to introduce the work of the task force a little.

When he reaches my table, I ask him what he plans to do about the lack of access to mental health care in Hong Kong. Private psychiatrists cost thousands of dollars every month, an amount out of reach to working-class patients; public healthcare is overwhelmed. *Yes, I understand completely,* Wong Yan Lung says. *The task force believes in prevention over cure— we're going to advocate for early detection of mental health issues, so the system doesn't become overburdened.*

He smiles, and gets up to swap over to another table of journalists. I don't challenge him, because I know he means well. The policy of focusing on primary care is supported by research and data: Less severe mental health care cases can be dealt with by general practitioners or family doctors, rather than getting funneled to psychiatrists right away. This way waiting times would shorten for patients, and psychiatrists could spend more time with each one. But "early detection" won't save me now, or anyone else who is already in the system. I wanted to ask Wong: *But what about those of us who are already there? How are you going to help me if I don't want to be a burden anymore?*

The David Trench Rehabilitation Centre is a glossy five-story building at the end of High Street in Sai Ying Pun, just as it forks into Bonham Road. Down the street is a Baroque building locals nicknamed the "High Street Haunted House"; it was built in 1892 as the Old Mental Hospital, and was rife with urban legends about ghost sightings. I started coming to this outpatient clinic in 2015, after the hospitalization. The private psychiatry fees of over HK$2,000 every two weeks were too unsustainable. My suicide attempt has fast-tracked me in the public hospital system: I didn't have to languish for over a year with no medication while waiting to be assigned to regular outpatient care, or be forced into financial ruin by the private healthcare system I cannot afford.

I enter through the door at the South Wing, and make my way to the counter to pay the consultation fees. It's nine A.M., and the clinic just opened for the day, so there's a long queue; a framed certificate on the wall tells me that the structure won the Quality Building Award in 2012. A boy starts singing behind me in the queue, and a woman with dark purple circles under her eyes chews something that looks like a mochi, and then spits it back out into a handkerchief. Another woman with a walking aid marches around the room, yelling out that she needs to lose weight.

The patients here are well enough to avoid hospitalization, but many think aloud, as if there's a filter removed. *I'm not like them—I only have depression,* I sometimes catch myself protesting weakly. In Esmé Weijun Wang's *The Collected Schizophrenias,* she writes, "Because I am capable of achievement, I find myself uncomfortable around those who are visibly psychotic and audibly disorganized. I'm uncomfortable because I don't want to be lumped in with the screaming man on the bus, or the woman who claims that she's the reincarnation of God. I'm uncomfortably uncomfortable because I know that these are my people in ways that those who have never experienced psychosis can't understand, and to shun them is to shun a large part of myself."

I briefly fantasize about flashing arbitrary markers of success when I'm at the clinic. *Next time,* I think to myself, *I'll bring along a framed panel of my university graduation certificates.* But who am I putting on this performance for? The patients, the doctors, or everyone else? I don't have to forge a kinship with these patients, but neither do I have to set myself apart from them. Wang wrote of a hierarchy in the ward she stayed at, one that favored depressives over schizophrenia patients. It is different at outpatient clinics in Hong Kong, where hundreds of patients push through the doors every day. The nurses and hospital staff do not play favorites with faces they forget. Each of us is arbitrarily placed on different points along the normalcy–sanity spectrum, but on this morning, we are here for one reason alone: We can't afford regular private mental health care. This is the great equalizer, whatever condition we have.

I wait for the registration staff to call me to my doctor's

office. "My doctor" is a mischaracterization because over the past five years, every two appointments I've been assigned a different psychiatrist. Sometimes it's because their rotation at psychiatry has ended, and other times because they've just left the public sector altogether to make more money in the private system. I'd go into their office, they'd ask me if I felt like dying lately, and once I say *no* they'd kick me out and give me exactly the same amount of meds as last time, despite my requests for a reduction.

The waiting room at David Trench is surrounded by weary nurses, signs that warn against unauthorized recording within hospital walls, posters that remind you that sometimes medical students sit in to observe sessions, and a notice board of thank-you cards with a pink label announcing "Appreciation makes lives better" fixed on top. An hour later, I still haven't seen the doctor yet; I didn't take sick leave, so I'm due back in the office soon. It's the first shift at the clinic, but there are already around thirty other patients. I pick out a leaflet from the shelf and start reading. One pamphlet recruiting patients for a study warns that *hi fun* [doing drugs] *kill my brain,* along with bad clip art of a person with jigsaw puzzles falling out of his cartoon brain over a puddle of rainbow poison. The first question in the FAQ section of the bipolar pamphlet asks: *Why do patients overspend?*

As a "stable patient," I come and replenish my medication only three times a year. The threat of withdrawal symptoms stops me from going off antidepressants on my own, but I don't want to rely on them forever, so I never miss a doctor's visit. Given the administrative work required to fit almost three hundred thousand patients into specific time slots, the date for your next appointment is given to you months in advance and it is almost impossible to reschedule. If you're absent for your assigned slot, you either have to get to the clinic early in the morning and start lining up for one of the limited walk-in spots for the day, or you have to restart the process for entering public healthcare again—meaning waiting up to hundreds of weeks. The system is not designed for anyone who needs to keep up with all the other demands of making a living in one of the most expensive cities in the world.

My number is called, and I see a new doctor again, in blue hospital scrubs with the Chinese characters for *doctor* sewn onto it. He asks after my weight, my appetite, my sleep quality. *Do you fight with people at work? Your record says that you're on Xanax—are you a nervous person? How are your energy levels during the day?* He fires off all of these questions in rapid succession in the first two minutes, and I'm out of his room in ten. I'm back at the shroff to pay for the medication: HK$30. The consultation fee was HK$80, so in total, I pay just a little over a hundred dollars every six months. I pick up the boxes of Remeron and Xanax from the pharmacy, and head off to work. I run down the steps of Upper Station Street, stopping only for a second to stare at a butterfly with midnight wings fluttering near a red fire hydrant, oblivious to the world.

When I get a common cold or conjunctivitis or even skin infections, I head down to my neighborhood pharmacy, where the same staff pack bright capsules into small bags I can take home for less than a hundred bucks. They stand before shelves spilling with shampoos and cans of milk formula, and nod as dozens of kaifongs and regulars describe their symptoms across the narrow counters. Within seconds they reach for the right shelf and hand them the medicinal creams or eye drops they need, along with the correct change. The pharmacists and I have an easy camaraderie; when they see me, they go, "又係你啊," "Oh my god, not again, what now?," and I tell them my latest ailments, laughing. The university clinic was free for students, but my first job didn't cover medical insurance. I have not been to a private family doctor for almost a decade.

The public healthcare system in Hong Kong won't break the bank or have nurses that demand to see your insurance documents before admitting you, but waiting times for the emergency room can be up to eight hours. When I worked as a reporter in a small newsroom, I filed copy in between waiting for X-rays at Queen Mary Hospital. Being near the public hospital gives me anxiety attacks: The space reminds me of the excruciating wait behind the curtains during my suicidal episodes, begging for a doctor to tend to me soon. While the public healthcare system is known for its high quality of care and low fees, it is also notorious for its long wait times, both for emergency services and for specialist clinics and surgery. But if you can't afford private hospital fees of thousands of dollars for a night, you just have to suck it up.

This wealth gap in the healthcare system is even more prominent with mental health care, which is often unaffordable and inaccessible. Apart from the difference in the amount I was paying for every public mental health appointment versus a private psychiatrist, which is less than HK$100 versus HK$2,000, I also have no medical insurance for mental health. Half of the population is not protected by any medical insurance plan, and many health plans explicitly state that they do not cover mental health care. In the past five years,

I've experimented with all kinds of help I could afford: public psychiatrists, free counseling at university, clinical psychology with the public hospital, a social worker assigned to me who checked in every two months, and help websites. None of the appointments were frequent or lasted long enough for a tangible impact to materialize. When my government-prescribed social worker, and then my clinical psychologist, both told me they were going to "close my case" soon because I was becoming more stable, I felt dumped. *I'm not okay yet!* I wanted to scream. *I still haven't worked through my abandonment issues, or my childhood traumas, or my affinity for codependent friendships! We aren't done here!*

Even well-paid expats struggle to navigate the system here, especially since health plans that covered mental health care in their home countries may not do so in Hong Kong. "It was a ridiculous experience. I could tell the psychologist had no experience with depression," a man told CNN. He paid HK$2,500 a session. Another British expat who used to receive free care under the National Health Service self-medicated with sleeping pills and alcohol in Hong Kong, because the HK$3,000 sessions became unsustainable. He passed away from suicide at the age of thirty.

Another long-standing problem is that there just aren't enough psychiatrists. A government census found that one in seven Hong Kongers live with mental health conditions, but there are only around four hundred psychiatrists in Hong Kong for a population of over seven million people, according to the specialist registry in the Medical Council of Hong Kong. When I ask a mental health professional about this, she explains that Hong Kong is a densely populated city, meaning that despite the low number of psychiatrists, mental health care is more geographically accessible than in countries that are spread out, like America. The number also does not take into account the network of mental health care professionals outside of psychiatrists, including social workers and clinical psychologists. But the overall lack of psychiatrists still manifests into long waits for ordinary residents who cannot afford private mental health care, and short consultation times with the doctor.

At public hospitals or outpatient clinics, the current system divides patients into three tiers—urgent, semi-urgent, and stable. Whether or not an individual is "stable" is determined only by a short triage session, and conditions can deteriorate rapidly in many cases. As of this writing, the waiting time is up to 123 weeks in one district in Hong Kong; even semi-urgent cases fetch a three-to-four-week wait. On average, patients get only ten minutes during each appointment, no matter what tier they fall under.

"It's not like we only want to spend ten minutes on a patient," a doctor training to become a psychiatrist in a public hospital in Kowloon tells me. Doctors like her have to see about thirty patients in one morning, including a "new case," a patient's first visit to the clinic, which usually takes between half an hour to an hour. "There is always an indirect cost; if they give one patient more time, then another gets less, and someone else would suffer," she says.

Wouldn't the poor conditions at public psychiatry wards deter more patients from receiving help? I ask, and she shrugs. The Kowloon hospital where she worked was worse than the hospitals I've been to. But the wards can't resemble resorts, otherwise, they could be abused by people who have no intention of leaving, she says.

The doctor has few colleagues: Psychiatry has limited openings for trainees, and is not particularly popular among prospective doctors. The lack of psychiatrists in Hong Kong is emblematic of the general shortage of doctors in the public sector. The two medical schools in Hong Kong produce fewer than five hundred doctors a year. Even though trainees are required to work in public hospitals first, they can elect to go private after a few years, where they would make more money for shorter hours, leaving the public system in a perpetual state of doctor shortage.

In 2020, spending on the public hospital system was increased; however, the government stated only in a noncommittal way that it would allocate resources to provide appropriate support to people suffering from mental distress—they did not specify in their budget the amount that would be earmarked for mental health. In the meantime, beds continue to overflow into the corridors at the public hospitals, and patients check their mailboxes every day for the official slip printed with an appointment date a hundred weeks away.

Hong Kong is a pressure cooker, people here like to say, shrugging. We fight to get into university, work inhumane hours at the office after graduation, then return home to our tiny apartments. Sometimes, people say this with the smug, self-assured tone of someone who believes they are superior for not having cracked under this pressure. But this is only half of the story. Mental health conditions cannot be wholly explained away by the rhythm in a city; my own depression was not triggered by lifestyle or social pressure. But the lack of quality, affordable healthcare means that we never receive the care required to leave the mental health care system; we remain as statistics on a spreadsheet as the number of new cases accumulate. The state of mental health in the city becomes a ticking time bomb, one that erupts into a full-blown crisis during a protest movement.

.   .   .

When I was first diagnosed with depression, I found few resources online, and had no one around me with whom I could speak about it apart from my writer boyfriend. Until recently, information was scarce and opaque, and googling didn't yield any real results. Because I was unembarrassed and clichéd about my pain on social media, I soon became the go-to person in my circle for where to get professional mental health help. I wasn't qualified to give out mental health advice, but I would send them scanned copies of the same list of psychiatrists I received from my school.

In 2017, when reporting a sexual assault by a man on the street who appeared mentally unwell, I found out that the police had internally used the term "傻人發現," meaning "idiot found," for categorizing cases involving mental health patients in the public. A year later, when the government tried to open a community mental health center in a public housing estate, five hundred residents signed a petition saying that they do not welcome people with mental health conditions. Although professionals in the field say that stigma has improved, statistics by a mental health NGO show that over 40 percent of Hong Kongers still think "lack of self-discipline and willpower" causes mental illness, and six in ten adults do not know where to seek mental health care aside from hospitals. Experts often warn that the real numbers of Hong Kongers with mental health conditions are even higher than the official figures, but cases are underreported due to social stigma. In the media's portrayal of mental health, even sympathetic stories are framed in a way that "others" interviewees, treating them as victims in tragic narratives or heroes who overcame an illness, rather than as everyday people experiencing something that could happen to anyone.

In recent years new resources have cropped up, and high-profile suicides such as the death of beloved singer-songwriter Ellen Loo have triggered conversations in the public realm about mental health. One young journalist who has been fighting to destigmatize the topic is Jasmine Leung, the twenty-three-year-old host of the mental health podcast *From the Wallflowers*. I found out about her podcast when I was on the hunt for personal stories about mental health in Hong Kong, which are still rare to come by. In one episode, Jasmine interviews a Hong Konger who talks about being committed to a psychiatric ward and describes details that are exactly like my own experience, down to the showers and trying to sleep amid screaming patients. No one else in my life has had this experience, and listening to the episode made me feel a little less alone.

Jasmine is a conversational and bubbly podcast host, discussing difficult topics with a light touch that is immediately endearing, a departure from the sob-story tropes local media usually employ for such stories. She interviews mental health professionals, but also speaks from the intimate perspective of someone who lives with mental health issues. The current diagnosis for Jasmine is dissociative disorder, which comes after years of symptoms including mild anorexia, panic attacks, and suicidal ideation. She has out-of-body experiences, and sometimes cannot differentiate between dreams and reality.

Jasmine tells me all of this with a smile that pulls her large eyes into crescents, her short bangs framing her bright face. She grew up in a middle-class family in the Tsuen Wan district, one of the first new towns in Hong Kong. Her mother wanted her to study a medicine-related subject, but she chose journalism at the University of Hong Kong instead, out of a rebellious spirit and a desire to learn the stories of other people. Her brother was studying in Australia, and at home, her parents fought constantly. Then her father had a stroke. While everyone else was crying, Jasmine stood in the corridor of the hospital, laughing. "I was very nervous, and didn't know what sort of reaction I could give. I wanted to calm others down, so they wouldn't be worried about me, and so I was laughing nonstop."

Next came the panic attacks on crowded trains, when she'd feel like the ceiling was collapsing on her. She canceled on her friends and stopped going sailing, fearing that the boat would sink, or that she would somehow lose her fingers. Her then-boyfriend convinced her to see a counsellor, and together, they took the Trans-Siberian Railway from Beijing through Russia to Finland. When she returned, she had a going-away birthday dinner with her family, before she flew off to Australia for study abroad. She cried for five hours, believing that she would never see her family again, because she thought she might kill herself. Her family tried to convince her to stay, but Jasmine went ahead with the exchange program. Her first suicide attempt was in Melbourne, when she took a knife from the kitchen and held it close to her, but fell asleep with the weapon. Shortly after, she was hospitalized.

When Jasmine returned to Hong Kong, she wanted to explore mental health "as a form of self-therapy," and came up with the idea for a podcast. Podcasts had gotten her through a period when she stopped speaking to people altogether. For her final project at journalism school, she pitched the idea of a podcast to her course adviser. "They told me it was too ambitious, that even making one episode would be challenging. That there was no way I could do it. I was furious. So I made nineteen episodes in one go. And that's it," she tells me. *From the Wallflowers* won two awards in the English category in the 2019 Mind HK Media Awards.

Years earlier, she had decided against seeking help in the public mental health system; the waiting times were too long, and she was concerned that it would leave a public file that would stain her record and affect future employment. But through the podcast, she has inadvertently announced to the whole world that she lives with mental health conditions. Jasmine is adamant that mental health stigma can be resolved through communication, that all it takes for society to become more accepting is some more time, and patience.

Jasmine's family initially did not support her decision to work on the podcast. There was a generational gap. "Back [when my mother was growing up], people felt like life was just about working hard and reaping the fruits of their labor. They didn't believe that these problems existed, but it was just that they weren't thinking about it. These problems have always been there. These days, we have the knowledge and language to talk about mental health," Jasmine says.

Eventually, she convinced her mother. In one of the episodes, the two of them have a heart-to-heart on tape. "In my generation, if people told me that you have mental [health] issues, we just thought you have crazy or abnormal behavior," her mother said. "Like, chi sin." Now she is trying to learn about the different types of conditions, and is supportive of her daughter's decision to help herself and help others via the podcast. Her advice to other parents is to always listen to their children instead of arguing with them. "Whatever happens, you must be on your children's side."

The recent social unrest in Hong Kong pushed our collective mental health states over the brink, renewing discussions about the lack of mental health care and our culture of silence around the topic. Protesters, witnesses, and journalists alike struggled with the unrelenting violence on the streets, the mass arrests and around-the-clock developments. During the protests, Jasmine freelanced for media outlets including *The Telegraph* and Agence France-Presse. She was good at separating work from everything else, but the effects lingered in her subconscious and her body after the events. She still refuses to visit the area near the university where a siege took place, and in quiet spaces she sometimes thinks she can still hear the sounds of crowds and protest chants.

During our conversation, Jasmine repeatedly mentions that she does not want to be a burden to people around her. I thought about how, after I became a news reporter, I scrubbed old blogs where I talked about depression. Journalism is cutthroat, and reporting on Hong Kong became more taxing on one's emotional health as freedoms declined; I wanted the editors at the publications to know that I could handle it. I knew what it was like to be terrified of being seen as a burden. But when Jasmine was reporting on the protests, she didn't hide her condition from her employers, because she wanted to be honest and a team player. She knows that she feels better when she acknowledges her own emotions and asks for help. Her colleagues and supervisors have been supportive, and they know that sometimes she might need to take a break. Jasmine did everything I didn't have the courage to do. And in return, the world told her it was okay to be vulnerable.

When I was at my most suicidal in 2015, I made a bucket list. I told myself I wasn't allowed to die until I had checked off the items. I took a photo of the page in my notebook and kept it in the favorites folder on my phone, so I could refer to it every few months.

> Go to Santorini
> Fall in love again
> Learn how to ride a bike
> Start a band
> Write a book

*I'm almost done with my list,* I say to my partner one evening recently. *Does that mean I'm allowed to die now?*

*No,* he says, exasperated. *It means you make a new list. And besides, you still don't know how to ride a bike.*

At least once a week in an online mental health support group with a little over a hundred members, a familiar crisis unfolds, usually in the early hours of the morning. The group on the messaging app Telegram arose out of the 2019 protests. Members chat with each other about side effects they're experiencing from taking tranquilizers, compare the number of times they've dropped out of university, and express their desire to bury themselves in a hole. But sometimes at three A.M., someone will tell the others that they are contemplating suicide. The effectiveness and efficiency of various suicide methods and what tools were required may be discussed. A suicide note may be left behind. Other members might chime in: *Me too.* But more often, someone will say, *Don't miss your doctor appointments, and go to the emergency room if you need to.*

The admin of the group once talked someone out of suicide while she was on holiday. She is a Hong Konger in her twenties working in the finance sector, formerly apolitical by her own description. But on June 12, 2019, when the police responded to a strike and occupation outside the Legislative Council with heavy-handed tear gas, she felt compelled to join the demonstrations. Four days later, she took part in her first major protest. Soon the continued exposure to scenes of violence began to have noticeable effects on her body. At one protest, the admin found herself hyperventilating when the protesters drifted past her making loud percussive noises meant to drum up morale. She ducked inside a 7-Eleven to catch her breath, and then the shop next door was teargassed. Then, in early August at a march in Tsuen Wan, she witnessed a group of thugs in white beating up protesters.

"I hesitated whether I should run up to help the crowd that was being pursued and attacked by the men with knives and wooden sticks and steel rods," she says. "But I had no weapons; I didn't know if they would assault me as well." A victim started bleeding, and someone yelled out for an ambulance. Some protesters on the scene were crying, saying that they had to take revenge. "I want to protect these people, but I also felt very helpless."

After the incident, she found it difficult to eat or move. She obsessed over questions like why Carrie Lam, a Catholic like herself, would turn her back on the people she was supposed to serve. Then she broke up with her boyfriend after he questioned the logic of protesters calling on others not to patronize pro-government and pro-police diners, and the need to "mix politics into everything." She was referred to a psychiatrist at the public hospital clinic, but was cautious about what she would tell the doctor, and asked them not to enter the details of her case into the computer record, in case mentioning her involvement in protests would get her in trouble. The admin's on 50 milligrams of Pristiq, which is used to treat major depressive disorders, and over the past year she's been on Seroquel, Xanax, Remeron, Diazepam, and Propranolol. She hasn't seen a single news clip or other multimedia news since the incident she witnessed, preferring to read updates in purely text form. She's planning on leaving Hong Kong.

Findings by researchers at the University of Hong Kong published in the medical journal *The Lancet* show that during the demonstrations that persisted through the second half of 2019, almost two million Hong Kong adults showed signs of post-traumatic stress disorder. As early as a week after the protest movement began, there was a suicide that was linked to the demonstrations. More followed: Sometimes they left behind notes before falling to their deaths. Fellow protesters laid flowers and built shrines. Experts voiced concerns that this could lead to a trend of "martyrdom" or copycat suicides—a mental health epidemic, some called it. But we didn't know how else to mourn. Journalists covering declining mental health in Hong Kong interviewed protesters who spoke of extreme fatigue, dissociative states—not feeling anything, "no pain, nothing"—during clashes with the police, and others who were desensitized to the cycles of violence. A suicide prevention research center director told *The*

*Guardian*: "Some of them are very young, very naïve, very pure in their hearts. They just throw themselves in. . . . They might not be psychologically mature enough. For them, the possible damage could be quite severe." Ex-lawmaker Claudia Mo said of the deaths: "It's not worth it. . . . Time is always on the young's side."

As of late 2020 the admin's group was still active, even though the pandemic put the brakes on weekly demonstrations. Ongoing protest-related arrests or court cases still trigger collective breakdowns within the group. Some stopped speaking to family members or were even kicked out of their flats as political divisions widened. These peer support groups fill a gap in the mental health services in Hong Kong, but professionals warn that without the presence of, say, social workers to redirect the conversations, members can spur each other on to perform dangerous acts. A psychologist tells me that current political developments will only complicate the city's struggle with mental health: The national security law has imposed a climate of fear that makes it difficult for students to trust their schools enough to confide in them, and businesses have been divided into "yellow" (pro-protest) and "blue" (pro-police). Hong Kongers who have taken part in protests sometimes pick from lists of trusted "yellow" psychiatrists, which imposes even more limitations to seeking help. If the mental health system was overloaded prior to the protests, the political crisis has stretched it to a breaking point.

At the time the protests began, my depression had been under control for two years. I was working an editing job with reasonable hours, and I had a room of my own with a window that faced a glorious tree. I was in a stable relationship. I'd just turned twenty-six. *This is the part where I finally get to enjoy my twenties,* I thought. Then came the demonstrations against the extradition bill: six months of marching in the rain, crying on the couch, checking up on my friends obsessively to see if they'd been hurt. In the evenings my partner and I would sit side by side, watching two different live streams of civilians screaming during "police clearance actions" as fumes of tear gas fogged up the screen on our separate computers, while writing or posting updates on Twitter or drowning in alcohol. Whenever I wasn't out protesting, I felt like a coward. I was terrified of being arrested, especially after friends who were lawyers told me they had seen cases of the police withholding mental health medication from those in detention over protest charges.

Events escalated, each new development bringing on more fitful nights. On the first day of October 2019, I woke up to a phone call from a friend asking urgently for a lawyer contact, since he suspected someone he knew had been arrested. On the same day, a police officer shot an eighteen-year-old protester point-blank, just missing the young man's heart. In November, a university student fell inside a car park and passed away. The circumstances surrounding his death were mysterious, but there had been a police operation nearby. During the peak of the protests, when young protesters in Hong Kong waged a battle with the police on a university campus for days, I stopped sleeping. On the rare occasions I did, I had dreams of being pursued by haunted figures, of being forced onto a train that took me to an ominous destination.

In 2008, the Hong Kong writer Lee Chi Leung published *A Room Without Myself,* a collection of essays that was billed as "an unapologetic retro/introspection of the author's personal history of manic depression and colonial upbringing." It won the Hong Kong Book Prize that year, and reading it in 2020 I was struck by the brutal honesty in his depictions of mental health, especially at a time when the population rarely discussed these matters in public, and treated mental conditions as a matter of shame. In a way, the book can be read as a 226-page explanation to those who've never crossed over to this side. Friends in my generation told me that the book had been revelatory when they were in their teens and early adult years, and was their first point of entry into understanding mental health, but in the collection of essays, Lee also writes about the 1992 Japanese film *March Comes in Like a Lion,* his travelogue to Taiwan, and the fervent anxiety he experienced over the monotony of Hong Kong life.

In Lee's book, I found a passage that almost echoed my own guilt over not doing enough for the protests: "Other people have fallen over during the chaos, and yet I couldn't even take care of myself. (Much of post-crisis trauma stems from guilt . . . and the failure to re-establish some semblance of order in life.)" This was from 2005—Lee was tear-gassed during the Hong Kong protests over the World Trade Organization conference, when Korean farmers flew into the city and occupied the streets over economic policies on rice pricing.

Each generation has faced its own set of social problems or political turmoil and, in turn, mental health crises. In 1989, the June 4 massacre in Beijing triggered a wave of grief in Hong Kong; in 2003, the SARS epidemic and the subsequent economic crisis led to a historically high suicide rate. Decade after decade, the people in Hong Kong have learned to live with fresh disappointments that are more devastating than the last. Imagine: You're in your late thirties, and you are one of the young activists who tried to save a village from being torn down, but nothing you do prevents the government from getting their way. You're in your twenties, living through the Umbrella Movement as a university student; you watch your closest friends get tear-gassed, then lose hope in the city when the protests do not result in the political change you fought for. You're eighteen, voting for the first time, and your candidate gets elected but then gets disqualified and jailed by the government. You're fourteen, and taking part in political activism for the first time, and even though you haven't done anything except hold placards and chant slogans all day, the government charges you with rioting. It always feels like the end of the world, only more so now than ever before.

During the worst months of the protests, my friends missed work, cried in public, posted morbid social media statuses about the uncertainty of Hong Kong's future. I knew we weren't just sad, but depressed: The blue colored all of our social interactions, our waking hours, our sleep. There wasn't a day when we could take a break without the weight of the arrested, injured protesters hanging over us. This was not a mutually abusive romantic relationship I could leave, or a depression that could be fixed by developing habits such as waking up earlier, exercising regularly, or getting more sun. This was my home and I could not opt out of caring about its future. The protests eventually died down with the arrival of the coronavirus pandemic, but the crackdown continued in more insidious ways: In mid-2020, China passed a law that would outlaw all dissent. The street battles are gone, but my insomnia persists. There is a heaviness in my system, remnants from those days that I cannot purge.

But there was also a surge of more people in my community speaking about mental health than before. It was impossible to claim that depression and anxiety were character flaws when everyone collectively experienced this grief that clouded our days. The demonstrations also fostered a practice of mutual support that destigmatized the idea of seeking help for mental health. Everyone was trying to make the people around them feel better; indie musicians led breathing exercises and ran chat sessions with young people who needed a tree hole to vent into. Artists and writers made zines that gave advice on managing emotions during turbulent times, and reminding fellow demonstrators known as 手足 (literally "your brothers- and sisters-in-arms") that "no one gets left behind," as per a popular protest slogan.

Grassroots organizations such as From Trauma to Transformation offered alternative ways of mental health support, such as talks on meditation and social trauma, and online workshops that catered to protesters with safety concerns. The group's cofounder tells me that when the Umbrella Movement ended in 2014, the psychological wounds were never properly attended to, and everyone went on with their lives as usual. In 2019, thousands were arrested in relation to the growing protests, and scenes of clashes were broadcast almost around the clock through social media. It left behind a significant population wrestling with milder symptoms of PTSD who may not necessarily seek clinical help. The trust between the people and institutions has been broken. "Since this involves collective trauma, we can't just pretend that counseling everyone so that they would be 'happier' would solve this. It's not a problem that exists on an individual level," she says.

At the indie bookstore Art and Culture Outreach, amid tables of zines and locally published nonfiction books, hundreds of Post-it Notes fill up several vertical wood panel displays, with messages like *I lack the courage to kill myself* and *My beloved*. They are part of an art exhibition titled *Natural Early Death*. The artist spoke to young adults born in 1992, to ask them whether they have ever contemplated suicide, and if so, what's stopped them from committing the act. The idea was born out of a question she had in 2018—*Is there a way to die that affects nobody?*—but it took on a new significance with the 2019 protests. Some notes are deceptively simple: "一個都不能少," as in, "We need everyone in this fight." Others are mini-memoirs: "I used to be a boy, and I hope to become a girl; when my first goal's accomplished, my next is to protect my family and friends so long as I live." One is blunt but poetic: "to outlive the regime."

Brian Leung, a now-exiled protester, said in an interview: "What unites Hong Kongers is pain." When I first read this, I understood it to mean that we'll always be hurting. But maybe Leung wanted to remind us that we're never alone. 見字飲水; drink water when you read this, and don't die. There would be no revolution if there is no one here alive to witness the day.

I'm still on antidepressants. Doctors don't usually use the word *recovered* with their patients; rather, they say *stable condition*. I'm not *formerly depressed,* but rather a *sometimes depressed* person. But if I kept looking over my shoulder, wary that my depression would return, or let the dread over Hong Kong's political future overtake my days, I would miss all the life that goes on in between. If I wanted to wait for my circumstances, my city, and this world to improve definitively before I resumed living, that day would never come. With the cards that we have been dealt, everything is going to be shit for a long time. Our lives are but collections of quiet moments amid the chaos: the watering thrill of spicy food, the rain that looks like coconut flakes from my window, the way the tree drapes itself over my street, speckling sunlight on the pavement. These present moments belong to us even if our futures do not.

And then it's October, the last shards of summer hanging over a still-blue sky. The third wave of the pandemic's just ended, and restaurants are cautiously pulling up their shutters again. The streets are calm, but maybe not for long. My next appointment at David Trench is in twelve weeks. I go for ramen by myself, slurping every last bit of the broth till I can see the bottom of the bowl. This year, I'll be brave enough to face winter.

I'm at the pier again. I walk along the fenceless rim of the waterfront. The horizon is smeared with streaks of orange, soft and vast over the silhouettes of islets. I sit at the edge, balancing a cup of coffee in between my knees and staining the pages of my book with salt. The border here is un-guarded. No one would even notice if I slid myself down into the water. But I don't. Today I want only to watch the waves break against the shore.

# PART III

# The Former International
# School Kid

A month after we hang out at a gig for the first time, the boy who later becomes my partner sneaks me onto his old campus late at night and gives me a tour. The school is almost exactly halfway between my father's flat on Farm Road and my partner's childhood home: We quickly find out that we grew up seven minutes away from each other, and share the same district councillor. *It's rumored that some of the rooms in the school were used as torture chambers by the Japanese during World War II,* he tells me as we sit down to face a sports court. The name of his school is King George V, and its predecessor opened in Hong Kong in 1894.

The boy and I bond over our love of music and our interest in Hong Kong politics, code-switching between English and Cantonese. This is spring 2016, and we are both in the process of trying to figure out our relationship to this place we grew up in but felt alienated from. He tells me he works in corporate investigations but wants to quit, maybe to go into journalism or law. I tell him that this will probably sound obnoxious as hell, but I'm trying out this new litmus test of whether my date knows the basics about Hong Kong's elections and protests.

Even then, there are subtle differences between us. He spent all of his life in international schools and then attended university overseas, whereas I made the switch back to the local education system in my teenage years. He is making twice my salary, while I have more access to the local community through my university classmates and through reporting, and less angst about my belated adult quest for belonging.

On our next few dates, we take walks by the sea and talk about growing up in the 2000s, when there were fewer crises in Hong Kong, less at stake in not being politically aware. During the Umbrella Movement in 2014, he had just returned to the city from London and would go down to the occupation site; I was away in Scotland. At the time, my university friends were getting tear-gassed and writing essays about the police's disproportionate use of force, and my ex–secondary school classmates were changing their profile pictures to that of a yellow ribbon, to show solidarity with the movement. My ex–international school classmates were silent.

After the movement, Hong Kong identity became intertwined with political activism, especially among the younger generation. Apolitical people are sometimes regarded as not true Hong Kongers, because only those affluent enough to leave would be able to ignore the most significant political movement in the city to date; this population overlaps significantly with international school graduates. My partner and I both want to prove to our peers that we are Hong Kongers—not international school kids.

. . .

I'm twenty-four, standing in line at the U.S. Consulate for my American tourist visa, to visit my friend in San Francisco. It's my first trip to the United States. The staff at the consulate ask me a couple of questions about my job, my family, my flat to make sure I'm not trying to smuggle in and then overstay. I answer them dutifully. *You say you've never been to the U.S.? Where did you get this accent from? Did you go to an international school?* I say *no,* catch myself, then *yes,* and eventually I just give up and say, *I think it's because I watched too much* Gossip Girl.

I'm not American, not even a little, but sometimes on holidays strangers will slide up to me as I'm sitting at a bar table trying to order ramen, to ask me what state I'm from. In Hong Kong, the accent makes new people I meet question whether my allegiance is with them—if I'd be out on the streets chanting slogans with them, or grumble about how the protests on my doorstep have interrupted their daily grocery route. They want to know if I'd stay here with them till all the life rafts on this sinking ship are gone, or fuck off at the first opportunity. *Are you really a Hong Konger?* is what they're asking.

I met Sarah at my first reporting job after graduation. Sarah, then, was a small and frightfully smart nineteen-year-old with a forest of full bangs tucked into her oversized glasses and a smile that hit you like the afternoon sun in winter. She could not recognize many local legislators at first, just as I had struggled to catch up during my first few months reporting, but she picked it up quickly. She wrote features about sex workers, and profiled trans activists and left-leaning activists.

Sarah was in her final year at her international secondary school in Hong Kong when this city she grew up in was swept up by the Umbrella Movement. She and a few friends started wearing yellow ribbons to school to express solidarity as the occupation began headlining every local, and then international, newspaper. At Sarah's school, however, it barely registered among the other students. "There were people asking us in September or October, 'What is happening, why is there so much traffic in Central?'" Sarah recalls. "Or they'd be like, 'Why are you wearing a yellow ribbon?,' and I'd think—'Are you stupid?'"

Her classmates were the kind to care more about starving kids in Cambodia than anything that was happening in Hong Kong, self-identifying as "global citizens." During protests here, while the rest of the city was tear-gassed, they posted photos of themselves on the beach. Others posted about protest movements abroad but were "radio silent about things happening on their doorstep." Sarah says that the idea of global citizenship among international school graduates denotes "a certain kind of people; people who have no roots because they're rooted everywhere have the privilege of not having to root themselves in the place they're at." That identity is a class marker of a global elite made up of the rich.

Sarah attended university overseas, where she wrote her dissertation on Hong Kong and began to "make myself local but in a way that's legible to me and my politics." During the 2019 protests, Sarah discreetly raised awareness of the protest movement through events and translating materials about the demonstration from abroad. Even though she was experiencing it from afar, the movement inadvertently helped her feel more connected to the local community through updates on the messaging app Telegram, which protesters used to mobilize and organize, as well as through live news streams.

When Sarah was working in another city abroad, she met a group of Hong Kong aunties through Telegram. One evening, when the protesters in Hong Kong were trapped inside the Polytechnic University, one woman had a breakdown and called the rest of them over, including Sarah. "We just watched the live stream together, in silence, even though we didn't know each other." Sarah says that part of her political activism was motivated, at least subconsciously, to try to find a Hong Kong that she could see herself belonging to.

"Having seen activism in other places—to call yourself part of the community requires certain choices and commitment. If you don't have that, you don't even deserve to be part of the community. I want to deserve to call myself part of the Hong Kong community, and I'm working on understanding what that involves."

These days, Sarah's also trying to be more generous with herself. "I used to feel really guilty and I'm still unpacking a lot of that, because it's the root of my anxieties, feeling like I can't truly call myself a Hong Konger." But it wasn't a helpful emotion, she says. And trying to position herself as the exceptional international school graduate who became politically conscious and doesn't go on yacht parties, at the end of the day, doesn't do anything. "You don't choose how you grow up or the structure of privilege you're in," Sarah says. "But you can choose to resist it and commit yourself to making things better."

. . .

In 2019, my partner started an online petition for international school kids to express their opposition toward the proposed extradition bill, which would eventually set into motion the major protests over the next couple of months. At the time, different petitions representing different groups were circulating on social media, all to protest the bill: There were petitions that were classified by district or religion or secondary school, that gathered the signatures of homemakers across Hong Kong or new immigrants from mainland China.

Some of the names his efforts garnered surprised him: People he had labeled as apolitical or even pro-Beijing signed his petition. Three months later, for a feature for an American magazine, I interviewed a friend of his, a lifestyle vlogger and an international school graduate who supported the protests. "On Instagram, a lot of people I follow or who are following me post about the protests, so I don't want to seem like one of those international school kids who doesn't really care. I do, but I have my own life outside of all of this. And I have a lot of friends on both sides, so I don't want to offend anyone," she told me. My partner and I both had friends who lived in the international school bubble for so long that they had no communities or bridges that would allow them to feel close to Hong Kong. He wanted to get his former classmates—international school graduates across age groups and different ethnicities who had been 離地, detached from reality—to get more involved.

By then, the protest movement had stepped up its efforts to be more inclusive, especially with traditionally marginalized communities. In October, the police sprayed a mosque in Tsim Sha Tsui with blue dye, angering the ethnic minority and Muslim communities. A day later, outside the Chungking Mansions, members of the ethnic minority community handed out bottles of water to protesters, and later organized cultural nights. Toward the end of the movement, the Hong Kong government deported an Indonesian migrant worker, Yuli Riswati, over her citizen journalism on the protests. At a rally my partner and I attended, Yuli addressed the crowd in Cantonese through a long-distance call, and told Hong Kong people to fight on. Domestic workers could never gain legal residency here because of discriminatory laws, and the ethnic minority community has long felt excluded from the rest of the population. The developments were a long-overdue step toward moving away from the idea that belonging to a place depended on your ethnicity or where you were born.

At times I wondered if my partner's project was even worth the time: International school graduates are such a small, privileged subset of the overall population that the stakes felt low. But because their privilege had allowed them to become prominent voices in the global discourse, their views and comments could be taken to be representative of the general Hong Kong population. Once I started working in media, and then art, I saw them everywhere. *Of course,* I thought when I first noticed. They—*we*—make up less than a tenth of Hong Kong, but are overrepresented in professions such as writing, journalism, and the arts. When international publishers and publications look for someone to give sound-bites on or write articles about Hong Kong, they won't care about their class background or whether they know the city well, so long as that person looks the part. Sometimes I read interviews with artists that describe the political situation with a noncommittal "There's just a lot of gray area," and other times I watch talented friends lose out again and again on top journalism positions to international school graduates with less experience but from a more privileged education background.

The majority of my ex–international school classmates no longer live in Hong Kong, and have gone on to higher education abroad, especially if their parents are expats who have moved on to their next posting. I keep in touch with only a few friends from that school. But on Instagram, I noticed an old classmate, James, using the reply and voting functions on Instagram stories as a platform for conversation, everything from debates over beauty standards to tactics used by protesters. Sometimes I'd see on his feed screen captures of news headlines, or on-the-ground updates of the lunchtime protests in Central, which were taking place weekly, sometimes daily, in the peak of the demonstrations, attended by well-dressed office workers in the business district.

James's parents are both Hong Kongers. His mother did not finish secondary school, while his father "collected degrees." His parents sent him to an international school to be "a bit more educated, well-read," but they also could not relate to his school experience. "My parents grew up quite poor," James tells me. "They can speak English, but my spoiled-brat attitude as a child basically told them their English was shit, and that hurt them for a very long time. I also saw that they avoided a lot of the parent-teacher stuff, because they felt they didn't fit in."

After primary school, James attended German Swiss International School: He says the student population was around two-tenths white, one-tenth East, South, or Southeast Asian, and the rest ethnically Chinese. The white students generally acted like they were superior, while scholarship kids from "more local" backgrounds—"you could tell from the way that they dressed, the way that they spent their money for lunch, or just the interests that they had, that they didn't really know how to fit in," he says.

His international school classmates would make fun of the way Hong Kongers speak English with an accent, and frequently said *That's so local* as though it were an insult; sometimes they'd refuse to go to a restaurant that looked dingy. But they also struggled with Chinese even though most were from Hong Kong, especially since they weren't allowed to speak any language that wasn't taught at the school, including Cantonese.

James took British A-levels, went on to study in London only to come down with seasonal depression, and dropped out before he finished his bachelor's. When he returned to Hong Kong, he started working at a company where the majority of the staff were Cantonese-speaking Hong Kongers, and he familiarized himself with the local slang. That year, he started going to the political gatherings on June 4 and July 1 for the first time, alone. At the 2019 protests, he flipped barricades near the legislature and was shot at by riot police with rubber bullets. When a major clash took place at a university around the corner from the menswear store he is partner of, the space opened itself up to protesters who needed sheltering. All of that makes him the one person I know from my former school who has taken part in the movement.

"I feel a lot of frustration at a lot of international school kids because—it's like I'm discriminating against a former version of myself," I say. "Maybe they just don't show it, but I just struggle to find them caring. I wonder if maybe they don't really have a stake in Hong Kong even though they've lived here all their lives. If you don't know what is happening in the place you live, you are benefitting from the economic and political system, but you're not playing your part as a resident."

"You know what grinds my gears?" James says. "People who say *Home Kong.*"

"And it's always accompanied by a picture of the harbor and the peak," I say.

"And yet they won't even know who their district councillor is," he adds. It's these people that irk him most, the people who claim to love a place by posting photos of their hike in Sai Kung, but aren't interested in becoming part of a community. "The international school experience is very much like the expat experience where you get the choice to care, but also you can live a life that's entirely detached," James says. "And it may not ever affect you, until it inconveniences you."

But James is sympathetic, because he remembers his own journey of finding his way back to Hong Kong. Being fluent in English has opened up doors for him, and he can now move in both spheres, but there's a part of him that feels like he doesn't belong anywhere. And while he acknowledges that some stereotypes about international school kids being spoiled and apolitical could be true, he believes that the graduates are also acting out of self-preservation, pragmatism, or fear, since many work corporate jobs that serve mainland Chinese clients.

"Growing up, until I made a conscious choice to care more and find out more about this city, I didn't really feel that this was home, either. I was away from what was 'local,'" he says. At local shops, he's been called stupid ABC (American-born Chinese) because of his accent, even though he isn't American. "A lot of international school kids don't feel a sense of belonging or welcome, even, and so it comes out as elitism sometimes. And they get discouraged from trying to get to know more about this place too."

"I struggle because I think that what they go through and the emotions they experience are legitimate," I say. But the exclusion faced by them isn't the same as how the people they call *locals* are shut out from opportunities by way of class. They have more resources to fit in, and being more proficient in English, will always have higher geographical and occupational mobility. Armed with foreign passports, they will always find it easier to flee in a time of political chaos.

James does not disagree with me. But he sees himself as a facilitator of sorts, and a bridge between the two worlds. "My hope is that people who are privileged become more involved in the conversation." Yes, people might get there on their own volition if they just try—"but it's weird how much an invitation helps." This doesn't have to mean that we excuse them their privilege, or feel the burden to educate them; but we could also think about the bridges we could build for and with them, rather than just blaming them for not "wanting" to try harder to get to know this place.

A year after our interview, two of our classmates organize a primary school reunion at their shop. I arrive half an hour late. "I already told everyone about how you're writing a book about how much you hate international school kids," James says, laughing.

"It's not a *whole* book on that," I say.

I had been dreading that meetup all week. I imagined it would be a night of comparing salaries, experiences at elite colleges, and everyone sizing each other up. Instead, we get drunk and stay to chat till one in the morning. I had spun my time in that school as a poor-little-me narrative of being bullied because of my class background, when really, almost every one of the dozen people at that gathering had been bullied by the cool kids to some extent, for all sorts of reasons. We are a crew of bastard kids, never fitting in anywhere, until we found communities that accepted us. I found mine in Hong Kong, and I know I am not the only one. Quietly hanging on the back of the shop door is a red fai chun, and drawn on the paper is a protest pig, waving its hands up ecstatically.

In August 2019, while the protests were ongoing, every evening at ten I would hear cries from outside my flat: Someone would say, *Fight for freedom!* And a chorus of voices would reply: *Stand with Hong Kong!* For around ten minutes, these chants would ring out from all directions, sometimes in Cantonese, sometimes in English. Every now and then, my partner and I would lean out the window and join in, shouting until our voices were hoarse. *Hong Kongers, add oil!* We formed these bonds of solidarity with strangers we never met, calling out into the void for one another. I've lived here all my life and did not once describe myself as a Hong Konger until my first extended trip away from home. *I'm from Hong Kong,* I told my multinational flatmates, my hosts in Turkey, the shisha place owner, not truly understanding what it meant. Where else could I be from? I have only known one home.

In 2020, an open letter from a graduating student at my partner's school, King George V, began circulating among other international school alumni in my network, and soon made the local news. The letter accused the school of perpetuating an environment of white supremacy, as well as homophobia and sexualization of female students. It said that the curriculum is overwhelmingly Eurocentric, and students were taught about Queen Elizabeth I, but not the detriments of colonization. The school and English Schools Foundation also foster the "complicity of sheltered students who are merely encouraged by the curriculum to be educated on 'real world issues' on a performative level, but deter students from actually taking a stance deemed too 'radical' or too 'political.'" The letter was eloquently written and intelligent, but noticeably absent were critiques of class or any mentions of the protests that took place in Hong Kong a year before.

Jeff and I met years ago; he reached out after I wrote a piece about a labor rights website, and since then we would run into each other at gigs. Jeff was an employee at an international school in Hong Kong. He attended the school in his teens—an Anglophone school where every other subject except Chinese class was taught in English, where *international* meant *Western,* and where American culture was especially valorized. He had classmates that were related to the families that run Hong Kong's biggest property developers. The curriculum was not designed to give room for students to study Hong Kong: "You can't read and study Hong Kong English or Chinese literature, nor can you study the history of Hong Kong." When Jeff was a student at Vassar College during the Umbrella Movement, he downloaded gigabytes of academic papers on Hong Kong to fill in the gaps of his education. He returned to work at his alma mater.

I want to speak to Jeff because I'm curious about what was happening in international schools during the 2019 protests, from someone who knows what it was like behind the scenes. Jeff tells me that during the protest movement, his school took an institutional stance of neutrality. "In practice, it meant not acknowledging the protest. Teachers are encouraged not to say anything about it." Even though some teachers were supportive of the protests and wouldn't necessarily get into trouble by speaking out in a personal capacity, job security fears also led them to self-censor, he says. Since he left, the space for international school students to learn about the city's political developments has shrunk further; official guidelines issued to teachers a year later instructed them "not to advocate for Hong Kong independence, illegal anti-government protests or any activity that sought to undermine the authority of either the central or Hong Kong governments."

Despite the school's position, students banded together and took it upon themselves to educate their fellow classmates. One student penned an essay on the 2019 protests in the school magazine, and in the caption to the piece on social media, highlighted how detachment and isolation from local society was written into international school culture. "We are sheltered from the politicised violence that has come to define daily life in the city, at a time when our peers elsewhere have been thrown, perhaps prematurely, into a frenetic struggle against authoritarianism and illiberalism. As students of the International Baccalaureate, our pretensions towards such lofty concepts as 'international-mindedness' and 'global citizenship' ring hollow in the face of our collective indifference towards acknowledging our role, peripheral though it may be, in Hong Kong's social upheaval."

An Instagram account from Jeff's school frequently posted protest-related news and essays submitted anonymously by other students. Many shared anecdotes about their classmates: One wrote that as local schools across Hong Kong organized human chains to express solidarity with the protests, students in his biology class "complained about the noise again." Another student described learning about the instances of police brutality, and said, "Never before had I felt such anger at the willful apathy my classmates displayed towards the political turmoil." But sometimes underneath posts like these, there were students who would defend the political neutrality principle as a way to "avoid commotions," while others at the school complained that posts like these "drag the school's reputation down." Others pointed out that the protesters have been violent, too.

"I think a lot of students, because they don't know much about Hong Kong to begin with, they are really attached to questions of whether the protesters are exhibiting decorum or civility," Jeff says. Jeff is no longer with the school and currently lives outside of Hong Kong, but he admits to feeling disappointed with some students: "The most upsetting thing is that the disengaged students are highly aware of the fact that they live in a bubble and realize it is problematic, yet somehow find reasons to remain committed to staying aloof." Then, a couple of days after our conversation, he softens. They are still students, after all. He needs to be patient, to allow them to grow and develop. "Conversing with students is a years-long endeavor, and honestly, some people I talk to have transformed for the better."

The narrative has always been that Hong Kong is a transitory city: People come and go, move on in search of better lives. I would have tried to do the same, if I had not found my people in Hong Kong. In university, I met lawyers who moonlighted as weekend farmers in Hong Kong's villages. I found former third-culture kids who also grew up on a diet of metal and emo, as well-versed in social justice in the United States as they are with issues surrounding land hegemony here. I got to know musicians, former protest leaders, activists for refugee rights, independent booksellers, other writers. Through them, I found a different version of the place I thought I had known, one I didn't want to run away from anymore.

But I know that the story could have gone another way: I could have become a person who would proudly tell people I'm *from +852,* but be barely able to describe the city without talking about Mong Kok or char siu rice. This city is no more than its mountaintop views, the quirky language with too many swear words, its nightlife and street food, if we do not make the place our own. For the generation that I grew up in, the internet has emerged as the most crucial space for building solidarity across geography: I thought I was a global citizen, the natural next step to being a former international school kid. But identifying as such doesn't absolve that responsibility to our immediate physical community—especially when that is where the consequences of our actions are most directly, discernibly felt.

What does it mean to belong to a place? I grew up knowing what it felt like to be abandoned; in my twenties, I found a home in my neighbors who are making self-funded community papers about our wondrous street corners, in the artists and musicians who are creating works in the most impossible of conditions, in friends who took over the streets and redefined activism. How do I explain the moments that feel so monumental to me: being at a hot-pot dinner with other journalists after a long week of news, a stranger gesturing frantically at me to get away from the police during a clash, passing a beer to an artist in the early hours of the morning at Bound? These are the people who taught me to no longer see a place as transitory, expendable. When we talk about the fight for Hong Kong, we pepper our discussions with keywords like *democracy* and *freedom,* or *basic moral responsibility,* when really we're just protesting for our friends' future, for their safety and well-being—especially the ones who will not be able to leave Hong Kong, and whose lives are so inextricably tied up with politics that they never had a choice over whether to care.

Belonging means the pull of a home so strong it will always be a part of you, wherever you are. I don't want to stand at a distance looking in, talking about how shitty this city is without taking part. I don't want to marvel at the skyline while refusing to understand the political developments behind the façade. I don't want to reap the economic benefits of the land only to leave before the storm. I'm still trying to understand what it means to be part of a place that nurtured me, to define what community means to us. But I know I've belonged to this city for a long time now.

# Language Traitors

We knew any changes wouldn't be so dramatic, that
they would come but they would be gradual. By and
large, they wouldn't attract the attention of the international media who would deem the news to be "too
local." In the end, it would fall upon us, the Hong
Kong media, to keep telling our stories.
—YUEN CHAN, "TELLING OUR OWN STORIES"

How do you write about the place you call home, in a language that is not your own?

In English-language literature and historical accounts of
Hong Kong, the story would typically begin on Possession
Street, an elevated patch of land where the British fleet first
landed. It would adopt the date of when we were ceded to
Britain as "the founding of Hong Kong." There would be
colonial imagery and references on every page: the former
governors, junk boats, Victorian-era buildings. It would
center naval officers and their children, foreign correspondents, or expats, and their privileged, glittery lives.

I did not want to write a book "about Hong Kong." Neither did I want to write stories about "my culture." I made the mistake once of misunderstanding "culture" and pitched stories about my musician friends to magazines and newspapers. This wasn't what editors were looking for. They wanted scenes with milk tea and mahjong and Ding Ding rides. When editors say "culture," they mean my Chineseness. They want to read about the fire dragon dance at Tai Hang, the hungry ghost festival, Hakka villages and ancestral rites. They like it when I tell them my mother is from Wuhan, and my father's side of the family came to Hong Kong in the 1950s from Hoiping. It's best if our family stories are somehow representative of the rest of the Hong Kong population. The clashing of cultures or a reckoning of our bastardized state make good anecdotes. Sections where you try to put forward arguments will likely be deleted. Too much "tell" and not enough "show." They want your life stories, not your opinions.

Maybe this isn't the book you expected to read: You wanted stories about "ordinary Hong Kongers," movers and teachers and finance workers and cleaners who all joined the protests in 2019. You might have thought there would be cameos by quaint, exoticized "everyday" characters: the salesperson with the headset selling cleaning products to a crowd of homemakers, the real estate agents that congregate near shopping malls, the elderly man at the pier in the lopsided white tank top that reveals exactly one nipple letting off a stream of all our swear words. These stories should be parables. They should ideally be about immigrants to Hong Kong at a representative enough cross section of history—the Sino-Japanese War, the Cultural Revolution, post 1997. Instead, I gave you this.

.    .    .

As a teenager and young adult, I wrote diary entries, blogs for my university, letters to lovers. My readers were always myself or the people around me; they looked like me and understood all my cultural references.

When I first started reporting, I wanted to write features about topics that were an important part of the local discourse but did not garner much attention in the English-language press. Some of these were hyperlocal stories: a computer crime law misused by the police to arrest protesters, a stretch of public space in Mong Kok dominated by loud middle-aged singers, a small website that reports exclusively on labor rights and strikes. I shadowed a community activist as she took participants on a walking heritage tour of Western District, and interviewed men who were spending the night in a temporary shelter on the coldest night of 2016. I woke up at seven A.M. for a seat in the courtroom during the trials of protest leaders, and cried back at home when they were given lengthy sentences.

I thought these stories were for Hong Kongers, but my editor, a Hong Kong resident from Britain, told me we should write the news as though we were explaining it to "a Texas grandfather." I learned to write for an imaginary white audience.

Some people don't even know where Hong Kong is, editors tell me. Explain, explain, explain. I got very good at writing context paragraphs. They contain no information of value to any Hong Kong reader. Sometimes, my eyes glaze over the lines even as I type them from memory.

*For seventy-nine days, protesters occupied major thoroughfares in Hong Kong's business and shopping districts to demand universal suffrage.*

*Under the One Country, Two Systems arrangement, Hong*

*Kong enjoys a high degree of autonomy until 2047, but freedoms are rapidly disappearing under Beijing's increasingly authoritarian rule.*

Hong Kong can be referred to as a *semi-autonomous region, international financial center,* or even *southern Chinese city.*

"*The Guardian* called it the 'Umbrella Revolution.' Imagine that: the name came from English-language voyeurism before it was translated back into Chinese on banners in the camps," observed Asian American writer Henry Wei Leung, who was in Hong Kong during the 2014 protests as a Fulbright scholar. During the movement, he had initially pitched a translation of Hong Kong writer Hon Lai Chu's essay "I Just Want to See the Sea" to an international journal and was accepted; it eventually declined to publish the essay, stating that the topic was no longer timely, and that it had "too much of an insider's perspective."

"Too much. They wanted a foreign gaze; they wanted a tour," he wrote. (It was eventually published in *The Offing.*)

Local reporters who work for international outlets stayed fixers or "news researchers" for a long time, doing most of the legwork, acting as de facto translators, and sometimes not even receiving an *additional reporting* byline at the end of the piece. Others who don't want to play this game freelanced, working with parachute journalists who flew in for protests. Rather than observing what is happening on the ground and then identifying stories, these foreign correspondents come with preexisting ideas of the story they want and ask journalists here to interview locals until they get that story.

Between the Umbrella Movement and the 2019 protests, journalists at international outlets told me that my hometown was boring, and editors told us that the stories we pitched were "too local." Subtext: There was no tear gas.

China watchers published endless pieces framing Hong Kong as a David and Goliath struggle against a global superpower, and were unable to speak of the city and the lives of its people except in terms of how Hong Kong was the battleground of the "new Cold War." Publications continue to act like the only time Hong Kongers deserve their own stories is when it's a narrative about our death.

I don't know if any Texas grandfathers have ever read my news stories about Hong Kong. But I do know this: When we cease to present a narrative comprehensible to Western audiences, we are forced out of the pages of the newspaper. We are wiped off the map. It is as if we do not exist.

In university, I was part of an English-language writing group that met up at a bar every week. I was twenty years old, and the members of the group, predominantly white men, were between half a decade to a couple of decades older. Afterward, we drank at tacky karaoke bars or pubs till three in the morning. The men were longtime expats or international school–educated Hong Kongers. None of them spoke a lick of Cantonese. Most had foreign passports and could leave the city anytime.

I don't think expats are precluded from being Hong Kong writers, if the city was instrumental in nurturing their creativity, if they helped us to see the place in a new way. But with the outsized representation of expats in English-language books set in Hong Kong, one would think the city is populated with no one but expats and a sprinkling of Hong Kong Chinese who exist as exoticized props. As poet Nicholas Wong once said, expatriate writing "is a part of English creative writing [in Hong Kong], but it cannot be the only part."

After the Umbrella Movement, I met up with one of the men from the writing group. We sat underneath the mid-level escalators in SoHo, drinking beers on benches splattered with pigeon shit. *Don't you think,* he said, *that writers took advantage of the international interest of the occupation movement to publish pieces that were frankly not that good?*

He wasn't entirely wrong. There are only so many ways you can spin scenes of crowded streets, riot police, and blue-orange tents. But when he said this, I know he wasn't thinking about his friends, who spent their years here as spectators, passersby, political tourists. They went down to occupation zones and patted themselves on the back, wrote grand pieces about mankind and read them at the open mics, then went back to running lifestyle blogs or going on boat trips or photographing their brunches at Aqua as everyone else continued to protest. He was thinking of local poets making a name for themselves in international literary circles for their work on the protests, writers who understood that the protests were a window to the world that would close as soon as international interest waned, who did not have the geographical mobility or white privilege his friends enjoyed. It is an exhausting, soul-draining exercise to write lovingly, despairingly, about the place you call home, only to have editors tell you that nobody really cares about Hong Kong, and to have your peers accuse you of profiting off the movement.

As I sipped on my beer, listening to him talk, I had a flashback to a time when these men attended a talk by another poet from Hong Kong, where she spoke about how the simplicity of language could work to your advantage in poetry. I was not at the event, but afterward at the weekly meeting, I overheard one of the men say, *She only said that because her English probably wasn't that good to begin with.*

At the time of the 2019 protests, I had left my job at the local news outlet and was no longer a full-time reporter. I still wrote features for magazines, and occasionally wrote opinion pieces that masqueraded as political commentary, but I could feel the gulf between what I was doing and the work of my journalist friends who were on the scene of the protests every day, getting pepper-sprayed on camera or beaten up by thugs. I wrote a blog post on Medium after the July 21 Yuen Long attack about my volatile emotional state. Although I had posted it only on my personal Facebook, it was widely shared by strangers. An editor connected me with *The New York Times,* and I wrote three essays for them about life amid protests and political changes in Hong Kong.

Other publications started messaging me, asking if I wanted to write something about "how it feels" whenever something significant happened in Hong Kong. I had accidentally written myself into a niche. Even though I was primarily a journalist before this, they wanted personal essays from me. *Fuck,* I told my partner, *I think I've become the sad correspondent for the Hong Kong protests.*

Sometimes, when I'm writing, I can hear the men in the writing group in my head. *She just got her book deal because she took advantage of the movement. Her writing is frankly not that good.*

I wasn't going to let them tell me what I could and could not write about my own city. If we want to write shit poems about Hong Kong, then let us write shit poems about Hong Kong. If I want to exploit my pain, then let me exploit it until my heart can no longer take it.

. . .

I have never studied in America or lived in New York City; from afar, I can only be a spectator of the "literary scene." My major publication bylines came through referrals from other Hong Kong–based writers and editors, or commissions from white editors who wanted to "have something on Hong Kong" for their magazine during the protests—in other words, a piece that could fill a quota. To this day, my body of work is found in more local and regional publications than international ones. Local and regional publications don't ask me to explain my city. They don't ask me to justify writing about the lives of my people. They let me write about what makes Hong Kong human, and not only what makes it different.

I was misled by the boom of books by Asian American writers in the late 2010s to believe that there might be more opportunities for Asian writers. I devoured these titles, felt vicarious joy for the success of these writers. But these opportunities were rarely extended to writers in Asia. When I first began pitching to overseas magazines and journals, I learned that there were publications that stated in their submission guidelines, "Do not send ideas about people and events in Asia unless they convey something about the Asian diaspora that resonates with the Asian American experience." Grants and fellowship opportunities that now prioritize POC writers are still rarely accessible to my friends and me in Hong Kong, either because we don't have the right citizenship or aren't based in Britain or the United States.

It is a disorienting experience to be an English-language writer from Asia; we are constantly mistaken for Asian American writers. On Twitter, I've been called "diaspora" or Asian American, even though I've only ever lived in Hong

Kong. I've been warned that I probably shouldn't write about Confucianism or stories about my grandmother, because it is a contested or tired topic in Asian American discourse. For a while, when social media was dominated by Asian Americans talking about how *Crazy Rich Asians* was a step forward for representation, my friends and I were privately bemoaning how the film essentially positioned Asian Americans as the underdogs, and people in Asia as privileged and filthy rich. It left me with a distinctly sour aftertaste, especially when my peers were barely surviving the political and economic realities of our cities.

As poet Nicholas Wong was publishing his second collection, *Crevasse,* NBC News listed him as an Asian American poet to watch. The article said his collection "shows how the experience of 'Asian American' can transcend place and language," then added, "Wong is currently based in Hong Kong." Wong writes in English, but he is not Asian American; he has never even lived in America. In an interview with translator Lucas Klein, Wong didn't seem to mind this mislabeling, but agreed that it was a strategic, political decision. It was Asian American writing that was on the rise, not writing by Asian writers.

When diasporic Asian writers move to their ancestors' countries, they become Asian correspondents for the American media companies they work for, and the stories of contemporary Asia are told through their lens rather than that of journalists who grew up in that place. Sometimes I get the feeling that we aren't real people to them, merely inhabitants of a place where the *real* story is one about how they reconnected with their ancestors' culture. Still, because I grew up reading English books by white authors, Asian American books made me feel seen, and I idolized these writers from afar.

At a journalists' drinks event a few years ago, I asked a diasporic Asian writer working for an international magazine why there weren't any Hong Kong writers in the Asia bureau, which was based here. *Well, because we don't just write about Hong Kong, but all of Asia,* she said. *Oh yeah, okay,* I said. On my walk home, my head swimming in a warm alcohol fuzz, I thought about what I didn't say: *Wait, so you get to write about anything you want, but writers from Hong Kong only ever get to write about Hong Kong?*

Sometimes I exasperate myself. Why was I always getting angry over how Hong Kong was being written about in Western media or books about lives of expats that become Amazon-produced series, when I could use that energy to write about, say, how contemporary Hong Kong bands like Kimberley Road Union and 小本生燈 are incorporating the poetry of 飲江 and 北島 in their lyrics? Why not instead analyze the oeuvre of writers such as Dung Kai Cheung, Wong Bik Wan, Hon Lai Chu, Yesi, Xi Xi, and others whose works have defined Hong Kong literature and were being translated in recent years? Had I internalized the idea that something was not part of the "discourse" unless it was in English, that a trend or phenomenon was not real until Western media covered it?

To be a language traitor is to live in a state where the language I hear around me every day and the voice I use to describe that reality are not one and the same. When interviewees give me quotes in Cantonese, I don't mark the quotes as translated, merely supply them in English; readers have no way of knowing what the interviewee really said verbatim. That dissonance I experience led me to a dilemma that each generation of writers of English in Hong Kong confronts every few years like clockwork. "Hong Kong is a Chinese city, full of Chinese people, and there is a Chinese language, with, of course, an incomparable literary tradition," English professor Douglas Kerr once wrote. "Why articulate a modern Hong Kong Chinese experience in a residual colonial English language brought to the China coast with the traders, the missionaries, and the gunboats of empire?"

To write in English, and, worse, to *choose* to write in English, the language of our colonizers, is an implicit betrayal of our mother tongue. English is still a deeply classist language in Hong Kong. The majority of English-language writers, if they are not white, are educated in private or international schools, and then go on to a liberal arts college or an Ivy League school. They are given top jobs in newsrooms and premium space in literary magazines, thus the opportunity to tell Hong Kong stories to the world. This dictates that the story of Hong Kong in the global discourse is necessarily told by people who likely never experienced being on the other end of the economic inequalities that run so deep in this city.

In English-language literature, books set in Hong Kong are limited to featuring characters of "mixed-race, jet-setting, upper-middle-class, work-hard-play-hard professionals," as one critic noted in a review of a prominent Hong Kong writer. By 2019, the writer, who is of this background herself, seemed mostly disappointed, annoyed at the city. Other writers have penned stories that adopted the tone of poverty porn when discussing working-class life, including characters such as cardboard grannies or drug addicts. The only exceptions to this narrow vision of Hong Kong are in the realm of poetry. Since Louise Ho, the trailblazer of English-language poetry, poets from a range of class backgrounds, including Tammy Ho Lai-Ming, Jennifer Wong, Nicholas Wong, Marco Yan, Mary Jean Chan, and Wawa, have adopted various strategies of incorporating the Chinese language and "local ethos" (intentionally or otherwise) into their poetry, pulling the two universes closer together.

The poet and academic Tammy Ho Lai-Ming has argued that there is space for writers to reshape the language using local sensibilities, make it "into Hong Kong" as the city inhabits "a third space between the coloniser and the dominant native culture." *Local* can be a vague but loaded descriptor, incapable of being defined yet simultaneously capable of being used for the purpose of exclusion. But I can see a Hong Kong that is endearingly familiar in the anarchist and storyteller Hung Jai Suk Suk 雄仔叔叔's bilingual poetry (translated by the author himself), when he writes about the outdoor classrooms in the Umbrella Movement: "First light / Morning lands on the streets / A breeze opens the door / To the fresh murmurs of / Trees, flyovers, bus stops." And in the poet Wawa's "Letter to a Future Daughter on the Occasion of the Fishball Revolution," when she writes, far away from Hong Kong, "I can't show you the trees I grew up with, the turtles I fed in ponds, the wet markets where I stood in a corner with my mother watching fish-stall vendors tear the skin off frogs. I can't teach you how to identify autumn's arrival by the nuance of a Hong Kong breeze, or what color of sunlight announces winter's visit." I turn to Nicholas Wong's poetry for all the darkly funny ways he pokes fun at Hong Kong ("If we anagram capitalism to *I am plastic*"), but also how he doesn't write about Hong Kong, resisting the temptation to act as though one has to represent the experiences of seven million people every time they write as a "Hong Kong poet."

Felix Chow, a twenty-year-old poet, told me that if English-language writers paid more attention to "the segregation between different social classes and geographical districts of Hong Kong" and expanded the subject matters of what is written about, it could be a direct way to destigmatize the language. He also believed that it would help for English-language writing to not be in "high" standardized English, but instead a version of Hong Kong English. "If people see other non-rich people writing stuff they identify with using English, they might feel more confident in writing themselves," he said. Poets like Felix and his peers could soon usher in a new generation of writers in Hong Kong that are much more attuned to the relationship between language and class.

Here's the thing you have to understand: I'm part of the problem. I don't believe that growing up working-class should automatically lend a writer an air of authenticity, because it does not necessarily indicate that one has meaningful engagement with a place. But I don't want to distance myself from privilege. If I gave you the impression that I had a shitty early twenties, it's because everyone my age in late-capitalist Hong Kong has had a shitty early twenties. I am not suddenly more representative of Hong Kong just because I offer you a little more than life in the Mid-Levels. The fact that my father could afford to send me to an international school guaranteed my fluency in English, and that in turn guaranteed upward mobility and continued privilege.

When I say I want to write for "us," as in the people of Hong Kong, I am living in a certain state of self-deception.

Ever since I started writing, I always felt the need to apologize for writing in English, which was by extension an apology for my privileged international school education. In secondary school, I sometimes wrote Facebook notes in English, and my classmates would cheerfully inform me that they wouldn't read them. They will likely never read this book unless it's translated into Chinese. Inexplicably, the Cantonese colloquialism for the English language is "chicken intestines." You're writing in chicken intestines again, they said. *Sorry sorry sorry,* I said to my classmates. *Sorry sorry sorry,* I said to an interviewee who said she used a dictionary to read my write-up, when I thought the writing style was already quite populist.

As a trilingual former international school kid, I've benefited precisely from this liminal space of being local enough to write stories that white writers can't, and "international" enough to write about Hong Kong for overseas readers. Even as I try to work through questions of how and what it means to write for a local audience, I know that my readership will probably be predominantly outside of Hong Kong. Whereas new works in Chinese and Cantonese add to the ever-growing canon of local stories about Hong Kong, writing in English is a constant negotiation with the question of what it means to "represent Hong Kong for a Western reader," an approach one editor suggested I take.

But how could a person, any person, write a single story that could embody this city and all its beautiful, chaotic contradictions? Do not read this and believe that I am the one who can give you the story of Hong Kong. Never trust anyone who holds themselves out as such.

· · ·

For so many who claim to love Hong Kong, the city has never existed outside of the archaic image of the Hong Kong cool. A good test is whether they can get through a conversation about Hong Kong without mentioning Wong Kar Wai, the auteur director who immortalized an old Hong Kong drenched in warm, flickering lights, a city inhabited with beautiful people wearing cheongsams or oversized coats, smoking cigarettes against a storefront, or looking at their own pixie-cut reflections in the escalators. A city always craning its neck for a lover that will never come.

Wong is arguably the most well-known director from the city, but his films are set in an imagined Hong Kong that embodied less what Hong Kong is than what voyeurs *wanted* us to look like—a chaotic city nestled within the Chungking Mansions, or the moody "mean streets of Mong Kok." You could read postcolonial anxiety in his work (the multiple appearances of the British National [Overseas] passport in *Happy Together;* the name of his movie *2046,* referring to the year before the complete resumption of Chinese rule in Hong Kong), but unlike other films that were released around the handover, his political themes are muted and subtle. Wong's films are defined by disappointment and disappearance, a negative space where everybody is waiting. It is unlikely that the filmmaker's works were ever intended to be *about* life in the city itself. None of this dampens the frustrated pleasure of watching star-crossed lovers whose faces are etched with permanent longing, but these characters nonetheless serve as blank canvases for viewers to project their own desires. His films delivered a "visual and spatial paradox" of Hong Kong that never existed, one that could be consumed by foreign audiences. But Wong's Hong Kong *aesthetics* should not be conflated with Hong Kong *culture.*

Why then, in the postcolonial era, are we still holding on to the notion that Wong Kar Wai's films were somehow representative of Hong Kong? A Beijing-based scholar wrote, in 2019: "Hong Kong once had a cachet that few cities could match: the home of Bruce Lee, Wong Kar-wai, and Eileen Chang—a bucket-list destination perched on a fault line of global politics. . . . But much of Hong Kong now feels about as exciting as a Chinese provincial capital." He asserts that the city "feels trapped in the 1980s." But this nostalgia-stained assessment is colonialist, suggesting that the heyday of Hong Kong came and went during its pre-handover era. It was the writer, not the city, that was trapped in the past.

Though films and English-language literature operate in different realms, both contribute to a specific imagination of Hong Kong, and the continual cultural obsession with these films is a gauge as to what types of representation of the city are favored over the others. What these critics are saying is, bring back the good cop/triad films of the 1980s and '90s that Tarantino would rip off, the golden era of Cantopop with Roman Tam and Anita Mui and Leslie Cheung. Few filmmakers have earned the overseas cult following of Wong Kar Wai, but directors such as Pang Ho Cheung and Johnnie To continue to deliver films that speak to local and international audiences, Pang with his brand of vulgar, playful Hong Kong humor; To for perpetuating and reinventing the city's legacy of action-crime films. (Interestingly, when Criterion Collection did a series on Wong Kar Wai in 2021, it commissioned only Asian Americans and Asian writers based in America, and not a single Hong Kong film writer, as though it barely mattered what people here thought about Wong.)

But the films of this past decade also depicted Hong Kong lives with so much cultural specificity that they were less translatable to foreign audiences, especially in the postcolonial era. Aesthetics could be consumed without context, but culture much less so. *The Way We Dance* (2013) based its story around street dancers in the city, while its sequel (2021) turned the focus to tensions between the industrial building subculture and gentrification in Hong Kong. *My Prince Edward* (2019) critiques the patriarchal culture and societal values surrounding the institution of weddings and marriage in Hong Kong, and *Suk Suk* (2019) features two closeted gay men who fall in love in their elderly age. *Ballad on the Shore* (2017) is about the disappearance of fishermen culture in this former "fishing village" of Hong Kong, while *Rhymes of Shui Hau* (2017) documents the folk songs in a South Lantau village in a language remembered now only by a handful of grandmothers. These stories touch on aspects of Hong Kong culture that resonate with local audiences, but may not immediately be appreciated by someone who has never lived in the city.

A series of independent films in the 2010s drew on lesser-known protest narratives, at a time when the resistance movement was gaining momentum. *Pseudo Secular* (2016) is a three-hour film based on the true events of 2011, when left-leaning activists in Hong Kong occupied the space underneath the HSBC building for almost a year. The documentary *Vanished Archives* (2017) looks into how public records are missing and thus offered an incomplete story of the 1967 riots in Hong Kong, while *No. 1 Chung Ying Street* (2018) generated heated debate on social media for trying to make parallels between the 1967 riots and land protests in the past decade. The films explored a side of Hong Kong protest culture outside of the Umbrella Movement, which was the dominant narrative in international media and English-language books at the time.

Outside of mainstream representations of Hong Kong, subcultures were taking shape on the streets, in industrial buildings, indie art spaces, and bookstores. All they needed were some writers.

Wilfred Chan and I met over Twitter. At the time, I was a reporter at *Hong Kong Free Press,* and Wilfred was a journalist for CNN International. Soon after we began talking, we realized we both had the idea of starting an English-language publication for Hong Kong writing. Our first meeting was over dumplings on Water Street. Wilfred's face is lined with a smile, and he always has a camera hanging over his chest. He told me how he went to school in New York City after a childhood in rainy Seattle, and used photography as a medium to investigate his relationship with Hong Kong. I told him that going to gigs in Hong Kong saved my life.

Soon, we were mourning the lack of good cultural reporting in Hong Kong. The few magazines that focused on culture had folded or shifted their focus to lists of "the best coffee shops in up-and-coming hipster neighborhoods" or "ten signs you're a real Hong Konger" (includes the item *Bubble tea is life*). They covered wellness and yoga with clienteles of rich white women and Hong Kong heirs and heiresses, but not gigs taking place every weekend or photography exhibitions in offbeat venues. Then there were magazines focused exclusively on the lives of white people in rich neighborhoods, such as the Mid-Levels or Sai Kung, that make you wonder if expats truly live in a parallel universe from the rest of Hong Kong.

Wilfred and I thought we could do better. We read back issues of *Muse,* a bilingual cultural magazine from the 2000s, and at times panicked over our foolhardiness, or asked ourselves why we thought we had the authority to do this. Wilfred is Hong Kong–American and hadn't lived here very long. I was twenty-four and had only recently started reading *The New Yorker.* But we went for it anyway. We learned how to make a website. We found a group of writers and photographers who were crazy enough to try this with us.

A year later, we launched *Still / Loud.* "We hope to be a space for young creatives and a shelter for overlooked stories," we wrote. We would write about culture without "the lifestyle shit." We would document a vanishing Hong Kong. We would profile musicians and artists without asking them the stock questions about what they thought of the protests, or what Hong Kong meant to them. We would take it for granted that their stories were worth writing about on their own terms. We would not force the "Cantonese is under threat from the Communist Party campaign for Mandarin hegemony" angle, or focus on the hip designers who recycled nostalgic aesthetics.

Since we were all bilingual, we could cover stories about events that were promoted or took place in Cantonese, but write about them in English, bringing them to a wider audience. If I'm honest, we also wanted to write ourselves *into* the creative scene, or at least feel adjacent to the community. And for two years, that's what we did. We wrote about trap artist Fotan Laiki on the cusp of newfound fame, anarchist book fairs, local films, Ren Hang, the story of *Muse* magazine, raids at Hidden Agenda. We became friends with our favorite musicians and zinemakers. The team met at cafés across the city and went to music festivals together.

In one of our first meetings at *Still / Loud,* writer Holmes Chan made a suggestion: that rather than transcribing the

Chinese terms into English phonetically, we should place the original Chinese characters next to the English text, no italics, no parentheses, because that would mark the Chinese as secondary. When someone uses phonetics such as *ng goi,* "You signal to the reader, via the literary presentation, that it is some kind of foreign body within the text," Holmes said. Typically, Hong Kong writers who write in English do not critically engage or challenge their chosen language. But when it comes to rendering dialogue, the seams that mark the difference between literary representation and reality will show, because the implicit understanding is that the person in the story is not in fact speaking in English, but Cantonese. But why was the writer writing in English? Was it enough to say, simply, that we, the writers, simply *wanted to* write in English, because we felt more comfortable with the language for one reason or another, and that comfort reflected our privilege?

I read Holmes's work years before we spoke for the first time. During Occupy Central, my friends shared a piece posted on Facebook by a fellow university student, analyzing the disproportionate use of force by the police during the first days of the movement using legal principles. That piece was written by Holmes. He was in the same literature and law program as me in school, but two years below, and was captain of the university's debate team.

Three years later, Holmes reached out and asked to meet up for coffee. We sat at our university's Starbucks as a line of students stretched out into the foyer. Holmes wears button-down shirts and sometimes speaks about the most casual of topics in the manner of listing well-rehearsed arguments to an imaginary debate judge. He had just returned from an exchange semester at Duke, which coincided with the election of Donald Trump. Holmes said he wanted to start writing professionally. I asked if he might be interested in joining *Still / Loud*. Over the years, we became good friends, taking turns sending each other our work for edits and feedback.

Holmes went to a traditional boys' school in Pokfulam that taught classes in English, right across from the University of Hong Kong campus. He developed an interest in writing early on. His parents saw it in a typically pragmatic, colonial way: good English, better job opportunities. Holmes didn't completely understand why he was drawn to writing, especially in English rather than Chinese, but soon it affected his pop culture consumption: He started watching *The Daily Show with Jon Stewart* and *The West Wing.* When he was a kid, he wrote stories that weren't defined by race, but were by default white, given that his literature consumption was all stories of white people. By the final years of secondary school, he was thinking to himself in English. Holmes studied law and literature, and, like me, became a reporter upon graduation rather than a lawyer. He has since written for an array of international publications.

"The original sin of the English language in Hong Kong is colonialism, and so, deliberately or not, people who write it must find an ongoing justification to exist; this is the tariff we pay for a seat at the table, to enter relevance," Holmes once wrote in a piece for *Still / Loud.* Unlike some other postcolonial regions, he tells me now, we have to accept that in Hong Kong, no matter how hard we work, how much we expand the market, Anglophone literature is always going to be in the minority. In colonial times, small does not equal powerless. Titles like *Gweilo: Memories of a Hong Kong Childhood* or *The World of Suzie Wong* use Hong Kong for export; these stories were not written for Hong Kong readers. "If you look at it strictly, they're not even part of Hong Kong's literary space, just an extension of the British literary space. The question then becomes, after colonialism, why the fuck do we still need you?"

After 1997, English-language literature remained a minority, and outward-facing. One Hong Kong book from the past decade, for instance, compares Hong Kong to New York City, a reference that assumes the reader is someone who already knows Manhattan and Brooklyn. In the Penguin Hong Kong series in 2016, five out of the seven authors were white men. Hong Kong's literature was written not for readers in the city, but for "an unseen diaspora, or some international connoisseur, peering at Hong Kong with anthropological detachment," Holmes argued in the piece.

"The common refrain is that Hong Kong people don't read English, but the problem is that they take that as the starting point of the Anglophone ecosystem—and therefore, they write for someone else. Hong Kong readers do not factor into their cultural output," he says. The result is that the Anglophone literature here gives him the sensation that he is *overhearing*. "It was the author speaking to somebody next to me about me, and I just happen to overhear this conversation, and of course the actual recipient of that conversation was a white guy. I was having myself explained back to me, but not directly to my face. The way to rectify that was to create a kind of writing voice that was speaking directly to me."

We ran into the same problem with *Still / Loud*. Throughout the course of running the magazine together, we never resolved the problem of audience. Who were we writing for? We said we wanted our pieces to be part of the local cultural ecosystem, to be read by Hong Kongers. But if that were the case, we would have written them in Chinese. Instead, we insisted that we weren't writing for white people, but ourselves. Even though we found readers in the local music and art scene, most readers were the Asian diaspora and international school graduates, which was nice but also not what we set out to do. In Hong Kong, white adjacency can be measured directly against your fluency in English. We wanted to build a bridge between the worlds with stories, but we were simply telling stories to the next most privileged class.

That doesn't mean that we could not work to expand the demographic of local readers for English writing, or write pieces that would appeal to them. Holmes says that if he wanted to write in English, he would try to justify the work's existence to a local audience. He would come to you instead. The typical Hong Kong reader does not really think about colonial baggage or resentment, he says. They aren't reading English, not as a fuck-you to English, but because it doesn't give them utility. We knew from our past experience that if an article on the same topic is available in Chinese, a local reader is almost always going to go for the path of least resistance. We would have to give them something they couldn't get anywhere else.

To consciously write for a Hong Kong reader requires configuring one's writing in a way that will make sense to them and developing a vernacular, Holmes says. This is not to infantilize the reader, or to treat them as a homogenous body, but to make them feel like they belong in the conversation. "I'm not interested in writing that is deliberately opaque or reclusive. Writing shouldn't be insular, or try to play at pretentiousness."

This means changing literary devices and strategies: one that doesn't slow down the pace of reading, doesn't put the brakes on a sentence, such that you have to look up a word in the dictionary or stomach a certain level of boredom or obscurity. Holmes wants to write in a way that makes the reading process as smooth, as frictionless, and as painless as possible. And with time, perhaps we can finally write our way out of clichés like how Hong Kong is a borrowed place living on borrowed time, and build ourselves into a new literary imagination.

We approached *Still / Loud* with the spirit of an experiment, and eventually like most experiments it failed. No one made any money from the publication. Everyone was a volunteer and had day jobs on the side. We never commissioned writers because we couldn't pay them; if they wanted to write, we invited them to join the team, so they would feel a sense of ownership. We knew that failing to monetize would bring sustainability issues in the long run, but we weren't prepared to have conversations about what ads were acceptable and what constituted selling out. We lasted two years. The publication ended the way publications always end: Writers felt underappreciated, editors were burned out and failed to support writers, and our arguments were unconstructive and toxic. We unceremoniously reached an unspoken decision to stop publishing around the time the protests in 2019 began.

These days, we're still writing, curating exhibitions, taking photographs, editing books, making zines, even though we don't do this together anymore. Wilfred lives in New York City and writes long features and commentaries for *The Nation*. Some of us are still friends. The publication will likely never be revived, although the archive of sixty-something profiles, features, and reviews still exists online. I have never been able to write about Hong Kong like that again: inward-looking, as part of and in a friendly, mutual give-and-take relationship with the creative scene, rather than writing to outsiders who always wanted me to give the artist profiles a stereotypical spin about what "made" them Hong Kong.

In 2020, Holmes put together and edited *Aftershock,* a book of firsthand accounts and essays from journalists during the 2019 movement. I was one of its contributors. In *Aftershock,* Holmes does not explain the events of 2019. For the anthology, one journalist writes about the death of student Chow Tsz Lok, who fell to his death near a protest site; another covers the Chinese University of Hong Kong protests as someone who lived on campus all his life; a third recalls tensions in the newsroom and over the dinner table. One reviewer wrote that it was a good book, but with the caveat that you had to already know what was happening in Hong Kong. It differs from the other Hong Kong protest books written in English, which offer few insights to readers who live here and already follow the news closely. Holmes prioritized the local readers.

"For Anglophone literature, to have a postcolonial future, to have *a* future, it needs to be read by present-day people, postcolonial subjects," Holmes says. "Whatever most successfully engages them and provokes them into some kind of interaction or dialogue, that is the way to go. At least it will not die. At least it will exist."

I sometimes joke that if Hong Kong were to be liberated, I could become a music writer instead. I could write about gigs my friend played at, how they sliced their fingers against the strings till their jeans were smeared with blood. I could profile bands and review albums, compare indie trends in Hong Kong, Taiwan, and China, write essays about how post-rock and shoegaze found an unexpected wave of popularity in East Asia. I do not want to write about only Hong Kong for the rest of my life. But at this moment, I know that there is nothing else I can write except this.

I am afraid that despite everything I claim, I have romanticized the city. I am still learning how not to reduce the people I love to stories, trading their lives for a coveted byline. There are other people whose stories are essential, but are missing here because I do not have the right to write for them. I cannot force my community into the story you want, and then return to them and live with the consequences of my untruthfulness. I am not here to exploit and then leave. If you promise to try to understand, I will exploit myself for you. But I will not apologize anymore.

I am no longer the young starry-eyed journalist waxing on about chronicling the slow death of the city. But I still believe in the work that my peers do: waking up early to position their cameras outside court for yet another political trial; writing about an artist, a neighborhood, a freshly exiled protester; pushing back against editorial pressure. They are the bridges that make the work of foreign correspondents here possible, the interpreters that bring the Hong Kong story into the pages of international newspapers. These days, they are doing their own stories.

We now live in a climate where censorship in mainstream local publishing dictates the stories that can be told, foreign publications make the call on what we can write about this place, and indie magazines fold and run out of steam from lack of resources. Yet there are still editors and makers who start homegrown publications that insist on telling these stories on their own terms. There are younger writers like Felix who are putting together poetry collections and wrestling with the question of what "local" writing means to them. When I talk to them at the many readings they are already attending and speaking at, they remind me of myself just a decade ago, desperately seeking books that set an example for what I wanted to write in the future.

One evening, as I stand among shelves of books at the independent bookstore Kubrick under its warm lights and soft piano music, I pick out collections of writing and photographs about the protests here, English-language anthologies by young poets, and small zines about overlooked urbanscapes or alternative lifestyles in Hong Kong. I think about the books I have received from activist friends that detail the lives of domestic workers back in their hometowns in Southeast Asia, the newspapers made by minority communities that are handed out at rallies for solidarity. At home, I flip through the book I received in the mail the other day, the anonymously edited poetry collection *Hong Kong Without Us,* so achingly beautiful in the way it captures the small, ephemeral moments and messages during the protest movement that would have disappeared if never archived: "The restaurant suddenly took in / a crowd dressed all in black. / Free dishes came endlessly out. / The police broke in / but only found teens / and neighbors, their outfits / changed, eating together."

Writing is not activism. Writing about a place cannot keep it from disappearing, and writing cannot replace the work of mutual care we have to do in the communities we inhabit. All the same, these documentations are all acts of resistance, of remembrance. Someday, when they tell us otherwise, we will revisit these accounts that challenge what they want us to believe. We will know what we cannot unknow.

# Welcome to the Factories

牛頭角的日出都看厭
時間不站在你身邊
沉迷過的樂隊解散了
—MY LITTLE AIRPORT, 《牛頭角青年》

The happiest moments of my life have taken place inside smoke-filled rooms burrowed deep within industrial buildings: at the many incarnations of Hidden Agenda in the East Kowloon district; at intimate private gigs organized by friends in their band practice spaces in San Po Kong; at secret parties hosted by anarchists who lived in these factories. These hazy gigs are a haven for teenagers with piercings and eyeliner from the 2000s, disaffected twenty-somethings who can roll cigarettes with one hand, musicians in dreads downing beers. Everyone looks vaguely familiar: The scene here is small, and the gigs recycle through a limited pool of people. There are the metalheads, the shoegazers, the post-rock introverts. They become my best friends, or familiar faces I nod at but never quite speak to, like acquaintances who went to the same church for a decade.

Every time a familiar song comes on, it takes me to a forgotten moment that has been secretly archived by my body. I think of music as a reservoir of tiny memories, memories that can evaporate but still be distilled into songs that hit like flash floods. Dancing to alt-J in my underwear, in that flat with the cool marble floors. My partner and I at Hidden Agenda, yelling secrets into each other's ears at the back to the music of Hong Kong indie pop outfit Thud. Catching the end of Sleep Party People's set on the grassy lawns at West Kowloon, watching a man in a Donnie Darko–lite mask surfing through the crowds in the November sun as the synth ignited the autumn air.

But music documents more than personal history: It is an archive of the times. Local indie darlings My Little Airport swearing at the chief executive, CY Leung, during the city's biggest music festival in 2014 as the city was forever changed by the Umbrella Movement. Tomii and his friends playing the Hong Kong protest anthem at the New Year's Eve countdown in 2019 at a cozy bar in To Kwa Wan, months before the national security law was passed and Covid-19 made such gatherings impossible. The audience yelling, "Revolution of our times" in Cantonese in between sets at these live houses, when you least expect it. The shows in obscure venues that have forced me to travel across Hong Kong and familiarize myself with their neighborhoods: Kwai Hing, Yau Tong, Fortress Hill. The mini festivals and parties at venues that have since closed. The bands that have broken up and gotten back together. The musicians who have since left Hong Kong.

I started writing about music before I learned how to write anything else. I went to gigs and reviewed them for a local website, and that became my entry point to the different scenes across Hong Kong in our abandoned factory buildings. I wore black to blend in with the dark venues, silently noting the different faces onstage and in the audience. *One day,* I thought, *I will get to know every one of you.*

I didn't become a music lover by choice. Music never stopped sputtering out of my father's elaborate home sound system in our three-hundred-square-foot living room. His records towered over me in tall piles: behind the television, on our coffee table, framing the mirror in the study. Sometimes I tripped over CDs. My father's taste in music was diverse: He listened to regional pop stars like Jacky Cheung and Faye Wong, but also Kraftwerk and New Order.

One of my earliest music memories is stumbling into the living room one afternoon as psychedelic guitars and choruses of children sing a haunting tune in unison: *We don't need no education / We don't need no thought control.* On the television, my father was watching processions of uniformed kids in grotesque masks fall one by one into a giant metal machine, which turns out to be a meat grinder: The children are turned into mince. *Hey! Teacher! Leave us kids alone!* I had nightmares for a week.

Music filled our flat, but my father never shared his interest with me, or talked about what drew him to these bands. In my late teens, during those long waits for bands to come onstage at shows, I would find myself humming along to familiar songs from the deejay's playlists, yet unable to name the musician. In university, when I returned to my childhood flat on the weekend, I murmured the names I now recognized in his collection. Echo and the Bunnymen. Bauhaus. The Clash. Talking Heads. They were all punk and post-punk-influenced bands. Shit, was my father secretly a punk? I tried to picture him in a black leather jacket, his hair shaggy and long, and failed. I've only ever seen him wear plaid and dress shirts.

My father is Rob from *High Fidelity*. He is a stereotype that would be made fun of on the internet today—someone who thinks their music taste is a substitute for having a personality. When we were on holiday as a kid, he set aside days to visit local record shops. Sometimes he brought cases of albums home. At Tower Records in Japan, he bought multiple copies of albums he already owned, because the special Japanese versions usually contain bonus tracks. I was exasperated. Where would we even put these records? Every corner of the flat was already overflowing with CDs. Sometimes he never even tore open the plastic to listen to them. I dismissed this as his hoarder tendencies; my generation grew up with iPods, mobile music libraries that fit inside our bags. And then, when I was twenty-three, I visited Amoeba Records in San Francisco, and found myself doing the exact same thing. I bought a dozen records at five U.S. dollars each, including Elliott Smith and the Raveonettes and Slint. I found an out-of-print copy of Slowdive's *Catch the Breeze,* and the definitive Tropicália record *Tropicália: ou Panis et Circencis,* for my partner. I held them in my arms and cradled them like a baby during the flight, because I didn't want to pay for extra baggage.

My father never studied outside of this city, but nevertheless developed an appetite for Western pop and rock. "When I was young, at the beginning of the 1980s, these British new wave, post-punk bands were coming to Hong Kong, and I felt perhaps one factor drawing them here was that we were a British colony," veteran music writer Yuen Chi Chung told me. Yuen ran a music magazine called *Music Colony Bi-weekly* between 1994 and 2004, scoring interviews with David Bowie and the Foo Fighters. Yuen said that if you wanted to be hip then, you'd listen to music from overseas—with Cantopop, meaning pop music sung in Cantonese, the dominant genre in Hong Kong at the time, there wasn't much variation or innovation with the music style.

But Western music was also much more mainstream during the colonial era: It was on the airwaves and on popular late-night TV shows like *Enjoy Yourself Tonight* 歡樂今宵. Hong Kong could tune in to the British Forces Broadcasting Service, the radio for the British Armed Forces, which sometimes played John Peel sessions. Even Yuen, a self-described "public housing kid with a modest background," became a music fanatic. Yuen speculated that with my father, who was a generation before him, music enlightenment could have come as early as the Beatles' 1964 legendary show at the Princess Theatre in Kowloon.

The last time my father and I went to see a show together was February 2017: Tangerine Dream, a German electronic group founded in the 1960s that my father played often at home, but was regarded as relatively obscure among my friends. By then he had already lost most of his eyesight and had to be led down the steps and into the hall. My father said he hadn't been to Hong Kong Baptist University for a show since the British band Siouxsie and the Banshees came in the 1980s. Yuen once recalled to me how, back then, the university banned rock shows at the AC Hall because rowdy music fans at Depeche Mode, Robert Plant, and other gigs frequently damaged the seats and the floor in excitement. My father ended up sleeping through the majority of the Tangerine Dream show.

After my father became legally blind and moved back to

the family tong lau, his record collection was packed away and kept in a refrigerated room at a mini-storage, Hong Kong's storage solution for small flats. He offered it to me once, and I laughed. I moved around so much that, until recently, everything I owned could be packed into three suitcases. My father and I stopped speaking in 2019. Tens of thousands of records are just sitting somewhere in an ex-factory warehouse unit in San Po Kong. No one has touched them for years.

When I found my own music in my teens, it was revelatory. My brother introduced me to metal, and soon it became a coping mechanism. After another of my father's tantrums, I held in the resentment that was blooming in my chest, and put on earphones and blasted Slipknot's "Psychosocial" until my ears rang. Being part of a band's fandom, with legions of other people who loved the band from all across the world and age groups, made me feel like I belonged to a secret family. On our Tumblrs, we reblogged music announcements and shared stories about how a song got us through the unforgiving time that was puberty.

I went to my first gig when I was seventeen: Hurts, an English electropop band, was playing at a music hall in Kowloon Bay. In the queue, I ran into a couple of students from my school in the year above me, to my surprise. No one in my year listened to anything but Cantopop, which during our era was often unimaginative and bland, and the lyrics were always about heartbreak and only heartbreak. I learned that there was a group of seniors who were hardcore music fans; one of them was NKCH. "It's not that pop is bad, it's just that there are more choices out there and people don't pay attention. With time, your tolerance towards different music goes up, and you lean towards the lesser known genres," NKCH told me when I interviewed him half a decade later. He and his friends run Zenegeist, a Facebook page that shares their favorite music to thousands of followers. The goal is not just to favor "indie" bands, but diversity, he explains.

I decided that I was destined to be in a band. The problem was that I didn't know what to do with a guitar or a bass or drums. I played the piano all through my childhood and teenage years but never got far. I haunted the "seeking bandmate" pages on local online forums, and eventually found a couple of dudes who were seeking a vocalist. We met up in an hourly rental space in a walkup building in Mong Kok, where the instruments were sticky with beer residue. For the first practice, we covered "Zombie" by the Cranberries, and Nirvana's "Come as You Are." It turned out that the bassist had just started learning the instrument and could not keep up, even though the Nirvana song was easy to play. We went to the McDonald's on Nathan Road afterward, ate chicken nuggets for hours, and chatted about our favorite bands, but never made plans to jam again.

But the drummer, Jason, kept making unexpected cameos in my life. He started working at Hidden Agenda as a sort of 打雜, meaning he pretty much did everything from babysitting bands to posting promotional flyers. But usually I'd find him behind the bar in a band tee, unscrewing caps from bottles or pulling the nozzle for draft beer into plastic cups. He would look up from his black-framed glasses and go, *Weiiiii,* with a smile as though we were old friends. I smiled back, handed him the cash, and disappeared into the crowd of writhing bodies as guitar sounds pulsed through the room.

Every time I learned the directions to Hidden Agenda, the beloved live-music venue moved to a new location. I was eighteen years old the first time I tried to find the elusive live house. Ngau Tau Kok is a labyrinth of factory buildings that crisscross into one another. My location services swerved wildly as I tried to find the right route, and I still couldn't locate the right street and then the right building. In the dark, they were all just faded and graffitied façades with air conditioners and exhaust fans protruding from their windows. The entrance could be at the back, or through the car park. Sometimes in factory buildings, lifts are ancient beings that refuse to budge if you don't pull the gates together properly. I tailed behind a girl in red lipstick, a fedora, and a long black dress until we reached a floor with dusty vending machines and band stickers splashed on wall surfaces. I could hear the music shaking even from inside the elevator, and knew I was at the right place.

That an indie scene exists at all in Hong Kong is a small miracle. The city did not encourage creativity or alternative lifestyles, especially art that operated outside of government institutions and art-funding bodies. When I grew up in the 2000s, no one around me was in a band or had any desire to be in one. My classmates and I were forced to learn a classical instrument at a young age, especially if we came from a middle-class family. But it wasn't to develop our artistic sensibilities or to encourage our creative expression; it just looked good on our school applications. My teachers instilled in me the idea that only two types of people became artists and creators: those who don't score well enough to attend regular universities, or kids with trust funds. *If you don't get into a university, that's pretty much the end of your life,* we would often hear from our teachers. It became the only truth we knew, etched into our heads. The priority was owning a flat, not making art. My secondary school friends came from working- or middle-class backgrounds: They were told that their future involved either supporting their families or making their middle-class families more middle-class. No one told us we had other alternatives.

Music didn't fit into the equation. When I found the industrial building scene and other young people who listened to obscure bands I had never heard of, I wondered, *Where did these people come from?* They had been there all along, but in a world I couldn't touch and didn't know existed, until I crossed over. They embodied a sense of freedom that felt more real to me than the then-abstract notion of "freedom" in Hong Kong we had to defend. They inhabited a Hong Kong that I could see myself in, showed me that a different life was possible.

Hidden Agenda was established by a group of music lovers in the late 2000s. Its most well-known cofounder is Hui Chung Wo, who opened a shop selling band tees from Thailand in Hong Kong when he was twenty, and later moved with some friends to live in an industrial building in Kwun Tong. Hui and his friends were music lovers, and realized the unit could double as a gig space. The live house wasn't founded in industrial buildings because of the cool aesthetics: Abandoned warehouses are affordable, spacious enough for shows, and far enough away from typical residences to avoid noise complaints. Over the past two decades, industrial buildings in our city have been indispensable to artists in need of space for installation works, dancers that jeté across converted rehearsal rooms, and indie makers. In the 1950s, postwar Hong Kong began to develop into a manufacturing city, focused on light and labor-intensive industries. The cost of land reclamation in Kwun Tong was low, and factory buildings sprouted from the land. But manufacturers began moving to mainland China in the 1980s due to favorable economic policies, competitive rents, and lower labor costs, leaving behind vacant buildings, now relics of the city's industrial past. So in moved the artists.

Today, there are still more than a thousand industrial buildings in Hong Kong. Different districts have different scenes: There are co-working spaces in factories in Kennedy Town; art galleries camp out in Wong Chuk Hang's buildings; and Fo Tan's former factories are home to the studios and workshops of many budding artists, given their proximity to the art school at the Chinese University of Hong Kong. Musicians favored Kwun Tong, and for a while in the 2000s and 2010s, it was a breeding ground for underground music. The artists and musicians in these scenes were not rich, upper-middle-class, overseas-educated bohemians; many were from working-class families, and lived in these factory units because they could not afford rent elsewhere. There were also activists who had been members of the post-'80s generation of protesters against land hegemony and village demolition.

Ahkok Wong, a musician-activist, estimated that at one point, there were over a thousand bands in three hundred or so factory buildings in Kwun Tong. He himself stayed in a unit with other friends in the adjacent neighborhood of Ngau Tau Kok for over six years. "We were musicians, photographers, designers, and street artists. We held dinner parties, screen printing workshops, film screenings, and even a boxing competition in the corridor," he wrote. His friends spray-painted "Kwun Tong Art District" onto a road sign, and hung up banners that said "Band Jai Village." In his book *caak3 seng1,* he chronicles his time in the factories, at times questioning the city's collective proclivity to enact arbitrary restrictions to freedom in small, everyday ways (regulating buskers, banning musical instruments on mass transit, forbidding performances unless permits are obtained). Perhaps he had not meant it as such, but I read these descriptions of factory life with reverence, romanticizing life in this creative, anarchist utopia.

Some stories from the factories are intergenerational. An indie band I followed closely in the 2010s is Murmur, whose handwritten set list is still taped to my closet. The father of Murmur's drummer was a fashion designer who has worked in Kwun Tong for thirty years; he passed on his love of music to his daughter, Monsha. He had a storeroom-workshop space in an industrial building in Kwun Tong, and when Murmur needed a space to practice, the studio became a rehearsal room. They also recorded their first album there.

But in the early 2010s, a government plan to gentrify the East Kowloon district soon drove up rents, and former vertical factories—rusty metal gates, exterior walls weeping with mold—were renovated into commercial buildings with glass windows. Soon, even Kwun Tong became too expensive for artists. Hidden Agenda stubbornly stayed put in the district, but in just a decade's time, the live house (and its rebranded successor) was forced to move four times before closing its doors in 2020 for good. At HA 4.0, its fourth incarnation, the venue had few traces of its gritty industrial roots left: The toilets were finally usable, and hipster-looking bare light bulbs hung from the ceiling. It was also less "underground": Rather than being burrowed deep within an industrial building, this venue was on the ground floor. But that also meant it was no longer under the radar. While raids were not unheard-of at previous incarnations of the live house, they were not yet high-profile. This time, the police made sure everyone knew they had an eye on the venue.

In March 2017, a food and hygiene officer posed as a concertgoer and attended a gig at Hidden Agenda. The venue was then raided by the authorities, who said operators were selling tickets without an entertainment license. It's almost impossible for Hidden Agenda to attain this license, because a warehouse's land lease dictates that it cannot be used for any purpose other than industrial and storage; venue cofounder Hui Chung Wo has repeatedly tried and failed. It also cannot modify the land-use conditions without obtaining the approval of the other tenants in the building.

The authorities always have ways of cracking down on alternative culture and indie music. In May of that year, my friend Lok, who fronts the bands Emptybottles and Wellsaid, was opening for Oxford indie rockers TTNG, when the British band was arrested for performing without a visa. "When [the police] arrived, they came with police dogs and riot shields," he told the radio the next day. "The audience . . . [felt] threatened and was saying that these measures were uncalled for. It was unnecessary; no one was being violent." A small group in the indie scene showed up to protest outside the police station in the area the following day, with a banner that said "Save Hidden Agenda." Eventually, more than half a year later, the band was told that the authorities would not formally charge them.

For two years, Hidden Agenda rebranded as a new live house called This Town Needs, a play on the former name of the Oxford band. It found new investors and continued to put on shows at a spacious second-floor venue in Yau Tong, overlooking the fishing village of Lei Yue Mun. But in February 2020, the venue announced that it would be closing its doors for good.

Why did law enforcement think it was necessary to crack down on a bunch of dancing, moshing kids, even arrest the performers and risk international notoriety? The simple answer is that Hong Kong officers have always been bureaucratic to the extreme, deviating from their by-the-book tendencies only for powerful groups they have had long relationships with. These industrial-building scenes clearly operated outside of the law, and that was reason enough. But sometimes I also think that they are afraid of us. It is not that Hong Kong musicians and gig goers would suddenly turn into violent mobs that demand to overthrow the government or challenge state power. It is that despite everything we had been brought up to believe about what is required to survive in this city, we forged a new path. We lived lives we chose for ourselves, even though we failed to comply and submit to what our adults and law officers and government leaders told us.

The closing of Hidden Agenda and the rapid gentrification of East Kowloon marked the end of an era. After the raids, many warehouse shows were driven further underground, and became private gigs altogether: Sai Ceong, a factory gig space on the other side of Hong Kong, adopts a members-only policy; other shows are so secretive that organizers spread the word through private messages rather than set up event pages on social media. A scene that was already niche has even fewer means to recruit new gig goers, and a new generation of music lovers will find it harder to discover bands that operate in the margins.

On the tomb-sweeping-day holiday in October, on the eleventh floor of an industrial building in Kwun Tong, musician Tomii Chan hugs a guitar close to his chest, tapping his foot along to an invisible beat as his bandmates pore over the digital stems of their new songs. The elevator is a beast that has to be manned by a dedicated operator, but the insides of the building are modern and sterile. The studio is warm with blue tones, light streaming through a small window: Resting underneath the drums is the exact same olive-colored IKEA carpet I have at home. Lining the walls are soundproof cotton blocks, and angry drumming from next door sometimes spills in. I sit on the couch as Tomii tinkers with a tune. "I told my bandmates, you must have gone mad to want to write about me."

Tomii's standard outfit is a denim jacket and a white shirt, with slick gelled hair like James Dean's. He and I met years ago, when I worked at an underground music showcase in university, first as an unpaid intern and then as a reviewer, door bitch, and social media manager. At the shows we organized, I stood at the door of the Backstage Live Restaurant in Central checking off names and sticking ticket sales into a money box, catching an occasional riff whenever someone opened the door for a smoke break and let the music waft out. Despite all the titles, my job consisted mostly of going through Facebook event pages and compiling long lists of all the gigs in town for the biweekly newsletter. It was there that I first learned the names of bands I would grow to love, venues that would become favorite haunts before abruptly shutting.

In the summer of 2014, Tomii and his first band, the funky, soulful Tri-Deuces, came into the recording studio at our offices for an interview. I followed his career with interest when he joined the indie band Stranded Whale. Now, after seven years of hanging out at the same gig spaces, we're friends: He's sat in my living room listening to vinyl records with me and my partner till three in the morning.

I had been hoping to catch them rehearsing, but for two hours they huddle over a MacBook, commenting on the songs in progress. The bassist, Thomas, turns off the overhead fluorescent lights and, for theatrical effect, points the warm lamp toward Ah Tin, who is whamming his fingers onto the synthesizer. Tomii's vocals come over the many speakers that litter the room—Fender amps stacked on top of one another, overhead speakers wedged at the corners of the ceiling. "Waiting for," he sings gently over rippling synths and a seesawing bass line. In between the songs, the bandmates light cigarettes.

Tomii first picked up an instrument when he was seven years old: The violin teacher in his primary school played the *Doraemon* theme song, and Tomii, an avid *Doraemon* fan, started taking lessons from him. Later, Tomii enrolled in a music secondary school—one of the only ones in the city— with a heavy religious background. His mother was a preacher, so his parents supported the decision. The school was very into classical music training: Tomii took composing, chorus, instrumental, and music appreciation classes Monday through Friday. It was a private school with almost eighty piano rooms, but he received a 50 percent discount due to his family's Christian background. For a while, Tomii, too, was devoted to serving God and praising him through music. One of his guitar teachers was a member of Hillsong United. But as he got older, the atmosphere felt more forced. There was a mandatory worship session every morning, and even a hymn-writing competition. He gradually drifted away from the religion.

In his senior year at school, he started listening to Oasis and John Lee Hooker, and taught himself the guitar. On the online forum hkbandmusic.com, Tomii put a band together, Tri-Deuces. For a while, they played indie venues and mainstream competitions. They won the regional Asian Beat competition in 2013, one of the many record shop/ instrument store–sponsored band contests at the time, but before they ever had a proper release, Tri-Deuces unceremoniously broke up. The creativity was fizzing out, and they lacked chemistry.

Tomii's second band, Stranded Whale, was more of a mainstream indie success. He met Jabin Law, his co-frontman, on the same online forum; Jabin listened to Jimi Hendrix and B. B. King, and they bonded over their music taste, jamming to Muddy Waters and other blues tunes. The other bandmates, Dean and Ah Hin, were in the same church workshop house band as Tomii back in 2010, when he was still going to church. Together they formed the indie folk band, which featured some jazzy elements. Stranded Whale's "Release the Swallow" and "Calling from the Higher Ground" were some of my favorite tunes from the mid-2010s band scene in Hong Kong: solid songwriting, a touch melancholic, and with none of the sickly bubblegum aftertaste that was prevalent among songs by local indie rock bands from the era.

Stranded Whale played at Clockenflap, Hong Kong's biggest festival, and toured Taiwan. But they struggled to find their place in the scene: Indie folk always lurked at the peripheries in Hong Kong, but never took off the way postrock and math rock did. The reception of their second album, which was more mature than their earlier works, was disappointingly lukewarm. Even as the band was starting to break up, Tomii was still writing new songs for them. "I was not in a position where I could make [Jabin] stay, to make the band stay." Tomii still shares a band room with his exbandmates. He is a multi-instrumentalist and doesn't need a band to write or release songs, but he misses the collaboration. "It feels less alone."

The pandemic year 2020 was especially difficult for Tomii, even without the band's breakup: a romantic relationship also ended, and he constantly fretted over his elderly parents' health. Even before this, Tomii was an anxious person: Sometimes it was so bad that he would get headaches, and he was always pulling his hair or fidgeting with something between his fingers. But when he played, he was at ease. He felt in control in a way that he didn't with other aspects of his life. The performance venue was his safe space. The pandemic made his usual coping mechanism of playing gigs impossible. Tomii began seeing a Chinese medicine doctor. He carried a little slip of paper in his wallet, a list of foods he should avoid for his health: okra, oolong tea, and even bananas. His bandmates suggested that maybe he could just quit drinking and smoking.

When I ask him about his future, Tomii goes quiet and lights a cigarette. Then he says, with hesitation: "Questions like this puzzle me every time, especially when I'm going through an existential crisis. Tomorrow becomes very far away, very obscure." Tomii will be thirty soon, and he worries about the fact that he still isn't financially independent. He's never made much money from his indie ventures: He has to fork out rent for the band practice space, and still lives with his working-class family. For a while, he worked as a session musician at weddings and pop concerts at Queen Elizabeth Stadium, for major Cantopop names such as Andy Hui and William So Wing Hong, and even televised singing competitions. He stopped around two years ago. "It was very tiring and boring, playing other people's songs. No one had any enthusiasm; it was like a nine-to-five job." These days, to make ends meet, he gives music lessons, produces albums for fellow musicians, and works part-time at cafés and co-working spaces.

The names of the tracks on Tomii's latest EP, *Replay,* resemble musings of someone undergoing a midlife crisis, such as "Old Ways" and "Regrets." Tomii knows his father wants him to secure a full-time day job, but he never gives Tomii a hard time. His parents remain supportive of his creative endeavors, which is rare in Hong Kong. They've gone to his shows in industrial buildings, the only gray-haired couple in a sea of giggly gig goers. Sometimes, late at night, Tomii listens to them gently chatting and chuckling in their bedroom through the open doors, and feels calm. He is their only child, and wants to be there for them for the last stretch of their lives.

Over the years, I've watched Tomii play a range of genres, either in his own work or on his friends' projects: indie folk, soul funk, emo. Most of his solo work is guitar-driven, blues-inspired tunes that feel like a warm hug of whiskey injected into your bloodstream on the coldest night of winter. "Unchain My Heart," always a crowd pleaser, is such an old-school love song you feel like someone must have already written it. He is not a euphoric rocker, and none of his music lends itself well to cathartic screams. But his music is emotional in its own measured way, and when he sings in his distinct accented English, you can hear it: It reeks of longing, and transports you to a time before this, to jazz lounges with murky lighting that disappeared decades ago. When Tomii plays, his shoulders are hunched over with a weight too heavy for this world, and, eyes downcast, he jerks along with his guitar as if it is wielding him instead.

For two years, he and his friend Andrew Wong, a designer and saxophonist, organized the Gloomy Island Blues Festival, to bring the blues to Hong Kong. Even though the city was previously enamored of rock 'n' roll, and the blues speak to a sense of disillusionment with life that should resonate with Hong Kongers, the genre does not receive much attention here. Tomii and Andrew drew in the local swing dance community and hosted a gig at the wooden houses in the fishing village of Tai O, a nod to Mississippi Delta Blues. Tomii wanted to introduce not only the music, but the context of the lives of Black musicians in America's Deep South, and how the blues were born out of oppression. Even though the historical contexts are completely different from Hong Kong today, the sentiments are close to Tomii's heart.

What often surprises me is Tomii's steadfastness. There is no doubt that he writes good songs and is immensely technically talented, but this city he grew up in just isn't a great place to be an independent musician. I sometimes wonder whether Tomii would fare better in another city with a musical history so rich he would not have to explain his references, where he would be appreciated by larger crowds. Tomii is not gimmicky; he never gratuitously throws in markers of Hong Kong in his lyrics to satisfy an imaginary international listener, and he does not market himself as embodying some sort of local ethos or spirit. He writes songs that feel true to him and never once considered a different career path. Music is the only thing he is good at, and this is the life he wants. I hear that so rarely in Hong Kong: that someone is living a life they want. It is enough for Tomii that he has the freedom to do what he loves; everything else was secondary. "I know I have it in me, I just need more time—or maybe a different place."

But even as he says this, he betrays a reluctance to leave his hometown and its people behind. Tomii's obsessive qualities and his inability to let go come through in his music. They are what drew me to his work: We are both people who clung on to genres that died before we were born, relationships we should have put to rest long ago, memories from past seasons that withered from our touch. "But in the end I hope that you can be / Living your life with satisfactory," Tomii sings in the last line of his EP, simply titled, "A Song for Moving Forward."

Tomii tells me that the name of this new band I'm visiting in the rehearsal space is 友誼永固 Friends Forever. It is so cheesy that I first think it is ironic, but Tomii is sincere. "So many of my bands have broken up. This time, I want us to be friends forever."

There is a My Little Airport song for every occasion, my friend Jesse says in his car, on our way to a gig. He connects his phone to the speaker, and the car is flooded with music from the beloved Hong Kong indie band. Jesse has been an MLA fan since university, but back then I could never get into the indie pop duo, finding them a little too twee. But in my midtwenties, their lyrics hit me in a new way. Jesse was right. No one else, not in literature or films, has captured the lives of young Hong Kongers in such an accurate, eloquent manner. My Little Airport wrote songs about a late night at a McDonald's ("Last night at McDonald's / White lights, Cantonese songs, and homeless people"), the view from the first row on the upper deck of a bus, and To Kwa Wan, the neighborhood I grew up in ("I hope that railway station / Will take even longer to build / I cannot afford even higher rents")—the lyrics here translated from Chinese. They sang some songs in English with a Hong Kong accent ("Victor, Fly Me to Stafford," and "I Don't Know How to Download Good Av Like Iris Does").

During protests, friends posted lyrics to their music: "There are rioting teenagers everywhere in the world / when will they show up in Hong Kong?" or their cover of a song by the local hip-hop outfit LMF, 今宵多珍重: "Take care tonight / Things might not look like this tomorrow." Their songs have chronicled several protest movements: There is "I can eat more ice cream tonight, imagine I'd be arrested tomorrow afternoon" and "Let's sleep on Connaught Road tonight." The song "Ms Ng" is a spoken-word piece that tells the story of a bank worker who went to Nathan Road after work, and found herself tear-gassed with other protesters in black, then vows to join the protests from then on.

My Little Airport's music, in particular its inability to be fully translated, is an example of how cultural and linguistic barriers to the act of listening manifest themselves in Hong Kong. Despite my attempts to translate some of their lyrics here from Cantonese, the essence of these intimate and exquisite, yet 鳩, lyrics is impossible to capture. They feel like soft inside jokes whispered into your ear just before bed, jokes only Cantonese speakers understand. The music scene in Hong Kong is already small and splintered off into different genres; sometimes language—whether a band sings in English or Chinese—is what draws different audiences. Venues like the Wanch, the Wan Chai pub with live music every night, attract all sorts of music lovers, and possibly every indie musician in Hong Kong has played there at some point; there are fewer non-Chinese faces in factory gig venues. Politics can also divide: There remains a crowd who grew up in the East Kowloon band scene that refuse to perform at Clockenflap, the music festival that, for a while, took place at the West Kowloon Cultural District managed by the government.

The other band that is quintessentially "Hong Kong" to me, on the other end of the spectrum, is An Id Signal 意色樓. If MLA is gentle and happy-sad, An Id Signal is for screaming till your voice breaks. Fronted by activist and musician Leung Wing Lai, who also goes by Ah Lai, the band grew out of the industrial building scene in the 2000s, along with the Hidden Agenda crew and "the wayward kids who didn't want to go home," Ah Lai once told me. They hung at bars and each other's band rehearsal spaces; eventually, Ah Lai moved into one of these spaces, too. An Id Signal's music is characterized by Ah Lai's tortured vocals, which screech and drag and sing the Cantonese lyrics, drifting between consonance and dissonance. In 2017, Ah Lai was jailed for 176 days over protesting the demolition of villages in the New Territories.

The scene that Ah Lai is part of organizes guerrilla shows during festivities—unannounced gigs underneath overpasses or at public waterfronts without performance permits. One

year, after the factory live house raids, the theme of the mid-
autumn show was "No Industrial Building, We'll Play on the
Streets." Hosting it underneath overpasses means that the
equipment will be protected if it rains, plus the government
organization that manages overpasses is usually slower to
react than the cops or the hygiene department.

People often ask me whether the music scene in Hong
Kong is "political": What they mean is, if the lyrics allude to
a spirit of resistance, or if the musicians are active protesters.
They do not understand that rebellion comes in the form of
organizing shows without obtaining permits, playing where
you were told you couldn't play, living how they don't want
you to live. In other words, we aren't supposed to exist at all.
And yet, here we are.

In a scene in *Mad World,* Tung (played by Shawn Yue) is
lying wide awake on his top bunk, unable to sleep. He walks
downstairs to the narrow entrance that houses his subdivided
flat, then breaks into a run, past one steel-rolling-shutter
storefront after another, as though he could leave a part of
himself behind if he just ran fast enough. "打開這幻象或約
定你為何需要逃走," sings a male voice, gentle but disembodied, like he is holding a vigil for the protagonist. When I
heard the music, I did something I normally would never do
in the cinema: I turned to my partner and whispered, "Do
you know who this musician is?"

The first time I met Wong Hin Yan in person was at an
industrial building art space screening of *Pseudo-Secular,* a
film based on the Occupy protest movement of 2011 in Hong
Kong. Hin Yan had been part of the occupation where activists camped underneath the HSBC building in Central for

almost a year; he also scored the film. At the screening, he took questions from the small audience, wearing a suit jacket too large for his thin frame, and socks underneath his sandals. And then, for a while, I saw him everywhere. A younger but barely different version of him was in an archival photograph: There he is in a skinhead cut and white undershirt, perched atop the Queen's Pier like a hawk guarding its nest. There are times when he dresses like a Chinese scholar from another dynasty who accidentally got beamed into his era.

Wong Hin Yan was born in Hong Kong, and grew up in an old public housing estate in Cheung Sha Wan. His father was a worker in a public utilities branch of the government, and his mother was a homemaker. "My upbringing was not particularly traumatic compared to many people," he tells me, then lets out a dry laugh. His family did not understand Hin Yan's artistic pursuits or social activism, but they learned to slowly accept it, and they got along fine. Hin Yan did not go to university, instead studying photography at a vocational school. When his fellow graduates became photojournalists, he freelanced as a graphic designer. He never considered music as a career. Rather, he fell into it when a friend introduced him to theater and asked him to play music for a production in 2005; by the 2010s Hin Yan was a full-time musician. These days, he introduces himself as musician, actor, and anarchist.

Hin Yan started making music when he was in his third year of secondary school, hitting notes on a midi simulator on his computer with his mouse. He played around with samples, bought knockoff music software, and messed around until he heard something that sounded good. He learned the electric guitar and joined a three-person improv band with his secondary school classmates. One bandmate was the indie film director Lam Sum; the other later became a monk.

But mostly Hin Yan played by himself, trying to learn how to compose songs, taking detours as a self-learner until he found something that moved him. A self-described loner, he writes his songs in his room in the Fo Tan industrial area, in the heart of the art village populated by Chinese University art students and graduates, where he has lived for almost a decade. "I live there because there are no band guys—I did that once in Ngau Tau Kok, and slept next to an amp when the musicians were rehearsing. I bought powerful earplugs but realized it was useless, because your whole body still vibrates." It was much quieter in Fo Tan, although space is still lacking: He can swivel and his guitar will hit something. He and his roommates have thought about moving to a village house when their lease is up, but it is unlikely their neighbors would tolerate the noise.

Hin Yan isn't a person who feels at ease with speaking to a large crowd, but he feeds off the response of the audience. Sometimes people call him a folk singer, which he is ambivalent about: "When you label yourself, you take away possibilities." But he's a big believer in fate, as in "我條命係咁." He puts himself through performances for a shot at sublimity. "Because there's a chance there that you could reach a very real, very beautiful moment. Maybe you can only have that twice or three times, but because you've seen it before, you know it's possible and you think, *Maybe this time it'll happen*. And so you put yourself into a situation which is difficult and annoying and embarrassing."

Over time, Hin Yan developed what became his "sound." The songs start off bare, anchored by just one acoustic instrument and Hin Yan singing over it, sometimes vocalizing himself, but there are sometimes douses of airy, monotone ringing and distorted guitar lines. His vocals oscillate between feverish chanting and soft whispers, like a haunted presence down a long-abandoned hallway of an industrial building. His songs could only have been written by someone whose first language was the complex, tonal Cantonese. Sometimes the music quivers, just for a second, within a note you weren't sure existed, a note that sounds in-between. I had been so thoroughly bored by the Cantopop scene over the past decade, its manufactured lyrics and vanilla pop stars, that I forgot Cantonese songs could sound like this.

In his adolescence, Hin Yan listened to Lou Reed incessantly, poring over his lyrics. His literary influences are on display in his songs: One is inspired by Liu Yichang's novel *The Drunkard,* and another by a poem from Yam Gong. His own Cantonese lyrics are poetic gut punches, precise with their imagery and stripped of redundancy: not being able to wake up a person who pretends to sleep, a reference to those who deliberately choose to be unenlightened during a time of political change. In other places, he sings of a moth that flies to the light, and finds its way to a burning heart.

The first song he wrote in the style he eventually grew into was 《轉念始於足下寸土》, in 2010. Hin Yan sings: "鐵一般的秩序是路障只會讓我們跌倒," "An ironlike order is a roadblock / it would only make us fall." At the time, he was involved with the protests against a high-speed rail connecting Hong Kong and China. Hin Yan was only eighteen years old when he became involved in social activism. He and his bandmates had heard about a place called "autonomous 8a," where you could learn guitar and jam for free. He started hanging around that space, which was a resource center for student and left-centric movements. "I was really young, and I thought, this is so cool. It was completely different from the life I knew—going to school, and consuming mainstream media and pop culture." The group of activists he befriended set up street booths to educate Hong Kongers about public space. His political philosophy was developed not through reading theory books, but a decade's worth of discussion sessions in these collectives with these friends.

On July 1, 2003, Hin Yan and his friends took part in the half-million-strong protest against the national security law. They brought drums and sang and danced on the streets. Toward the end of the march, the police told them that the protest had officially ended, and that they should leave. But Hin Yan's friends wanted to keep going up to the central government office. Twenty or so of them ended up being sandwiched by the police, and two were taken away. "It was an incredible experience because the next day, everyone was just talking about the number of people on the streets and the civic awareness everyone demonstrated, and we had this story that everyone forgot about." Very early on, he developed a distrust toward the police. "I realized that when they were wearing that uniform, they were no longer a normal person, and I cannot have any expectations towards them."

Over the past decade, he lived through three political turning points: 2010, when the modes of protests expanded past just attending annual marches to the religious rite–like prostrating walk, which he took part in; 2014, the Umbrella Movement, when he watched his close activist friends viciously attacked and smeared by a growing localist movement that had grown tired of this now-older generation of post-'80s activists; and 2019. "I think every generation of social movement—they must have that idea that they're doing something new, there's something the world doesn't know and they're there to challenge them with their ideas." His own emotions were more muted in 2019, because he had lost faith in the regime years ago, and had been angry for a long time. Hin Yan describes it as "the ultimate battle to the death," a notion that he is conflicted over. A fire had been lit and was now burning, but it was unclear how long it could burn for.

Hin Yan and his friends are the type to advocate for the concept of 快樂抗爭 happy resistance. This concept underpins the more subtle forms of rebellion in the music scene, and introduces party elements into the solemn struggle. Long-term resistances rely on positive emotions, too, rather than just anger. In 2019, he was part of the drum crew, beating and cheering on everyone else as they marched along with the crowd. "This is such a small place, a small group of people, doing something that could affect the whole world—we all knew that we won't have the energy to keep going." He started leading breathing exercises in live videos he posted on social media, at a time when many were suffering from panic attacks watching news live streams of police crackdowns. In an old interview, Hin Yan said that what was most important to him was to "reduce suffering" for other people. His personal goal, since 2019, has been to escape the cycle of reincarnation. He doesn't expect the physical world to change too much, and he's sick of playing the game. His freedom came in a form of spirituality that shook materiality. He pauses, and then says, "終極離地啦."

During the 2019 movement, Hin Yan remixed a rant by an uncle in a roast meat shop who had let out a chain of vulgarities at the authorities and expressed support for the anti-extradition movement. Later, he wrote new Cantonese lyrics for a Chilean song, "El pueblo unido jamás será vencido," and recorded it with a group of friends at the live house Sai Ceong. His lyrics read like a call to arms:

新界人！九龍人！團結唔會被打沉！
(New Territories folks! People of Kowloon! We won't sink if we are united!)
離島人！港島人！團結唔會被打沉！
(Islanders! Hong Kong Islanders! We won't sink if we are united!)
自己人！自己人！團結唔會被打沉！
(Our own people! Our own people! We won't sink if we are united!)

But it is another one of Hin Yan's songs from that period of time that stayed with me. On the day that the national security law was announced, he posted on Facebook, "Take a deep breath when you read this." It was a song called "Bread and Rose" that he wrote for the play *The Phenomenon of Man: REVOLVER 2021,* although the Chinese title 《聽搖滾的北京猿人 2021》 is named after a song by deceased Chinese rocker Zhang Ju. The play follows several intersecting storylines at different moments of revolution across history and time: Hin Yan plays a priest in Beijing before the Second World War, writing a book about human evolution. "The world is about to collapse / It is already not the first time / The glass fragments that split open / taught me the meaning of the stinging pain." Hin Yan sings from the depths of a well, imploring us to persevere as the flames lick our flesh.

. . .

Sometimes, it can get lonely. I am at a gig again at mid-autumn. Another secret industrial building in Kwai Hing. Lok is fast asleep on the couch on the roof, even though he is slated to play a set in half an hour. I'm clutching tiny bottles of wine, which I empty at alarming speed. My partner and I stand at the edge of the building, staring at the strange moon above us, strange because this part of town is quiet and it is glowing too bright. I know how the rest of the night will go. I mouth along to the songs, because they are our friends and we know every song our friends made, at least I think they're our friends, even though at first it is a parasocial relationship, me watching them, them watching me watch them. I try to avoid eye contact with those strangers–not–strangers, gig regulars we've seen around for at least half a decade and yet have never said hi to, probably too late to be friends now. I get drunk and get a cab home, and the next day I wake up with a sharp pain in my hip and rust stains on my pants. Three months later, another band bites the dust. Someone is leaving Hong Kong or they've gotten fed up, playing venue after venue after venue, still no big break.

A David Boring gig always has the mood of a secret party that is counting down the destruction of humanity. "KILL TIME TILL THE END ARRIVES," the band chants, and something primal is triggered in the audience. Standing beneath the exposed water pipes in a warehouse, Laujan death-stares the audience and screams into the mic, the hostility congealing into something palpable in the sweat-stenched air. The audience rises and falls with the rhythm, at one with its urgent beat. The day after a show, I'm always bedridden from the violent dancing, but something has lifted. It occurs to me that this is the closest I'll ever be to feeling religious.

It is difficult to remember a time when Laujan was not in David Boring, because David Boring only truly became David Boring after she joined. In 2013, when I was working at the indie music showcase and hunting for new bands to play at our gigs, my university's music club recommended David Boring to me. A year later, I saw the founding members of the band perform for the first time: Their noisy, punk-inspired music was a clear departure from the genres of the local indie scene at the time, but they were still an amateur university band that role-played rockers onstage. Over the years, they found their sound: Industrial at its core, the songs were anchored by ghostly melodies, veering toward somber ballads in one section and feral screeching in the next. Their guitars sometimes resembled the singsong of a nightmarish clown daring you to step into the dark. I was obsessed.

My first interview with David Boring was in early 2016, when every member agreed that the addition of Laujan was the catalyst for the band in its current form. Laujan joined the band at guitarist Jason Cheung's invitation after their vocalist left to study abroad. Laujan wasn't sure if he was serious at first; she didn't write or play music. We meet up again in 2020 to chat. "I never thought of being anyone, anything. I think I'm always quite private, and I have no ambition of being famous—if anything I hate being recognized, hate being in the limelight," she says at a burger joint in Sheung Wan, smoothing out her dip-dyed blond ends. But she was attracted to art forms that could justify the way she was feeling, especially when they weren't emotions that could be easily articulated, and she found her way to film, literature, and music.

"I think I was angry pretty early on in life," Laujan tells me. She wears a leopard-print shirt, her eyes smeared in streaks of red, and orders a bunless burger. As we speak, switching back and forth between English and Cantonese, her tongue piercing peeks out in flashes. Laujan has a distinct English accent I can't quite place, a defining characteristic of her vocals. She attended a boarding school in Dorset for two years, and later spent another two years in London for her master's in architecture. She was the most rebellious among her Hong Kong friends—all good kids. She had a difficult childhood even though on paper they were a perfect middle-class family, and her parents split up when she was eighteen. In university, she started trying to rebel against things she didn't like about the establishment, but also the virtues she was taught growing up: being filial, respecting your elders.

Laujan emerged as the natural front woman. Laujan still doesn't consider herself a "musician," even after all these years, but her stage presence is arresting and ferocious, and she growls in tight metallic long-sleeved tops, cheongsams, a Little Red Riding Hood–esque dress, sheer black one-pieces that border on BDSM clothing. Unlike her reserved bandmates, she writes long poetic posts on social media after their gigs. "It is not a good show for us unless at least one member of the band has a public meltdown," one of these read. She is a perfectionist, and runs the band in a "military" way. Under her leadership, they embark on mildly ridiculous projects, such as renovating their new band room in a Kwun Tong industrial building themselves. (They celebrated with a small, private gig surrounded by their moss green walls and carpeted floors.)

In 2017, they put out their first full-length album, *Unnatural Objects and Their Humans,* a brooding, conceptual piece set in a dystopia not unlike Hong Kong. The songs discuss internalized oppression ("It takes cowardice to push on through this game / It takes madness to stay sane"), the loosefucks 老屎忽 sitting at the top of a hierarchical society ("I like the way you vote for lies / I like how you have rapey eyes"), and the mundanity of death ("No memories, no emotions / No pleasure, no pain"). The album is in shocking pink, and the liner notes are accompanied with dry diagrams about the codependent, toxic relationship between Unnatural Objects, Their Humans, and The Machine. The mix could not capture the feverish energy of their live shows, but the twelve tracks presented a coherent vision of a Hong Kong seen through their morbid, nihilist lens. Jason's disembodied vocals often followed Laujan's, manipulated so that the sound resembles a machine regurgitating its commands. Before the songs descend into noise, they are preceded by eerie, gorgeous dual guitar harmonies, a tantalizing bass line, and drums that could take down walls.

As the band's lyricist, Laujan painstakingly crafted a story for each song, which paints apocalyptic landscapes and chronicles a different marginalized character in society (Susie Exciting with her razor blade; Brian Emo, modeled after their founding drummer, Stan Chik, who "was told that hope would keep him sane / But it's hope that gives him all the pain"). She describes writing as a process of "documenting a narrative," leaning on horror because the genre uses an uncomfortable sentiment to tap into nuanced psychoanalyses and socially unacceptable topics.

Laujan hates it when people disrespect vocalists, because she takes her role so seriously. At every gig, the songs compel her to stretch her cords in all directions. Her voice can be earnest, monotonous, or even childlike. When she first started out, music veterans told her that she needed to take singing lessons, and said there were things they had to do to survive in the scene: befriend the right people, play shows with this or that organizer. She thought, surely they could do it themselves, on their own terms. The set of rules in the indie scene was bullshit. They organized their own shows and embraced the DIY aesthetic. Laujan trusted that they would be rewarded for their stubbornness.

And they were. Even though they still played to small, niche audiences, opportunities came that were unprecedented for a Hong Kong band. Nobody in David Boring except Laujan, whose mother was an ardent fan of Anthony Bourdain, knew who the chef and food personality was. They appeared in the Hong Kong episode of *Parts Unknown,* where they took him to Sun Hing, the late-night dim sum restaurant that was a favorite among HKU students. Bourdain lifts a piece of custard bun with his green chopsticks. Laujan says that they talked for a long time about music and the no-wave scene, although, after editing, the narrative became one of the typical stories in the media about how young people in Hong Kong are struggling. A couple of days after the episode aired, Bourdain died by suicide. "It was really unreal," Laujan muses. "It's easy to be oblivious to another person's mental health state. I have issues that even my closest friends are not aware of." In the clip the band posted, they said: "This is a difficult but profound watch for us, the ridiculous but heart-warming memory of Anthony plus the full crew being in our grubby band room, watching us beating each other up in amusement, is still vivid."

A year later, David Boring played at South by Southwest

and Baby's All Right, a first for a band from Hong Kong. There was little press coverage back home. "No one from Hong Kong gave a shit about all this. Maybe I'm just being pessimistic, but I think people don't like us, or we're being blacklisted," she says, laughing. When they returned, a local organization that "nurtures young talent" including musicians reached out to them, saying that they now fit the criteria for their program. Laujan ended up confronting them, asking where they'd been when they needed help, and casting doubt about how they were treating musicians with the attitude of cram schools for students. Not letting independent musicians develop in an organic way would end up only hurting the ecosystem and the bands.

David Boring is probably bored of this by now, but interviews with them never fail to mention that the band members are all "professionals"—Jason is a doctor, former members Dave and Stan are both engineers, and Laujan is an architect. The band practices around their irregular schedules, on tomb-sweeping day, Valentine's Day, the dragon boat festival, and is self-disciplined, efficient, and organized. That interview angle hints at a cultural fascination with white-collar workers who tear off their buttoned shirts only to emerge as artist-superheroes in a hypercapitalist society. But not fitting into the slasher-musician-living-in-an-industrial-building stereotype also invited scorn from their peers. One told them they couldn't be punk because they all had proper jobs. "That's bullshit. If we're still going by that standard, no one in Hong Kong is a true anarchist, no one has the authority to do anything on punk, because we're all part of the system."

The only member from the band's original lineup is Jason. The old lineup fought every other practice, and when the band played they visibly emanated pain; Stan, teeth

bared, bashed the drums as though they were his worst
enemy. Now, with the new members, it is much easier to
write songs. But sometimes Laujan misses that conflict and
energy. These days, David Boring is signed to an indie label
in London, which is rare for bands from Hong Kong; most
local musicians fail to receive much attention from audiences
outside the city.

David Boring is sometimes referred to as the angry voice
of a generation, and Laujan admits that it might be because
they never shed the youthful will to express desperation. In
2021, the band added more characters to their horror-story
universe: Jane Pain, Nancy Nightmare. Laujan likes how
naming a song after a person creates a certain kind of sinister
uncanniness. These are stories of characters from a first-
person point of view, characters you might be judgmental of
if you encounter them in real life, but she wants to view
them with sympathy, show how they respond to a harsh
world. "In a way they're victims, but there might be a chance
that the trauma is of their own doing." That trauma or experience is always based in Hong Kong, and it is always a
Hong Kong–based character, even if that is not expressly
mentioned. The band trusts that everyone who is from Hong
Kong will understand the context of the songs. But Laujan
does not want David Boring to be seen as a representative of
Hong Kong. And even given the latent political nature of
their work, she is wary of political art. "Political art has the
power to elevate—almost like a war cry to a movement. But
if you're making bad art, people shouldn't come out to support the art because of the message."

In 2019, there were times when it felt like the end times
that David Boring had sung about had arrived. At the height
of the protests, I reserved every weekend for marching in

some different district in Hong Kong, and each Monday, I showed up to my office job as usual. Then, Covid-19 hit in early 2020, and a few months later the national security law was enacted. I ask Laujan how this has affected her art. "Because I've been pessimistic and skeptical most of my life, it's always been bad times. For me, the world has always been fucked up. But there's just always enough distractions for people to ignore the fucked-up-ness. The past year was not as difficult for me as it was for many of my peers, but that nihilism itself is scary and sinister. If anything, I feel like it's more honest, because everyone's recognizing that the world is fucked up."

I wasn't dealing with the developments as well as Laujan. I had nowhere to direct my pent-up despondency, and gigs were my only outlet and means of catharsis. During the protests, I saw David Boring twice, first at the Fringe Club in Central, and then at Eaton Hotel, where they hosted a show titled "PAIN." The band hold themselves out as inapproachable haters, but despite their aggressive music, Laujan tells me that the band "set out to heal." As the mechanical, whirring distortion of the guitars clashes into the climax that is "I Can't," the crowd stomps and shudders as though undergoing an exorcism. The band shrieks and twists as the world burns, and a wound in me spills out then closes.

Bands break up everywhere, all the time. Their music disappears into the ash heap of history, resurfacing only in a gecko-shit-covered corner of a record store still standing even when the city itself is gone. My favorite slowcore band, Carissa's Wierd, was an underground cult favorite in the 1990s Seattle scene, but never signed to a major record label or found commercial success, and eventually disbanded. But at least their catalog remained on the internet, and after the members bought back the rights, they reissued the records. The remnants of defunct Hong Kong bands have few traces anywhere, sometimes not even on Bandcamp or YouTube. In 2020, Hong Kong photographer Vic Shing established a photo archive of over a decade's worth of shows he dedicatedly documented. But hearing that wrong note screech through the amp, or laughing as the guitarist winces at the feedback, watching the bassist swing his hips, or crowding outside a club to smoke cigarettes after the show—they belong to specific moments in time and can never be replicated.

Every music fan across the world and throughout the history of time has a sappy story about how music saved their life. Here's mine: When I was in remission from depression, the loud music drowned out everything in my head. Leaning against the shaking walls of a crumbling room in an industrial village gave me a brief respite from pain, a magical couple of hours where nothing was shitty even though everything was shitty. The melodies cut through my cloudy thoughts. I have cheered and cried and screamed at these shows, the only space that allowed for a full spectrum of my emotions. Standing in the second row and mouthing the lyrics to the song, I found out that if the music was loud enough, I wouldn't be able to hear the noises in my own head. Nothing I tried later in life—meditating, drinking, praying—worked better than this.

The musicians thrashing their instruments underneath an overpass during a pouring mid-autumn, or the tiny mosh pits in a warehouse, are as much a part of the city's history as the crowds on the street. They blossomed in Hong Kong under impossible conditions, climbing out of torn fences and sprouting from cement. I can move to Berlin or Seattle or Manchester, and there would be better music, a more supportive scene, and cheaper shows, and still I would never root for their success the way I do with these people in Hong Kong who grew up with me in my twenties, showed me what it meant to live free. We are always so attuned to loss in this city: We say, *remember to archive, remember to remember.* When the day comes for us to gently trace the contours of the city with nostalgia, do not forget these people and their music. We relegate them to memories before their time. What I would give to not have to remember; to find these scenes in the fringes in the most unforgiving of times, still thriving, alive.

# A City in Purgatory

念念不忘，必有迴響；有燈就有人.
　　—《一代宗師》

We'll be back.
　　—A BANNER IN 2014, DURING THE LAST DAYS
　　　OF OCCUPY

We are back.
　　—A BANNER IN 2019, ON THE FIFTH
　　　ANNIVERSARY OF OCCUPY

By all accounts, I am the most useless protester there is. You wouldn't want me on your team. I have a deformed hip that has plagued me for over half a decade, and forty-five minutes into a peaceful march, I will likely be hunting for a surface—the pavement in front of a shuttered shop, the asphalt road, a rusty barricade—to sit down on. When the police fire tear gas right next to me, I accept fate.

It is summer, autumn, winter. The skies are pale and the crickets rest. The dry wind brushes our cheeks, flaking our skin. A different street corner, but the scene is the same. The smoke clouds my vision and smothers my senses. I can't run, so instead I stand there and cough into my mask. I know it is time for me to go when everyone starts screaming and bolting in the opposite direction, away from the riot police charging forward with their rubber bullets.

When I'm home, cocooned on my sofa and watching live streams of other people getting tear-gassed, I tell myself, *I'll write instead.* Surely there's a way for me to play my part. But what is writing good for when we can't write a way out of this darkest timeline?

When I was fifteen, my Chinese history teacher played the class a documentary of the June 4 massacre—the government's response to a student-led democracy movement in China in 1989. By then, the devastating Cultural Revolution had ended more than a decade ago, and it was a time when artists and activists had just begun experimenting with new forms of creativity. Every year on the anniversary of the 1989 event, that teacher would talk about June 4 in the morning assembly, imploring us never to forget. My uncle, a Chinese history and culture teacher at another school, kept dusty volumes of books on June 4 in the bookshelves at my grandmother's place, but I never touched them. I only knew that it began as a student-led protest, that it was a historical incident routinely denied by the Communist government, and that it sparked an emigration wave among the educated middle-class population in Hong Kong. They wanted to leave the city before it would be taken over by Communist China in 1997.

On the projector, we saw students piling into the streets

and the squares of Beijing with hand-painted signs, chunky glasses resting on their fresh faces. Some protesters passed out from a hunger strike, and more students and everyday citizens rode their bikes in. When the tanks rolled into Tiananmen Square and the gunfire scorched the night, we let out audible sobs in the dimmed classroom. At recess, the other students in our year stared in discomfort: Why was everyone from the 4A classroom crying? We were in a daze, unable to speak. What kind of government does that to its own children?

A year later, I attended the anniversary vigil at Victoria Park for the first time. It falls during the nascent summer; the violent rain would coat the streets with a layer of glistening wet paint, the city so still as though it is holding its breath. The vigils are notoriously conservative, boring even: Every year, the organizers lead the crowd in a chant, the Tiananmen mothers or other activists speak, and then everyone sings exactly the same songs. The program has remained the same over the decades. But that first time when I was sixteen, seeing a replica of the Goddess of Democracy statue up close, watching the bottoms of our white paper cups pool with candle wax, and learning the words to the 自由花 song, I understood what it meant to belong to a group of people who understood that remembering itself is an act of defiance. In Hong Kong, after the bloody crackdown in Tiananmen Square, journalists who covered the incident came together to publish a four-hundred-page book called *People Will Not Forget*.

At my final year in grade school, a new principal came. She introduced a series of reforms that included having the students make announcements at assembly in Mandarin instead of Cantonese, and organized school trips to Yunnan. She was quoted in an article saying that she believed students should "understand the culture of their motherland" and "serve the people of Hong Kong and mainland China." Soon, rumors from our own teachers and even alumni of the school she previously served as principal began circulating that she was 紅底, pro-Communist. Longtime teachers began tendering their resignations.

Another rumor was that she had tried to prevent our Chinese history teacher from her annual speech about the June 4 movement. As students, we were kept in the dark about what went down. All I remember is that year, at my last June 4 morning assembly ever, our principal glowered from the side of the corridor as my Chinese history teacher walked over to the balcony and addressed the students. *Do not forget,* she said.

I've met many people at vigils over the years. Children who were carried on shoulders by their parents, photojournalists who knew exactly which roof to go to for the best candlelit crowd shot, former Chinese dissidents who have found a home in this city, Guangzhou natives who discreetly came for the commemoration. They come holding withering umbrellas, even as the rain slaps the pavements and mutes everything in the air, singing "無論雨怎麼打自由仍是會開花." *Freedom blossoms no matter how hard it rains.*

But there's one person I think about the most: a girl I met that first time I attended who sat next to me during the whole vigil. She had honey-colored skin and round eyes, sported a black tee and a top knot, and was only ten years old. Because my parents never took me to any protest, I had assumed that everyone else's parents were just like mine. I still think about her because she would be precisely the age of the most active protesters in 2019, waging street battles with the police as though they had nothing to lose.

Every year, even more than two decades after Tiananmen, the people of Hong Kong still gathered on that evening, their faces illuminated by soft candlelight in a packed sports court. By the time I was in university, Hong Kong was already a city defined by its constant protest marches and rallies. They became marked dates on our political calendar: on New Year's Day, on June 4, on July 1, on October 1 marking China's national day, people hit the streets year after year with dedication. They were regular protests, sometimes with specific political demands or in solidarity with a political development—for the release of Chinese dissident Liu Xiaobo, or for universal suffrage, or for the resignation of a chief executive. Taking place in parallel were smaller protests against the demolition of villages, or a particular street or historical structure, led by artists and "post-'80s" activists.

Before Xi Jinping came into power in 2013, we believed that the threat to Hong Kong's political institutions and everyday life would at least be slow to materialize. Universal suffrage, as had been promised, was still on the table. The stakes were lower and the sense of urgency was less pronounced. In 2012, student leaders such as Joshua Wong were successful in getting the government to shelve a plan to introduce a pro-Chinese, patriotic curriculum in schools. But a new generation that had grown up after the handover in 1997 was realizing that the Communist Party could take away our culture and semi-democratic institutions without even breaking a sweat. The promise of universal suffrage felt more improbable with each passing year: China showed no indication of budging on the issue. Maybe it was time to escalate things. This was the lineage of protests that the 2014 Umbrella Movement hailed from, and when the occupation took place, it brought together generations of protesters, activists, and regular people.

The Umbrella Movement was premised on anger, but also hope. It was an escalation from the usual marches with their vague themes of resistance, and involved a broader demographic than the left-leaning movements in the 2010s. Young truck drivers protested alongside photographers, office clerks, and hairdressers, building a small protest village on the streets of one of Hong Kong's busiest business districts. Protesters slept in tents, participated in hunger strikes, and took nightsticks to the head. Still, after seventy-nine days, political change eluded the city. It became clear that the promise of democracy would never materialize, that it was likely never intended to be kept.

After the Umbrella Movement, a depression swept over my generation. The protest leaders splintered after bitter ideological rows. Some students in my university were outspoken and radical during the occupation, then went on to become investment bankers and never posted about politics again. If Hong Kong was going to shit, they could at least be winners in the cesspool. I was not depressed. I felt guilty for missing the movement because I had been away in Scotland, but I was also idealistic and naïve. I was ready to throw myself into "doing something for Hong Kong." I got a job as a reporter at a new post-Umbrella media outlet. I figured that if I wanted a crash course on the city, there was no better way to do that than by being sneered at by sources for not having done enough homework on the history of their political parties, or trying to navigate insider jokes on the community Facebook pages or online forums. Unlike my interviewees, which included veteran protesters who learned to demonstrate alongside Korean farmers, and labor activists who joined the strike of the dockworkers when they were still students, I didn't have dramatic moments of political enlightenment. I was not forced into caring after having witnessed a friend bear the brunt of police brutality. I was just ready to finally become a part of the city that raised me.

Even though Umbrella failed to realize top-down political reforms, activism in neighborhoods and communities was beginning to grow. Organizers realized that for everyday Hong Kongers to care about the vague, abstract question of Hong Kong's political future, they first have to have a stake in their own surroundings and take notice of how politics shape their reality. Activists formed shadow district councils and monitored public spending. Journalists reported on the subtle shifts toward localism among young people. University students protested when the pro-Beijing council refused a top job to a professor who taught me human rights in law school.

We knew that it was only a matter of time before the crackdown began. We knew the script that the Communist Party followed. But for a brief moment, we let ourselves believe that we could bring about change so long as we kept going.

When I missed Umbrella, everyone told me I had missed out on a once-in-a-lifetime political movement. Hong Kong has always been a city of protest, but we had never protested so hard: for almost three months, eighty-seven rounds of tear gas, three districts. By the time I returned to Hong Kong after my exchange semester, the Lennon Wall outside the legislature, a mosaic of sticky notes scribbled with political messages and words of solidarity, had been taken down. I never got to see with my own eyes the tents jutting out of Harcourt Road, the activists giving lectures in mobile class-rooms, or the students making trips down to occupation sites in their uniforms. People had lost steam; plus, they said, the government had learned its lesson and would make sure oc-cupations like it would never break out again.

For a time, they were right. At the protests I covered after 2014, the turnouts were often abysmal: There was usually just a smattering of maybe fifty eccentric regulars and opposition lawmakers. Weak chants of slogans and half-heartedly drawn banners. The organizers for these gatherings were generally older, conservative democrats, and they failed to engage the disillusioned, younger protesters who took part in the Um-brella Movement. The press outnumbered the attendees. We often left early, knowing there would not be any escalation.

Five years later, on the morning of Wednesday, June 12, 2019, I walk past my office and instead take the train to Ad-miralty. A few days ago, my partner and I were at a march where a million protesters had unexpectedly turned up to oppose a proposed law that would allow "criminals" to be extradited to China. Under the one country, two systems arrangement, Hong Kong's and China's legal systems were separate; we operated under the common law system, with basic safeguards such as the right to a fair trial and bail. Dem-ocrats and activists began sounding the alarm that this could further collapse the borders between Hong Kong and China.

A citywide strike was called for June 12, when a second reading of the bill would take place.

That morning, a swarm of demonstrators in black tees has already taken over Harcourt Road; supply stations have been set up and stocked with yellow hard hats, red-white-and-blue bags, and boxes of bottled water. It is a well-rehearsed routine: It has been five years, but they have not forgotten.

A brief spell of rain comes down, and I walk around in a trance, nodding when I run into familiar faces. I climb up the footbridge and look down. For a moment, I feel like the city truly belongs to the people in the most literal sense—the roads, the overpasses, even the government buildings. They said nothing like this would happen again after Umbrella, yet here we are. Water barriers and barricades are conjured and moved out onto the road. My partner finishes a law clinic session with a client and joins me at Admiralty in a suit and tie.

At around three P.M., things escalate. On Tim Wa Avenue, protesters advance and riot police storm forward with rubber bullets and tear gas. Far away from the front line, at the footbridge near Admiralty Centre, we begin choking on tear gas. Next to me, a young woman throws up. We pass a man who is doubled over near the railings, and give him water. When he looks up, I realize it is a friend from university.

The police block the footbridge on the end where it leads to the legislature. The only other exits are escalators, where protesters trickle down slowly because of how packed it is on the ground level. If the police keep advancing, there would be a stampede. "屌！唔好推啊！" *Fuck, don't push!* everyone yells. There is mayhem everywhere I turn. About half an hour later, my partner and I finally get off the bridge and head home. Four days later, we are back on the streets, this time at a protest march that will draw two million, dressed in all black to commemorate a fallen protester.

A month later, my partner and I have just landed in Hong Kong from a trip to Japan when our phones flood with news notifications the moment our signal returns. A group of white-shirted thugs has beaten up protesters, journalists, and civilians in a train station in Yuen Long. In our suitcases in the overhead compartment are boxes of matcha snacks, Cup Noodles, and a sapphire engagement ring in a red box. We had gotten engaged three days earlier.

We drag ourselves through the airport in silence, one hand on the trolley and the other refreshing the news feed every few seconds. These men had connections to local mobs, and the police didn't show up in time. A pro-Beijing politician is later seen shaking hands with the attackers. The attack was clearly planned to intimidate Hong Kongers against protesting the extradition bill at the time.

On the train to Kowloon Station, I ask my partner if he thinks we will have to leave Hong Kong one day. We previously said we were both committed to staying here till the end. For the first time, I wonder if the day will come when the city will change so irrevocably that I can no longer bear being here.

In August, the air takes on a life of its own. The winds weep with so much moisture that it often feels suffocating. On one of those days, I welcome a sweaty handyman into my flat. The tanned, smiling, thirty-something stranger, whom I found on a local household-repair version of "seeking arrangements," is there to dismantle a spare bed that I am hoping to sell.

As he removes the nails from the bed frame, he asks, "So you've been out on the streets, eh?"

I take a step back, immediately suspicious. "What gave it away?"

"There's a yellow hard hat by your sofa," he says, laughing. "Don't worry, I'm out every other week, too. I'm with the first aid. Just doing what I can."

While he smokes a cigarette in my kitchen, we chat about the protests. "My son keeps asking me to explain why the police are beating people up," he tells me. "Even the children know there's something wrong."

It's been only two months, but I can barely remember what my days were like before the protests began. My "real" life—the one where I show up to work every morning, have a drink in the evening with friends, hide underneath the covers reading a book at night or call a handyman for odd jobs—exists in a parallel universe, one in which the city isn't burning. On the weekends, I enter that other world—the one in which I head out wearing safety gear, my hard hat and face mask in place—to witness the thousands marching and then go home to watch live feeds of the news late at night.

It feels as if those two worlds do not converge. I don't know most of my fellow protesters. Except for a few close friends, most of the people I see on a day-to-day basis are not those I'd turn to for discussions about politics: The topic is too heavy for small talk. So on Monday mornings, I have no idea which of my colleagues also got tear-gassed the night before. Or if the grandmother who lives across the road was the same one I saw offering snacks to hungry demonstrators.

On weekends, parts of the city transform into a battle-field. The riot police take their formations, and the metal barricades on the sides of the roads are coated with pepper spray residue. On weekdays, the graffiti seems out of place as the streets are again filled with office workers, all of them hurrying somewhere.

Once in a while, something pierces through the illusion. At a demonstration in Sheung Wan, a couple of streets down from where I live, a protester in black grabs my arm.

"Hey! You recognize me? I was in the same class as you in law school!"

I don't. "Maybe if you took off your mask?" I suggest. "I can't tell who you are just from the eyes. Though you probably shouldn't take it off now." Fifteen minutes later, we are hit by tear gas, and he dissolves into the crowd.

Eventually, the worlds begin colliding. We construct these boundaries to remain anonymous, fearing retaliation at our workplaces or to avoid confrontations among friends and family members with different political views, but the walls won't hold and the spaces bleed into one another. One night, I meet friends for dinner at Causeway Bay, one of Hong Kong's busiest shopping districts. When we leave the restaurant, there are police charging at protesters. The huge bill-board outside the department store, usually flashing with ads for designer bags or beauty products, is switched off. I have never seen those streets so dark at night. That evening, I step over a pool of blood at the subway station as I take the train home.

October 2019. It is raining, and my feet are pruning inside my sneakers. Today, we are protesting against the government invoking emergency laws and placing a ban on face masks, which it says is to prevent protesters from avoiding detection. (Just a few months later, Hong Kong would reverse that ban in the heat of the pandemic, and make face masks compulsory.) I stand on the streets of Wan Chai, alone except for a few fellow marchers who skitter away every few minutes to avoid the riot police. I want to go home but I stay, to pretend I'm not useless to the movement.

Even though I am still writing about the protests, I don't want to put on a press vest for a license to be on the scene, not when frontline journalist friends have been living on rice balls and three hours of sleep. Protesters have sacrificed their relationships, their health, their futures; as for me, the sight of a police officer is enough to send my heart rate off the charts. The truth is that all through 2019, I never once got close enough to be in direct contact with the police, to be on the receiving end of their blows; they merely brushed past me.

I duck into an art bookstore and sit down, surrounded by crates of vinyl records and expensive photography books. When I head out again, the girl in the shop tells me to stay safe. She thinks I'm brave, but I don't deserve it. I haven't been out on the streets enough, out of the fear that my limbs would not be able to carry me away in time. Positing myself on social media as a source for the Hong Kong movement made me feel like a phony. All of us are somewhere on the spectrum of cowardice. Some of us admit it. None of us know how to deal with the guilt.

A protester I interviewed tells me that during the Umbrella Movement in 2014, she was still a university student, and could only afford to buy bottles of water for fellow protesters. Now that she's financially independent, she can do more. She has so little to lose compared to the students who are protesting. When more frontline protesters were arrested, she saw it as her duty to step forward. She doesn't want to leave Hong Kong; she's worried how the city would fare in the hands of apolitical "Hong Kong pigs." At times she's scared; she has been repeatedly saved from the riot police by people she calls the "real" braves. She sounds real brave to me.

"Do you think you'll ever reach a point where you'll have done enough to not feel guilty anymore?" I ask.

She hesitates for a second. "No."

When I worked as a reporter, I installed ten different news apps and allowed push notifications on all of them, so I could constantly keep an eye on breaking updates. When the alerts began seeping into my dreams during the protests, I finally turned on time-out mode at midnight so that I wouldn't have a panic attack in bed. Instead, I delayed the inevitable to the morning, when I would wake up to these headlines: "Hong Kong University Student Dies Following Fall Near Police Operation"; "Hong Kong Police Shoot Protester Amid Clashes"; "Hong Kong Riot Police Fire Tear Gas Near University Campus."

My phone buzzes and it's a friend telling me he has been injured while covering the protests. Or I find out that a secondary school classmate was arrested the night before. We sneak in moments of quiet in between the clashes on the streets. We go to the movies and order too much popcorn. We have dinner with friends who understand, and we don't post photos of our food. When we accidentally manage to spend a day without feeling overwhelmed, it feels stolen.

What is the point of doing anything when you don't know whether your city has a future?

Still, life goes on. It is a reluctant but sometimes welcome distraction from being glued to Twitter and the news 24/7, like the possessed. From living in some dark-timeline version of Hong Kong: students trapped inside a besieged university, sending notes to their loved ones in case they die at the scene; politicians attacked in broad daylight; shops shuttered and the air acrid and burned.

People often characterize depression as a lack of hope or vitality, but I associate it more with a restlessness, an inability to feel at peace. You're on the couch watching Netflix in furry pajamas, clutching a mug of hot tea, and you think, maybe the problem is that you aren't getting out of the flat enough. You throw on jeans and head down to the bar, but after half a drink you want to run home. You repeat this routine a couple of times before you realize the problem isn't where you are.

After Umbrella, the depression that overtook the city was one that eventually manifested in apathy. The people finally realized that Beijing had never meant to live up to its promise of granting democracy to Hong Kong, that no amount of protesting would change this. In Chinese, you would call this 死心: that all hope was gone and your heart has literally died. The depression eventually subsided and the people came back out. But in 2019, the depression feels like the end of the world. The cityscape has been so utterly transformed by the presence of riot police that you no longer recognize your own streets. You only want people around you to be safe amid the violence.

By December, it is impossible to leave our flats without first checking which areas are being tear-gassed at that moment. In the malls, protesters opt for the most PG-13 protest tactic: singing "Glory to Hong Kong," the unofficial anthem of the resistance. You can get pepper-sprayed for singing. You can't even do your Christmas shopping without possibly being pinned down onto the polished marble floor. Paramedics wear reindeer headbands and riot police circle pink Christmas trees.

On the first day of 2020, my university friends and I meet up for lunch at Tin Hau, then join the annual New Year's Day march. The protesters carry monster-sized posters and banners over their heads that say "FIVE DEMANDS" and 毋忘承諾 並肩同行. We are outside Victoria Park when a masked protester, a girl younger than me, starts screaming at demonstrators to get into the park, which would help with the official head count numbers. Years of marching have taught us that once you entered the park, you could be stuck there for hours: Crowd control makes it nearly impossible to move forward. When she sees us taking the route that forks away from the park, she yells directly at me. *If you're already out then what's the point if you're not going to even make it COUNT and instead you're going to jump the queue?*

I look down and walk away, fuming. Because of my hip, my legs will give out and I won't be able to march at all after standing in the park for hours. *You don't even KNOW me,* I want to scream back. But I don't, because I'm despondent and desperate and so is she.

We get as far as Wan Chai before the police suddenly announce at around five-thirty P.M. that the march is illegal. None of us have protective gear with us that day, and we aren't ready for clashes. We turn into streets swarming with riot police, then backtrack into another street lined with more officers. Protesters are told to leave, but several streets are blocked. There is only one thing to do at this stage, if we don't want to be rounded up and made to kneel on the ground as they take down our personal details. We pretend that we just *happen* to be in the area. We go into a Southeast Asian restaurant and order beef rendang and satays, sitting in silence with other ashen-faced families as, outside the glass windows, the police run past every few minutes.

When the pandemic hits, the government imposes social distancing rules that further limit public gatherings. You can be ticketed for standing in a group, even if you aren't explicitly protesting. In certain districts that are regular protest hot spots, police deployment is so heavy it is impossible to walk anywhere without being stopped, and areas are cordoned off in advance. But people still come, chanting slogans in flimsy surgical masks or building barricades in full protest gear, an ebb and flow that takes the streets one instant, and scatters and retreats the next.

In May 2020, China announces that it is drafting a national security law for Hong Kong. Within two months, the law is implemented, even though no one in Hong Kong, not even the government or legislature, has seen what the provisions contain. Before the law is enacted, political parties disband, social media personalities lock or delete their accounts, and some activists quietly leave the city.

With the national security law in effect, I become too terrified to go to a proper protest. I might never get to go to a protest in Hong Kong again. If I had known this, I would have listened to that girl screaming at me. I would have made it count.

· · ·

*We're* so *far back in the queue of people to arrest—we're nobodies. They're not going to go after us,* we told ourselves. Let's not give in to the fearmongering. The best we can do is to keep doing everything as though nothing has changed, as though the law does not exist. Still, on the night of the law, I write down a series of if-I-get-arrested steps for my partner, names of editors and nonprofit executives he should contact, lawyers I trust, the passwords to my accounts.

The law outlaws four crimes—secession, subversion, terrorism, and collusion with foreign forces—but even the slogan "Liberate Hong Kong" could be considered secessionist. Talking to foreign politicians may be "collusion with foreign forces," and pro-democracy politicians organizing a primary election is "subversion." The police could show up if your shop prominently displayed pro-protest materials. Within the first year, more than a hundred people are arrested under the law; you never know when something is illegal until the pro-Beijing papers or the government announce it, sometimes until someone is arrested. The police don't even have to charge you officially to confiscate your passport, and you likely will not be granted bail. Maximum sentence is life imprisonment.

I think back to a few years ago, when a series of bureaucratic hurdles led me to renounce my British National (Overseas) (BNO) passport status to renew my Singapore passport, and then subsequently also lose my Singaporean citizenship. I applied for a Hong Kong passport instead, despite my father's warning: "The city is going down the drain—best get out while you can." That year, in a *New York Times* interview, Anson Chan had said: "We have to think about people here who have no alternatives. They are not rich like some people in Hong Kong who, if things go wrong, can just up and go elsewhere. For many people they don't have this choice." Back then, I gave little thought to my decision to leave myself with no choice. I was twenty-one years old and had little concept of what passports could do in a time of crisis. It was also before Britain would decide to grant visas and potential residency to BNO passport holders in the aftermath of the national security law.

Because of the pandemic, my partner and I had been putting off planning our wedding. But when the law passed, we hastily put together a small ceremony on my friend's sixty-square-foot balcony, to get the legal proceedings over and done with. My partner has foreign citizenship, and I can apply to be a dependent only if we have been married for over two years. The option for me to leave when necessary could be back on the table.

The morning we sign our marriage license, the *Apple Daily* newsroom is raided by the police. If you squint at the photographs from reports about the raid, you can spot a lawyer in a suit who looks like a cheerful bear. He is a well-respected solicitor I met while interning for a refugee rights lawyer in university. Later, as a reporter, I texted him for updates about political cases I couldn't personally attend in court. Sometimes, at mid-autumn or Chinese New Year, he sent me cute e-cards on WhatsApp that wished me happy holidays. He is to be our civil celebrant that evening.

And then, as I am smearing eye shadow onto my lids, another news alert comes. An acquaintance has just been arrested under the national security law. I repeat our friend's name over and over in our empty flat. Then I pull the white dress over my head.

When our lawyer shows up, on time, my partner and I apologize profusely. "We know you've been busy today."

"Don't be silly, this is a joyous occasion," he says, gracious as ever.

I say my vow: "I will always show up for you, whether we are living in freedom or in fear, Hong Kong or elsewhere." And then we are married. The date of our anniversary is also a day the media forever remembers as a "crackdown."


It is easy to find the words to mourn the loss of a person: We miss their idiosyncrasies, we tell funny stories about them, we anguish over how we'll never get another call from them. Losing a city is much more intangible. I don't know where to find the language to describe the grief I feel when I walk through the city and see phantoms of riot police spilling from the escalators of the malls and street corners, the gray smear of the crudely covered-up protest graffiti in the underpasses and tunnels, or the torn down "democracy wall" at my alma mater, where, though once open to the public, now a security guard asks for my ID at the gate.

Buoyed by this law, the government begin implementing changes in all facets of life. It makes plans to introduce patriotic syllabi in classrooms, and restructure the legislative and chief executive elections so that they are even less democratic. Anyone working in public service is made to sign an allegiance oath, which sounds okay at first until you realize they mean you can never publicly say anything sympathetic to the protest movement ever again. The police set up a national security branch. Pro-Beijing papers complain about the art in the city's museums and collections that is not politically correct enough, like that of Ai Weiwei.

On Twitter, someone writes: "It's absolutely not that bad for the average Hong Konger, who is not a dissident or an activist. That is 99 percent of the population. All freedoms that I want to enjoy are still intact. I still can do anything I want to do, go anywhere I want to go, say anything I want to say."

After the national security law is enacted, every week brings about multiple new developments. Some high-profile figures—perhaps these "dissidents"—receive the most press coverage, but so much more is happening. Eight graduating students are arrested for holding up signs at their own university demanding the release of Hong Kongers detained in mainland China. A teacher is barred permanently from the profession for simply carrying out a class session that discussed pro-independence activists. A man is arrested for having "Liberate Hong Kong" stickers on the gate of his own flat. Are they not "average Hong Kongers"?

I knew what he meant, though. There are people who will forever be protected from this law because of their views, or their lack of stakes. Meanwhile, friends and former protesters around me have begun fleeing the city. We often speak of Hong Kong *disappearing* as the doomsday scenario, as though the city would submerge underwater like Atlantis. It is much more likely that one day in the near future, the Hong Kong cityscape will physically be unchanged, but there will be nobody here that remembers the place that once existed. This is what I fear most: The skyscrapers remain intact, the countryside hikes still beautiful, and our harbor rippling with night lights; you can still go to work and tweet dumb shit and outwardly you can't tell that anything is wrong, but the only ones left are those who believe this is the best version of Hong Kong there could ever be.

.   .   .

At a ramen store in Tsim Sha Tsui, after shopping for wedding bands, my partner and I sit down at a bar table and scan the leaflets of protest artwork and yellow Post-it Notes on the wall. We have been eating exclusively at these yellow diners since the demonstrations in 2019. This division of restaurants and shops into yellow and blue—pro- and anti-protest respectively—began as a boycott of chain stores with owners that declared their support for the police and the government. Among them are popular chains such as Starbucks and Yoshinoya; even though the discounted caramel lattes at the on-campus Starbucks and cheap one-person hot-pot sets at Yoshinoya had been an integral part of my diet since university, I haven't stepped inside either of these restaurants since 2019.

The rationale is to redirect resources to the movement in small everyday ways, but to say that we do this solely to contribute to pro-protest businesses is inaccurate. We are not doing this out of a freedom of choice, but a lack of freedom from fear. When we are outside and I start talking to my partner about a development in the news, he will shush me, and I'll feel a surge of annoyance. Why are we censoring ourselves before anyone censors us?

But I know why. The police have set up hotlines for Hong Kongers to report on one another, and you no longer know which strangers in your neighborhood you can trust. There are eyes everywhere. Posts in support of the movement, on private social media accounts, have been screen-capped and circulated on the internet; it could cost you your job. It isn't safe to talk about politics just anywhere now.

In anticipation of the national security law, some yellow shops removed their protest posters and stickers from their window displays and walls, though sometimes you can still see discreet protest pigs on the corner of a table. Earlier that day, my partner and I went to the history museum, and caught its *Hong Kong Story* permanent exhibition just before the museum announced that it would be closed for a "temporary revamp," presumably to update its materials to fit into the Communist narrative. At the stall next to me in the ramen shop, two girls are talking about their friend who was arrested during the demonstrations and has an upcoming court date. I dunk a piece of char siu into the thick tsukemen soup and suddenly feel exhausted.

If you leave Hong Kong as an adult, you are required to make an official declaration of your "permanent departure from Hong Kong," at least if you want your money back. The government has been taking a not-insignificant chunk of our paychecks every month for our retirement fund, and this declaration is required to withdraw thousands of dollars' worth of "accrued benefits." This departure has to be a *once-in-a-lifetime* event. Part of the declaration reads:

> I, [name of the claimant], [Hong Kong Identity Card/Passport No.] of [address of the claimant], solemnly and sincerely declare that:
>
> I departed/will depart* from Hong Kong on [dd/mm/yyyy] to reside elsewhere with no intention of returning for employment or to resettle in Hong Kong as a permanent resident.

Even those fortunate enough to secure a home elsewhere don't get to just *leave* this city. They have to pack their books and coats into boxes, host a week of farewell dinners, have a good cry at their local diner where the uncle always remembers their order, and then formally declare that they're *not coming back*. Writer Evan Fowler, who left Hong Kong in 2018, said of the bureaucratic process of declaring your departure: "Emotive morning. Gave my oath declaring I'm leaving HK. Six others in the room. One stumbled with emotion. All Cantonese. All lower-middle-class families in their 30s-40s. Room empty of articles but for a bottle of disinfectant."

Fleeing is different. When you flee, your retirement fund is the last thing on your mind. All you want is out. When the ex-lawmaker Ted Hui left Hong Kong in December 2020 in self-exile, he and his family's bank accounts were frozen in retaliation, for "money laundering."

"I have a personal belief: going into exile is not emigration," he wrote. "I will never emigrate, Hong Kong is my home and I can never put down roots anywhere else. . . . I would rather be adrift, and wait for the day when I can return home. I would definitely come home, weep and hug everyone at [the protest zone at] the bottom of the pot." After my partner read Hui's statement, he ran a bath and cried for the first time in years.

Just before the Christmas holidays in 2020, my colleagues at the arts archive and I do a tarot reading session in the office with my friend Bernadette. Because she is too good, I normally refrain from asking her anything. My family's history has taught me that sometimes, it's best not to know too much about your own future. But this evening, I couldn't help myself. Everyone wants to know the answer to only one question: Would we be leaving Hong Kong?

My editor draws a couple of cards, at her request. "You'll leave—but it'll be for your daughter." She's a two-year-old feisty edamame-loving bundle of joy. "And your memories of her in this city will not be the same as her memories of the city."

"You'll be leaving too," she says to me. I'm already tearing up. She sees snow, and white people, she tells me. "But London is so *cold*," I complain. "Why can't I just move to Taiwan?" Should I start comparing models of light-treatment lamps now, for my seasonal affective disorder?

A third colleague picks out a few cards. All three of us had drawn the Tower: a burning tower that represents chaos, destruction, crisis. She'll be leaving, too.

"Maybe we can reverse-colonize Britain," I say, still crying.

"Remember, I've been drawing the World for you," Bernadette says.

In 2017, I watched from the front row when they sent Joshua Wong, Nathan Law, and Alex Chow to jail for their roles in the Umbrella Movement. They were given jail terms of six to eight months on appeal, despite having already served community service as per their magistrates' court ruling. Just before court, I snapped a picture of the student leaders from where I was standing at the press area. It is a close-up of a group of young people who had, not that long ago, been mere teenagers. Lester Shum has his arms around a smiling Nathan Law and Alex Chow while Tiffany Yuen looks on wistfully; Joshua Wong is staring at something further ahead. They knew what was coming, but looked, at least for a split second, almost at peace. Behind them, a flood of photographers are in position.

Eventually, before they finished serving their sentences, the Court of Final Appeal overturned that previous ruling, and released the three. Outside the court, I sighed in relief. I was grateful that they were out, but also that this court saga was over. It had been many days of sudden court appearances, lining up early on cold winter mornings for a seat inside the courtroom—if you were late, you could sit only in the gallery outside—transcribing dense legal speak, and holding our breath as we waited for the verdict or sentence. Finally, this was over, or so I thought at the time.

A few months later, I went to the second anniversary celebration of Demosisto, the political party formed by Law, Wong, and other former Scholarism activists. The event was at a banquet hall in Whampoa in Kowloon, and almost every opposition politician attended. I smoked a cigarette with Long Hair—the socialist politician Leung Kwok Hung—then sat at my reporters' table, drinking free beer and watching a group of the boys dance onstage in pink shirts. The dance was so ridiculous, so poorly choreographed, that you couldn't help but laugh. You suddenly remembered that these were all just kids. Not one of them was older than thirty.

Now Alex Chow lives in the United States, and it's unclear if he'll return. Nathan Law left for the United Kingdom before the national security law came into effect, and has been put onto a wanted list; he is in exile. Joshua Wong is in jail, again, this time for an "unauthorized protest" outside the police headquarters in 2019.

After the jailings of Agnes Chow, Joshua Wong, and Ivan Lam in 2020, *Stand News* did a video interview with the remaining Demosisto members. "When was the last time all of you were in the same room?" the interviewer asked. It was when they were in the public gallery, watching court trials. They didn't even make plans to meet up—they just all happened to be there.

"Even if we can't do much at the moment, you have to take care of yourself," one of them said. "One day, we'll meet on the streets again."

"We might be moving," an ex-colleague tells me, laying down coasters and sauces on the table for hot pot. "Probably in the next couple of months or so."

"Wait, what?" I say. This is the first I am hearing of it. They had just been married for a few months and had recently moved into a new apartment in Hong Kong Island East.

"She doesn't feel safe here anymore," he says, gesturing to his wife. Even if it might be years before it truly becomes dangerous for them, living in a place where you cannot sleep every night out of anxiety is too overwhelming. "They're getting closer and closer." The couple have close friends in human rights and political circles, and work in relevant fields. It's the randomness of the national security law arrests that scares them: You never know who will be next. If it's your turn, they can arrest you over any minor statement you've made in the past, then confiscate your travel documents, even without a formal charge. And then it's over: It's too late to leave at that stage.

During the 2019 protests, I had written "記住緊守崗位，同中共鬥長命," as a reminder to myself. *"We should all keep doing what we're doing, and outlive the Communist Party."* But now, carrying on means that if you want to continue to speak or teach or write or protest, you have to brace yourself for jail or exile. You have to hedge your bets as to how far you can go without becoming a target, how long you can stay before leaving becomes impossible. You have to prepare yourself for the inevitable scenario that everyone you love will either be behind bars or thousands of miles away.

It's the final few hours of 2020. My partner and I are at the couple's flat, with Holmes and his girlfriend, and the friend who was arrested the day I got married. His passport has been confiscated, and he is now reporting to the police station every couple of weeks.

Over the next few hours, we become so engrossed in our board games that we forget to look at the clock. "Uh, guys, there's only twenty seconds left till 2021," my ex-colleague says. "I think we should start counting down now. It's almost time."

"I'm not ready," I announce.

How much time do we all have left? I don't know if I'll ever leave. But I do know that I'm now less certain I'll be here forever. For now, I'd like to stay for as long as is possible, knowing one day it won't be possible anymore. There are still so many places in Hong Kong that I've never been to, districts I've dismissed as dull residential areas. I come across a local YouTube channel, launched in the midst of the pandemic, that shows Hong Kongers taking a walk and exploring their own neighborhoods. A nondescript office building in Kwun Tong with lights cascading down, spiral staircases, and urban parks where you least expect them, the curving slopes that define our cityscape. One evening, my friend Adrian takes me on a motorbike ride through Hong Kong Island, from North Point to the Western District pier, then up the Victoria Road where the night tastes like damp soil. We park on a stretch of pavement next to the waterfront, a corner of Hong Kong away from the light pollution, so dark I can see the stars.

My partner and I make a resolution to visit a new place in Hong Kong every week. We take ferries to outlying islands, where abandoned stone hedges crack with foliage, a single gravestone is enveloped by bare trees. We eat fish and chips at Stanley on a day when the seaside town feels like the windswept Brighton, trying to imagine what the place would look like if the property developers had not put an H&M in a Victorian-era building. We head back to the area near the University of Hong Kong, where the incoming freshmen have much more on their minds than whether they can survive at orientation camp. We go home to Tai Ping Shan, where the streets always smell of bread and fresh laundry. We breathe in the air of every inch of this city.

A person can mean so many different things when they say they love a place.


On that last day of 2020, a crowd gathers in Tsim Sha Tsui, near the cultural center and the clock tower, for the countdown. They wear LED bunny headbands flashing in purple and pink, and face masks stamped with festive prints. The fireworks were canceled because of the pandemic, but the waterfront is anything but quiet. The sea of people chant "Liberate Hong Kong, Revolution of Our Times." They break into a chorus of "Glory to Hong Kong."

Hong Kong is dead, the new law wiped out the resistance, everyone said, and yet. Across the harbor, the lights are still on.

Incensed, the police announce on the loudspeakers, *The slogan that you just chanted violates the national security law.* The crowd boos. The police shine flashlights into the faces of the crowd. *Who chanted?* the officers bark.

They still don't understand that it was all of us.

# Acknowledgments

This book exists because of Marie Pantojan and Clare Mao. Thank you for fighting for this book on my behalf. Thank you for your pep talks, guidance, and feedback. I still can't believe I got to write the book I wanted to write; thank you for making this possible.

I'm eternally grateful to all the interviewees who took the time to speak to me and trusted me with your stories; I hope I have done you justice.

Thank you to my fellow writers and journalists, artists and musicians, for giving me a creative community in Hong Kong and beyond, but especially Holmes Chan, Wilfred Chan, Michael CW Chiu, Koel Chu, and everyone else at *Still / Loud;* Kaitlin Chan and Ysabelle Cheung; Kris Cheng and Angela Lee; Tomii Chan and Sum Lok-kei; Charlotte Mui, Emily Wong, and my friends at Asia Art Archive; and the outstanding reporters from *Aftershock* (sum dei ho!). Special thanks, once again, to Lok and Kris for reading and fact-checking the book; all errors are mine alone.

Thank you to Paul C. Fermin, for being a mentor and friend. Thank you to Wong Chi Chung at HKU's General

Education Unit, for all that you do for students at the university.

I would not have been alive to write this book if it were not for these people: Jessica, Nicole, Adrienne, Angelo, Rose, Lamlam, Sherman, Callum. All the gig buddies, ex-flatmates, and chosen family in my life who have been given pseudonyms in this book, you know who you are. To my brother, Zung.

Thank you to Tiffany Sia, for her insights and guidance, and for offering a space to sit down and write for a week at Speculative Place.

Thank you to the editors who took a chance on me, especially Jyoti Thottam at *The New York Times,* Zoher Abdoolcarim, and C. R. Foster of *The Rumpus,* Mimi Wong at *The Offing,* Emanuele Berry at *This American Life,* Anne Henochowicz at the *Los Angeles Review of Books China Channel,* and Tom Grundy at *Hong Kong Free Press.*

I am indebted to Alice Poon and Liber Research Community for housing research; *From the Factories* and Ahkok Wong for their documentation on the history of industrial building music; Lee Chi Leung, whose book made so many Hong Kongers with mental health conditions, including myself, feel less alone; the English-language writers in Hong Kong who have paved the way; and the musicians and bands who let me write about them when I was a nobody.

Thank you to everyone who read my TinyLetters; a few of the sections in this book first appeared in these emails I sent out to fewer than a hundred readers. Thank you to the tree at Blake Garden.

My grandmother, 嫲嫲: Thank you for raising me. I miss you every day.

Finally, thank you to Elson, for giving me a home. You

get the last line in the acknowledgments. That's a better promise than our wedding vows.

Sections of "A City in Purgatory" first appeared in *The New York Times* as essays, revised and adapted for this book: "The Mask I Wear on the Weekends," "Living in Dark Mode," and "Life in Hong Kong Has Always Been Impossible." Two anecdotes first appeared in "The Lonely Island," a segment for *This American Life*.

# Notes

## Preface

xi **over 90 percent of the population in Hong Kong:** "Hong Kong—the Facts," Government of the Hong Kong Special Administrative Region, https://www.gov.hk/en/about/abouthk /facts.htm.

xiv **Mainstream media had pronounced Hong Kong dead:** Louis Kraar and Joe McGowan, "The Death of Hong Kong," *Fortune,* June 26, 1995, https://archive.fortune.com/magazines /fortune/fortune_archive/1995/06/26/203948/index.htm.

xv **rid itself of all opposition lawmakers:** Tony Cheung and Jeffie Lam, "Mass Resignation of Hong Kong Opposition Lawmakers After Beijing Rules on Disqualification," *South China Morning Post,* November 11, 2020, https://www.scmp.com /news/hong-kong/politics/article/3109454/mass-resignation -hong-kong-opposition-lawmakers-after.

xv **shut down the city's biggest pro-democracy newspaper:** "Apple Daily: Hong Kong Pro-Democracy Paper Announces Closure," BBC, June 23, 2021, https://www.bbc.com/news /world-asia-china-57578926.

xv **promote former cops:** Kari Soo Lindberg, Chloe Lo, and Iain Marlow, "Ex-Cop Named Hong Kong's No. 2 as China Prioritizes Security," *Bloomberg,* June 25, 2021, https://www .bloomberg.com/news/articles/2021-06-25/hong-kong-s-top -security-official-set-to-become-city-s-no-2.

## A Map of Hong Kong, 2021

4    **just wanted to see the sea:** Hon Lai Chu, "I Just Want to See the Sea," trans. Henry Wei Leung with Louise Law, *The Offing,* May 19, 2015, https://theoffingmag.com/essay/i-just-want-to -see-the-sea/.

4    **brothels:** Adam White, "The Wild Western: What to Do in Shek Tong Tsui," *HK Magazine,* March 19, 2015, https://www .scmp.com/magazines/hk-magazine/article/2036954/wild -western-what-do-shek-tong-tsui.

4    **an apparition of Anita Mui:** A reference to the movie *Rouge* (1987), directed by Stanley Kwan, in which Mui's ghost waits for her lover, played by Leslie Cheung, on Hill Road.

5    **the apparently corrupt building management committee:** Karen Cheung, "Residents Revolt: Meet the Communities Fighting Bid-Rigging and Mismanagement in Hong Kong's Residential Buildings," *Hong Kong Free Press,* April 1, 2018, https://hongkongfp.com/2018/04/01/residents-revolt-meet -communities-fighting-bid-rigging-mismanagement-hong -kongs-residential-buildings/.

6    **multiplying the late-night noise complaints:** Karen Cheung, "In Hong Kong's Increasingly Gentrified Western District, Residents Beg Bars for a Good Night's Sleep," *Hong Kong Free Press,* April 29, 2018, https://hongkongfp.com/2018 /04/29/hong-kongs-increasingly-gentrified-western-district -residents-beg-bars-good-nights-sleep/.

9    **"I think Hong Kong people lack culture":** Lung Ying-tai and Andreas Walther, *Dear Andreas* (Taiwan: 天下雜誌, 2007).

10   **the concept of the third place:** Ray Oldenburg, *The Great Good Place: Cafés, Coffee Shops, Bookstores, Bars, Hair Salons, and Other Hangouts at the Heart of a Community* (Boston: Da Capo Press, 1999).

11   **Daniel Lee and his two partners:** "讀賣書人：序言書室 小眾交流 以書聚賢 [The Niche Discussions at Hong Kong Reader: Gathering Good People Through Books]," *MingPao Canada,* March 7, 2014, http://www.mingpaocanada.com/tor /htm/News/20140307/HK-gfk1_er.htm.

12   **for nominal rent:** Karen Cheung and Chelsea Ma, "Art Should Not Be Sensible: In Conversation with May Fung," Asia

Art Archive, October 18, 2020, https://aaa.org.hk/en/ideas/ideas/art-should-not-be-sensible-in-conversation-with-may-fung/type/conversations.

12 **"Financially, I really couldn't hang on":** "Club 71 to Close This Month," Associated Press, October 18, 2020, https://www.thestandard.com.hk/breaking-news/section/4/157633/Club-71-to-close-this-month.

13 **starred in a film as herself:** A reference to her appearance in the film *Memories to Choke On, Drinks to Wash Them Down* (2019), directed by Ming-Kai Leung and Kate Reilly.

15 **"the world's ten coolest neighborhoods":** Maureen O'Hare and Lilit Marcus, "The World's 10 Coolest Neighborhoods, According to *Time Out*," CNN, October 6, 2020, https://edition.cnn.com/travel/article/world-10-coolest-neighborhoods-time-out-2020/index.html.

15 **"Sham Shui Po Is the New Brooklyn":** Elva Pang, "Sham Shui Po Is the New Brooklyn," *Obscura,* April 24, 2020, https://www.obscura-magazine.com/all/stories/misc/sham-shui-po-is-the-new-brooklyn/.

15 **The Wedding Card Street in Wan Chai:** Hermina Wong, "Wedding Card St to Be Turned into 'First Class Shopping' District, Developers Accused of Backtracking," *Hong Kong Free Press,* February 1, 2016, https://hongkongfp.com/2016/02/01/wedding-card-st-to-be-turned-into-first-class-shopping-district-developers-accused-of-backtracking/.

17 **they were considered non-indigenous:** "HK Male Indigenous Villagers' Small House Rights Restored," *The Standard,* January 13, 2021, https://www.thestandard.com.hk/breaking-news/section/4/163332/HK-male-indigenous-villagers%E2%80%99-small-house-rights-restored.

18 **made way for pharmacies stocked with milk formula:** Karen Cheung, "Hong Kong–China Tension: Sheung Shui, a Frontline Town," Al Jazeera English, July 1, 2017, https://www.aljazeera.com/features/2017/7/1/hong-kong-china-tension-sheung-shui-a-frontline-town.

19 **The slogan is derived:** Ryan Ho Kilpatrick, "Localist Leader Arrested at 'Reclaim Sheung Shui' Protest," *Hong Kong Free Press,* September 7, 2015, https://hongkongfp.com/2015/09/07/localist-leader-arrested-at-reclaim-sheung-shui-protest/.

21 **closed my pier off to the public:** Kathleen Magramo, "Hong Kong's 'Instagram Pier' Closed to the Public by Officials Reportedly Citing Covid-19 Concerns," *South China Morning Post,* March 1, 2021, https://www.scmp.com/news/hong-kong /society/article/3123607/hong-kongs-instagram-pier-closed -public-officials-reportedly.

21 **teachers barred:** Rhoda Kwan, "Two More Teachers Banned from Hong Kong Schools Over Links to 'Social Turmoil,'" *Hong Kong Free Press,* May 4, 2021, https://hongkongfp.com /2021/05/04/two-more-teachers-banned-from-hong-kong -schools-over-links-to-social-turmoil/.

## Part I

### 1997

26 《鳳閣恩仇未了情》: A Cantonese opera duet named "Romance of the Phoenix Chamber."

27 **"spiritual pollution":** "Teresa Teng; Taiwanese Pop Singer," *Los Angeles Times,* May 21, 1995, https://www.latimes.com /archives/la-xpm-1995-05-21-mn-4448-story.html.

27 **Keith Yuen announces solemnly:** "集體回憶九七年 (1) [Collective memories of 1997, Part 1]," *YouTube,* https://www .youtube.com/watch?v=LUvHxq1HGzU.

28 **"The whole thing seemed strangely devoid of passion":** Yuen Chan, "Telling Our Own Stories," Throwing Pebbles, July 1, 2017, https://www.yuenchan.org/2017/07/telling-our -own-stories/.

28 **"washing away of the century-long humiliation":** Kinling Lo, "Handover Politics? I Was More Worried About the Rain, Hong Kong Tram Driver Recalls," *South China Morning Post,* June 23, 2017, https://www.scmp.com/news/hong-kong /education-community/article/2099527/handover-politics-i -was-more-worried-about-rain.

30 **"The disbanded soldiers":** Esther M. K. Cheung, "In Search of the Ghostly in Urban Spaces," in *Fruit Chan's "Made in Hong Kong"* (Hong Kong: Hong Kong University Press, 2009).

31 **"Serving two masters":** Oscar Ho, "The History of Lo Ting," in Driving Lantau: Whisper of an Island, ed. Lo Yin Shan (Hong Kong: MCCM Creations, 2012), 171–77.

31 **creating an alternate history:** Mickey Lee, "Back to the Fu-

ture: Contemporary Art and the Hong Kong Handover," *IDEAS Journal,* June 2, 2017.

## Parallel Universes

62   **established in 1967** and **"without regard to race or religion":** "Ordinance & Regulation," English Schools Foundation, https://www.esf.edu.hk/about-esf/ordinance/.

62   *Our mission is to inspire creativity:* "Vision and Mission," English Schools Foundation, https://www.esf.edu.hk/vision-and -mission/.

62   **make up only about 7 percent:** "Statistical Highlights: Education," Research Office, Legislative Council Secretariat, June 19, 2018, https://www.legco.gov.hk/research-publications /english/1718issh30-international-schools-in-hong-kong -20180619-e.pdf.

63   **75 percent local students:** Chan Ho-him, "Many International Schools in Hong Kong Fail to Meet the '70 Per Cent Rule' for Non-Local Students," *South China Morning Post,* April 7, 2020, https://www.scmp.com/news/hong-kong/education /article/3078856/many-international-schools-hong-kong-fail -meet-70-cent.

69   **competitive public and private schools:** Although the schools are referred to here as "public" and "private," the official categorizations in Hong Kong include government and aided schools (public), direct subsidy scheme schools (between public and private), private schools, private international schools, and English Schools Foundation schools.

71   **ranked Band 1:** Band 1 is the top tier for academic prestige, and its students are most likely to be offered a place in university. The majority of Band 2 and 3 schools teach in Chinese. International schools are outside of this system entirely.

71   **elite local private schools:** Many of these schools operate under the "direct subsidy scheme"; examples include St. Paul's Co-educational College, the Diocesan Boys' School, and Heep Yunn School.

74   **around HK$80,000 a year:** ESF school fees were HK$78,600 a year in the school year 2003–04, according to the Education and Manpower Bureau's report, https://www.aud.gov.hk/pdf _e/e43cho4.pdf. One international school charged up to, on

average, HK\$130,316 per annum, in the same school year. In 2021–22, ESF school fees are HK\$133,800 for the lower secondary level: https://www.esf.edu.hk/school-fees/.

76 **"there was little discussion of Hong Kong news":** Nannerl Yau and Jennifer Leung, "Best of Both Worlds?," *Varsity,* March 31, 2017, http://varsity.com.cuhk.edu.hk/index.php /2017/03/international-school-students-language-barrier.

80 **a fifteen-year-old boy is organizing protests:** Ada Lee, "Scholarism's Joshua Wong Embodies Anti-National Education Body's Energy," *South China Morning Post,* September 10, 2012, https://www.scmp.com/news/hong-kong/article/1032923 /scholarisms-joshua-wong-embodies-anti-national-education -bodys-energy.

# PART II
## 2003

85 **Liu Jianlun; China already had knowledge; and 299 people will have died:** Ilaria Maria Sala, "Hong Kong's Coronavirus Panic Buying Isn't Hysteria, It's Unresolved Trauma," *Quartz,* February 12, 2020, https://qz.com/1798974/how-sars -trauma-made-hong-kong-distrust-beijing/.

86 *The Miracle Box:* Referring to 天作之盒, a 2004 movie directed by Adrian Kwan about Joanna Tse and her work.

87 **studied at Leeds:** John Carney, "Fans Commemorate 10th Anniversary of Leslie Cheung's Death," *South China Morning Post,* March 31, 2013, https://www.scmp.com/news/hong-kong /article/1203541/fans-commemorate-10th-anniversary-leslie -cheungs-death.

87 **placing second at an Asian music contest:** "Mr Leslie Cheung Kwok Wing," Avenue of Stars, https://www .avenueofstars.com.hk/en/mr-leslie-cheung-kwok-wing/.

89 *I had believed that Canada was a heaven:* "哥哥點解叫哥哥? 十件張國榮你或許想知道的事 [Why Is Gor Gor Called Gor Gor? Ten Things Leslie Cheung Might Have Wanted You to Know]," *Sky Post,* March 29, 2019, https://skypost.ulifestyle .com.hk/article/2311703/【繼續為你鍾情】哥哥點解叫哥哥? 十件張國榮你或許想知道的事.

90 **beautiful yet already spectral:** In the film *Rouge,* Anita is in a

black cheongsam, a flower clip in her hair red as her lips; she died of cancer just months after Leslie's suicide, in December 2003.

90 **Leslie in a black see-through shirt:** Referring to his performance in Hong Kong in 2000 or 2001, as seen on YouTube, https://www.youtube.com/watch?v=xitNQi1ELiI.

90 *Remember remember remember:* "新聞檔案-03年董太「千祈千祈千祈，洗手洗手洗手," YouTube, March 13, 2020, https://www.youtube.com/watch?v=cphtFFEKEPo.

90 **proposed a national security bill:** "National Security (Legislative Provisions) Bill to Be Introduced into LegCo," Government Information Centre, February 24, 2003, https://www.info.gov.hk/gia/general/200302/24/0224159.htm.

92 *It's easy to leave:* "行政長官公布向中央請辭談話全文 [Chief Executive's Remarks on His Resignation]," Government Information Centre, March 10, 2005, https://www.info.gov.hk/gia/general/200503/10/03100238.htm.

## Twenty-two Roommates

99 **eight thousand of them are over 115 feet high:** Christopher DeWolf, "The Vertical City, Part I: How Hong Kong Grew Up," *Zolima City Mag,* October 6, 2016, https://zolimacitymag.com/vertical-city-part-i-how-hong-kong-grew-up/.

99 **two hundred square feet per capita:** "Improving Average Living Floor Area per Person," Government of the HKSAR, June 20, 2018, https://www.info.gov.hk/gia/general/201806/20/P2018062000367.htm.

99 **Nearly half of the city's flats:** Pearl Liu and Joanna Lam, "Nearly Half of Hong Kong Flats Rent for US$2,550 a Month—70 Percent of Median Household Income," *South China Morning Post,* August 20, 2018, https://www.scmp.com/business/article/2160554/nearly-half-hk-flats-rent-us2550-month-70-cent-median-household-income.

100 **An HK$5,100 "private" bed space:** Grace Tsoi, "Hong Kong Riled by Latest Tiny 'Space Capsule' Homes," BBC, October 26, 2016, https://www.bbc.com/news/world-asia-china-37759409.

100 **being able to purchase a flat:** Thomas Peter, "Frustration of Surviving Pricey Hong Kong Stirs Protest Anger," Reuters,

July 4, 2019, https://www.reuters.com/article/us-hongkong
-extradition-youngpeople-idUSKCN1TY30K.

100 **subdivided flats:** Naomi Ng, "Coffin Cubicles, Caged Homes
and Subdivisions . . . Life Inside Hong Kong's Grim Low Income Housing," *South China Morning Post,* September 26, 2016,
https://www.scmp.com/news/hong-kong/education
-community/article/2022430/theyre-just-us-exhibition
-shines-light-hong-kongs.

100 **headlines say:** Alexandra Stevenson and Jin Wu, "Tiny Apartments and Punishing Work Hours: The Economic Roots of
Hong Kong's Protests," *The New York Times,* July 22, 2019,
https://www.nytimes.com/interactive/2019/07/22/world
/asia/hong-kong-housing-inequality.html.

100 **"He spends half his $1,300":** Angus Watson, Ben Wedeman,
and Eric Cheung, "He Spends Half His $1,300 Monthly Salary
on Rent. This Is Why He's Fighting for a Fairer Hong Kong,"
CNN, August 17, 2019, https://edition.cnn.com/2019/08/17
/asia/hong-kong-protester-economy-intl-hnk/index.html.

100 **controlled by tycoons:** Elaine Yu, "Hong Kong's Oligarchy,"
*Dissent,* April 1, 2015, https://www.dissentmagazine.org/online
_articles/hong-kongs-oligarchy.

100 **selling land to property developers:** The land system in
Hong Kong is leasehold, meaning that the government owns
the title to all land. The land is "sold" via leasehold grants in
public auctions or tenders.

100 **"The reality of a draining public coffer":** Alice Poon,
*Land and the Ruling Class in Hong Kong* (Singapore, Hong Kong:
Enrich Professional Publishing, 2011), 113.

101 **"property tycoons and their close associates":** Ibid., 15.

101 **unethically and illegally so:** In 2008, a former lands secretary
received a lucrative post-retirement offer to work for the New
World Development subsidiary, one of the major developers in
Hong Kong, and relented only after controversy arose over the
conflict of interest. And then, in 2014, the former boss of one
of Hong Kong's biggest developers, Sun Hung Kai Properties,
was sentenced to five years in jail for misconduct after bribing a
former chief secretary.

102 **often present data to debunk:** Liber Research Community,
"Hong Kong Land Research," https://liber-research.com/en
/research-categories-en/land-supply/.

102 **have not improved:** Liu Hsiuwen and Kit Tang, "Where I Sleep," *Bloomberg Businessweek Chinese Edition,* October 3, 2018.

103 **45 percent:** Hong Kong Housing Authority, Government of the HKSAR, "Housing in Figures 2020," https://www.thb.gov .hk/eng/psp/publications/housing/HIF2020.pdf.

109 **public rental housing is over five years:** "Number of Applications and Average Waiting Time for Public Rental Housing," Hong Kong Housing Authority, May 11, 2021, https:// www.housingauthority.gov.hk/en/about-us/publications-and -statistics/prh-applications-average-waiting-time/index.html.

110 **Richard Nixon was in Hong Kong:** Christopher DeWolf, "Hong Kong's Modern Heritage, Part III: Choi Hung, The Rainbow Estate," *Zolima City Mag,* March 20, 2019, https:// zolimacitymag.com/hong-kongs-modern-heritage-part-iii -choi-hung-the-rainbow-estate/.

117 **one big capitalist playground:** Liu Hsiuwen, "【採訪後記】161 呎的日與夜 ['Where I Sleep': Post-Interview Notes]," *Medium,* October 11, 2018.

121 **have been known to deploy triads:** Former lawmaker Eddie Chu, who brought this issue to light, later received death threats warning him to stay out of the Wang Chau controversy.

121 **lived a quiet, self-sustainable life:** Wang Chau Green Belt Development Concern Group, 何處是吾家 [Where Is My Home?] (Hong Kong: BLEU Publications, 2018).

122 **"We can't afford to buy a flat":** "Video: Hong Kong Villagers Resist Eviction as Demolition Arrives in Wang Chau," *Hong Kong Free Press,* July 31, 2020, https://hongkongfp.com /2020/07/31/video-hong-kong-villagers-resist-eviction-as -demolition-arrives-in-wang-chau/.

124 **gaa yau:** "Add oil," a Hong Kong English phrase for showing support and encouragement.

126 ***The Wall Street Journal* interviews:** Lucy Craymer, "Coronavirus Prompts a Whole City to Try Home Schooling," *The Wall Street Journal,* February 26, 2020, https://www.wsj.com/articles /coronavirus-prompts-a-whole-city-to-try-home-schooling -11582734458.

127 **going for HK$5.3 million:** Price on Midland Realty website, accessed October 2020, https://www.midland.com.hk/en/.

2014

132 **the election system is designed to favor:** The Legislative
Council elections feature both geographical constituencies and
functional constituencies; only candidates for the former are
directly elected by Hong Kong people. In functional constituencies, lawmakers are chosen by various sectors such as tourism
and insurance, but the voters are sometimes not people but
companies with vested interests, meaning the votes are controlled by directors and owners. These sectors are traditionally
dominated by pro-Beijing candidates. See also Kris Cheng,
"Explainer: How Hong Kong's Legislature Was Broken, Long
Before Protesters Invaded the Complex," *Hong Kong Free Press,*
July 7, 2019, https://hongkongfp.com/2019/07/07/explainer
-hong-kongs-legislature-broken-long-protesters-invaded
-complex/.

133 **"comprehensive jurisdiction":** "Beijing Emphasises Its
Total Control Over Hong Kong in White Paper," *South China
Morning Post,* June 10, 2014, https://www.scmp.com/news
/hong-kong/article/1529300/beijing-reasserts-its-total-control
-over-hong-kong-white-paper.

133 **More than 787,000 people:** Chris Buckley, "Hong Kong Poll
Turnout Buoys Democracy Activists," *The New York Times,*
June 29, 2014, http://www.nytimes.com/2014/06/30/world
/asia/turnout-for-unofficial-vote-in-hong-kong-cheers
-democracy-advocates.html.

133 **forces a vote on the preliminary funding:** "香港立法會通
過東北發展區撥款引爆爭議 [Hong Kong Legislative Coun-
cil Passes Preliminary Funding on Northeast New Territories
Plans, Causing Controversy]," BBC, June 27, 2014, https://
www.bbc.com/zhongwen/trad/china/2014/06/140627_hkg
_nt_protest.

135 **five hundred demonstrators:** "佔領被捕 511人中的3個平
凡人 [Three Ordinary People Out of the 511 Arrested at the
Occupation]," *Ming Pao,* July 6, 2014, https://news.mingpao
.com/pns/港聞/article/20140706/s00002/1404583988799
/佔領被捕-511人中的3個平凡人.

135 **China issues a decision for the election** and **"love the
country and love Hong Kong":** "Decision of the Standing
Committee of the National People's Congress on Issues Relat-

ing to the Selection of the Chief Executive of the Hong Kong Special Administrative Region by Universal Suffrage and on the Method for Forming the Legislative Council of the Hong Kong Special Administrative Region in the Year 2016," http://www .2017.gov.hk/filemanager/template/en/doc/20140831b.pdf.

135 **"Hong Kong is now entering a new era":** Tripti Lahiri, "A Refresher Course on Hong Kong's 2014 Umbrella Movement," *Quartz,* September 27, 2019, https://qz.com/1714897 /what-was-hong-kongs-umbrella-movement-about/.

137 **holds a press conference:** "梁振英記者會：佔中是違法 行為 [CY Leung Press Conference: Occupy Central Is Illegal]," BBC, September 28, 2014, https://www.bbc.com/zhongwen /trad/china/2014/09/140928_hk_presser.

137 **dark corner in Admiralty by seven cops:** Kris Cheng, "Seven Police Officers Charged with Beating Occupy Protester Charged One Year On," *Hong Kong Free Press,* October 15, 2015, https://hongkongfp.com/2015/10/15/breaking-seven-police -officers-who-allegedly-beat-up-occupy-protester-charged/.

138 *We're the generation chosen by the times:* Lily Kuo, Heather Timmons, and Jason Karaian, "The Hong Kong government-protester sit-down finally took place—and nobody is satisfied," *Quartz,* October 21, 2014, https://qz.com/284510/the-hong -kong-government-protester-sit-down-is-finally-taking-place -and-streaming-live/.

## Through the Fog

141 **synonymous with mental health:** The image of Castle Peak persisted in the popular imagination as a sort of dungeon-like asylum, although it underwent renovation in 2006 and has since been rebranded as a pleasant, comfortable space.

149 *If you don't sign a voluntary admission form:* Mental health professionals I speak to tell me that, in practice, this is something doctors usually say in order to convince patients to sign themselves in under section 30, which sets out the conditions for a voluntary patient to be admitted and apply to leave a mental health facility. Under section 31 of the Mental Health Ordinance: "An application may be made to a District Judge or magistrate for an order for the detention of a patient for observation on the grounds that the patient—(a) is suffering from mental disorder of a nature or degree which warrants his deten-

tion in a mental hospital for observation (or for observation followed by medical treatment) for at least a limited period; and (b) ought to be so detained in the interests of his own health or safety or with a view to the protection of other persons."

150 **narrowly avoided jail:** Esmé Weijun Wang, *The Collected Schizophrenias* (Minneapolis: Graywolf Press, 2019): "There are inevitable parallels between involuntary hospitalization and incarceration. In both circumstances, a confined person's ability to control their life and their body is dramatically reduced; they are at the mercy of those in control; they must behave in prescribed ways to acquire privileges and eventually, perhaps, to be released."

153 *Mad World:* A 2016 Hong Kong film directed by Wong Chun, about the relationship between a man with bipolar disorder and his father.

154 **every ten days:** Lu Ningmin and Liang Rongxuan, "平均每9.3日一青年人自殺 [One Teenager Takes Their Own Life Every 9.3 Days]", *HK01,* December 27, 2017, https://www.hk01.com/突發/141085/2017回顧-平均每9-3日一青年人自殺-數據解構為何踏上不歸路/.

154 **76 percent:** Simone McCarthy, "Is Anyone Listening? Hong Kong Educators and Counsellors Call for More Attention to Rising Student Suicide Rates," *South China Morning Post,* December 29, 2018, https://www.scmp.com/news/hong-kong/health-environment/article/2179694/anyone-listening-hong-kong-educators-and and https://csrp.hku.hk/wp-content/uploads/2018/09/2018WSPD_press_release_tc.pdf.

154 **"regarded as 'losers' ":** Cherie Chan, "Why Are Hong Kong Students Committing Suicide?" *Deutsche Welle,* April 13, 2017, https://www.dw.com/en/why-are-hong-kong-students-committing-suicide/a-38414311.

154 **Shiu Ka Chun addresses:** Karen Cheung, "Social Welfare Lawmaker Slams Chief Executive for Neglecting Student Suicides in Policy Address," *Hong Kong Free Press,* October 13, 2017, https://hongkongfp.com/2017/10/13/social-welfare-lawmaker-slams-chief-executive-neglecting-student-suicides-policy-address/.

155 **"No need for such emotional language":** "邵家臻提學童自殺　質問「人命值幾多錢」　林鄭稱一直關注: 不需用激動語氣講 [Shiu Ka-chun Mentions Student Suicides; Questions 'How Much Are Lives Worth?'; Carrie Lam Claims Con-

tinued Concern: 'There's No Need for Such Emotional Language']," *Ming Pao,* October 12, 2017, https://news.mingpao .com/ins/港聞/article/20171012/s00001/1507777911686/【短片-特首答問會】邵家臻提學童自殺-質問「人命值幾多錢」-林鄭稱一直關注-不需用激動語氣講.

157  **"Because I am capable of achievement":** Esmé Weijun Wang, "High Functioning," in *The Collected Schizophrenias* (Minneapolis: Graywolf Press, 2019).

158  **almost three hundred thousand patients:** Government of the Hong Kong Special Administrative Region, "LCQ10: Mental Health Services," press release, April 28, 2021, https:// www.info.gov.hk/gia/general/202104/28/P2021042800469 .htm.

159  **kaifongs:** A colloquial term that refers to residents of the same neighborhood.

160  **but waiting times:** Zheng Cuibi, "伊院急症室輪候逾8小時全港逾5000人次到急症求診 [Around 5,000 Hong Kongers Seek Medical Assistance at Emergency Room, Waiting Time for A&E Around Eight Hours]," *HK01,* December 6, 2019, https://www.hk01.com/社會新聞/406820/冬季流感-伊院急症室輪候逾8小時-全港逾5000人次到急症求診.

160  **not protected by any medical insurance plan:** "Prepare for Medical Expenses," AIA Hong Kong, https://www.aia.com .hk/en/life-challenges/medical.html, citing "Thematic Household Survey Report No. 63," Census and Statistics Department, Government of the HKSAR, December 2017.

160  **do not cover mental health care:** "醫保多不保精神病 投保時宜小心看清條款 [Most Medical Insurance Does Not Cover Mental Health; Read Terms Carefully Before Purchase]," *Ming Pao,* August 7, 2018, https://www.mpfinance.com/php /daily2.php?node=1533581266225&issue=20180807.

161  **Another British expat:** Marian Liu, "The Secret Burden of Mental Illness in Hong Kong," CNN, April 29, 2018, https:// edition.cnn.com/2018/04/29/health/mental-health-suicide -hong-kong-asia/index.html.

161  **one in seven Hong Kongers:** "Statistical Highlights—Mental Health Services," https://www.legco.gov.hk/research-publications /english/1617issh29-mental-health-services-20170626-e.pdf.

161  **around four hundred psychiatrists in Hong Kong:** "Registered Medical Practitioners on the General Register and the

Specialist Register: Specialist Registration—Psychiatry," Medical Council of Hong Kong, April 2017, https://www.mchk.org.hk/english/list_register/list.php?type=S&fromlist=Y&advancedsearch=Y&regno=S24.

163 **allocate resources to provide appropriate support:** "Budget Speech," Government of the HKSAR, *The 2020-21 Budget,* https://www.budget.gov.hk/2020/eng/budget11.html.

164 **five hundred residents signed a petition:** "李慧筠, 精神中心落戶拗足五年 區議員: 唔反對咪幫緊佢 [Five Years of Debates Over Location of Mental Health Center; District Councillor: 'I Am Helping by Not Objecting']," *HK01,* August 23, 2018, https://www.hk01.com/社區專題/226012/被厭惡設施2-精神中心落戶拗足五年-區議員-唔反對咪幫緊佢.

164 **six in ten adults:** "Mental Health in Hong Kong," Mind HK, https://www.mind.org.hk/mental-health-in-hong-kong/.

171 **almost two million:** "Hong Kong: Nearly a Third of Adults Report PTSD Symptoms—Study," Agence France-Presse, January 10, 2020, https://www.theguardian.com/world/2020/jan/10/hong-kong-nearly-a-third-of-adults-report-ptsd-symptoms-study.

171 **there was a suicide:** Lily Kuo, "'Society Is Suffering': Hong Kong Protests Spark Mental Health Crisis," *The Guardian,* October 22, 2019, https://www.theguardian.com/society/2019/oct/22/society-is-suffering-hong-kong-protests-spark-mental-health-crisis.

171 **"no pain, nothing":** Rhea Mogul, "PTSD and Protests: How the Violence on Hong Kong's Streets Impacts Mental Health," *Hong Kong Free Press,* December 15, 2019, https://hongkongfp.com/2019/12/15/ptsd-protests-violence-hong-kongs-streets-impacts-mental-health/.

172 **"Some of them are very young":** Kuo, "'Society Is Suffering.'"

172 **"It's not worth it":** Alice Su, Twitter, July 2, 2019, https://twitter.com/aliceysu/status/1145914531689979905.

174 **"Other people have fallen over during the chaos":** Lee Chi Leung, *A Room Without Myself* (Hong Kong: Kubrick, 2008), 159.

176 **Artists and writers made zines:** Karen Cheung, "Off the Shelf: Somewhere, Someone Just Wanted to Let You Know," *IDEAS Journal,* January 24, 2020, https://aaa.org.hk/en/ideas

/ideas/off-the-shelf-somewhere-someone-just-wanted-to-let
-you-know.

177 **"What unites Hong Kongers is pain":** Gwyneth Ho Kwai
Lam, "【專訪】屬於每一人的共同體　梁繼平：真正連結
香港人的，是痛苦 (Leung Kai Ping: What Truly Unites
Hong Kongers Is Pain)," *Stand News,* October 18, 2019, https://
www.thestandnews.com/politics/專訪-一個共同體的誕
生-梁繼平-真正連結香港人的-是痛苦.

## PART III
### The Former International School Kid

181 *used as torture chambers:* "History of Schools During the Japanese Occupation," *South China Morning Post,* May 23, 2010,
https://www.scmp.com/article/715085/history-schools-during
-japanese-occupation.

181 **its predecessor opened in Hong Kong in 1894:** King
George V School, "History," https://www.kgv.edu.hk/history/.

186 **"On Instagram, a lot of people I follow":** Karen Cheung,
" 'Tear Gas on One Street and Civilians Walking on Another,' "
*The California Sunday Magazine,* November 14, 2019, https://
story.californiasunday.com/hong-kong-protests-photos/.

186 **sprayed a mosque in Tsim Sha Tsui with blue dye:** Kris
Cheng and Jennifer Creery, "Video: Hong Kong Police Accused of Targeting Mosque with Water Cannon Blue Dye as
Communities Conduct Clean-Up," *Hong Kong Free Press,* October 20, 2019, https://hongkongfp.com/2019/10/20/hong-kong
-police-accused-targeting-mosque-water-cannon-blue-dye
-communities-conduct-clean/.

187 **deported an Indonesian migrant worker:** Holmes Chan,
"Indonesian Migrant Worker Who Covered Hong Kong Protests Detained for 28 Days, Faces Deportation Over Visa Issue,"
*Hong Kong Free Press,* December 1, 2019, https://hongkongfp
.com/2019/12/01/indonesian-migrant-worker-wrote-hong
-kong-protests-detained-28-days-faces-deportation/.

192 **an open letter:** Rhea Mogul, "Hong Kong Student Calls Out
Racism at International School Via Change.org Petition," *Young
Post,* June 23, 2020, https://www.scmp.com/yp/discover/news
/hong-kong/article/3090297/hong-kong-student-calls-out
-racism-international-school.

194 **"not to advocate for Hong Kong independence":** Chan Ho-him, "National Security Law: Keep Views on Hong Kong Politics to Yourself, International School Group Warns Teachers in New Guidelines," *South China Morning Post,* September 4, 2020, https://www.scmp.com/news/hong-kong /education/article/3100266/national-security-law-keep-views -hong-kong-politics.

## Language Traitors

198 **first landed:** John M. Carroll, *A Concise History of Hong Kong* (Lanham, MD: Rowman & Littlefield, 2007).

201 **"*The Guardian* called it the 'Umbrella Revolution'":** Henry Wei Leung, "Ruins Above Water," *Drunken Boat,* https:// d7.drunkenboat.com/db23/nonfiction/henry-wei-leung; see also Henry Wei Leung, *Goddess of Democracy: An Occupy Lyric* (Oakland, Calif.: Omnidawn, 2017).

202 **"new Cold War":** Gideon Rachman, "Hong Kong Is a Flashpoint in the New Cold War," *Financial Times,* July 29, 2019, https://www.ft.com/content/ca123574-b1d7-11e9-8cb2 -799a3a8cf37b.

202 **I don't think expats are precluded:** *Expats,* here and throughout the book, refers to people who've moved to Hong Kong from countries such as the UK, the United States, Australia, and Singapore, usually to work in white-collar jobs or as English teachers.

202 **outsized representation of expats in English-language books:** John Lanchester, *Fragrant Harbour* (London: Faber, 2002); Naoise Dolan, *Exciting Times* (New York: Ecco, 2020); Janice Y. K. Lee, *The Expatriates* (New York: Viking, 2016).

203 **profiting off the movement:** In Hong Kong, protesters started calling profiting off the movement "eating blood mantous," named after Lu Xun's story "Medicine," in which the blood of revolutionaries is made into mantou buns to cure the sickness of children, generally used in Hong Kong to refer to those who profit off the protest movement.

205 **"Do not send ideas about people":** Submission guidelines for *Hyphen* magazine, https://hyphenmag.submittable.com/submit.

206 **NBC News listed him:** Frances Kai-Hwa Wang, "National Poetry Month: Asian-American Poets to Watch," *NBC News,*

April 24, 2015, nbcnews.com/news/asian-america/national-poetry
-month-asian-american-poets-watch-n345766.

206 **In an interview with translator Lucas Klein:** Nicholas
Wong and Lucas Klein, "一個香港男生的非母語寫作 [A
Hong Kong Boy's Non-Mother-Tongue Writings]," *The Initium,* October 7, 2016, https://theinitium.com/article/20161007
-culture-poems-crevasse-nicholas-lucas/.

207 **made me feel seen:** Karen Cheung, "Jenny Zhang's Female
Gaze," *Los Angeles Review of Books China Channel,* January 9,
2019, https://chinachannel.org/2019/01/09/jenny-zhang/.

207 **"Hong Kong is a Chinese city":** Douglas Kerr, "Louise Ho
and the Local Turn: The Place of English Poetry in Hong
Kong," in *Hong Kong Culture: Word and Image,* ed. Kam Louie
(Hong Kong: Hong Kong University Press, 2010), 75–96, cited
in Tammy Ho Lai-Ming, "Can We Say Hong Kong?," *Asian
Review of Books,* February 3, 2017, https://asianreviewofbooks
.com/content/can-we-say-hong-kong/.

208 **"mixed-race, jet-setting":** Michael Tsang, "Is Hong Kong
Losing One of Its Finest Anglophone Fiction Writers?: Xu Xi's
*Insignificance,*" Cha Journal Blog, March 27, 2019, https://
chajournal.blog/2019/03/27/insignificance/.

209 **"local ethos":** Tammy Ho Lai-Ming, "Writing Hong Kong's
Ethos," in *Cultural Conflict in Hong Kong* (Singapore: Palgrave
Macmillan, 2018).

209 **"a third space":** Tammy Ho Lai-Ming, citing Rey Chow and
Douglas Kerr, "Can We Say Hong Kong?," *The Offing,* January
17, 2017, https://theoffingmag.com/enumerate/can-say-hong
-kong/.

209 **"First light / Morning lands on the streets":** Yuen Che
Hung, *Are You Still Writing Poetry* (Hong Kong: MCCM Creations, 2017).

209 **"I can't show you the trees":** Lo Mei Wa, "Letter to a Future Daughter on the Occasion of the 'Fishball Revolution,'"
*Guernica,* February 29, 2016, https://www.guernicamag.com
/lo-mei-wa-letter-to-a-future-daughter-on-the-occasion-of
-the-fishball-revolution/.

212 **"mean streets of Mong Kok":** Ackbar Abbas, *Hong Kong:
Culture and the Politics of Disappearance* (Minneapolis: University
of Minnesota Press, 1997).

216 **"We hope to be a space for young creatives":** "Why We're Doing This," *Still / Loud,* February 9, 2017, https://still-loud .com/2017/02/09/the-still-loud-founders-discuss-still-loud/.

224 **"The restaurant suddenly took in":** *Hong Kong Without Us: A People's Poetry* (Athens, Ga.: University of Georgia Press, 2021), 29.

### Welcome to the Factories

226 **swearing at the chief executive, CY Leung:** "My Little Airport—梁振英．屌你！(請不要在深水埗賣旗) @ Clock- enflap 2014 [My Little Airport—Leung Chun Ying, Fuck You @ Clockenflap 2014]," YouTube, https://www.youtube.com /watch?v=4ninWjojxeQ.

231 **when I interviewed him half a decade later:** Karen Cheung, Vivian Yeung, Kylie Lee, and Wilfred Chan, "The Hong Kongers Trying to Start an Indie Music Revolution on Facebook," *Still / Loud,* March 22, 2017, https://still-loud .com/2017/03/22/zenegeist-hong-kong-indie-music -facebook/.

232 **indie scene exists at all in Hong Kong is a small miracle:** For the purposes of simplifying the discussion, throughout this chapter, "indie scene" and "underground scene" are used inter- changeably, but many Hong Kong bands play music that could be categorized as indie, but are not actually "underground," playing mostly mainstream shows and appearing on radio rather than operating within the industrial building system.

234 **manufacturers began moving to mainland China in the 1980s:** "Commanding Heights," PBS, https://www.pbs.org /wgbh/commandingheights/lo/countries/hk/hk_full.html.

235 **"a boxing competition in the corridor":** Mak Hoisan Anson, ed., *From the Factories* 我們來自工廈 (Hong Kong: Kai- tak, Centre for Research and Development, Academy of Visual Arts, Hong Kong Baptist University, 2014).

235 **"Band Jai Village":** Ahkok Wong, "《我們來自工廈》新 書出版 [New Book Publication: 'From the Factories']," *InMedia,* August 13, 2014, https://www.inmediahk.net/node/1025247.

235 **recorded their first album there:** Mak, *From the Factories* 我們來自工廈.

235 **a government plan:** The plan was called "Energizing Kowloon East." "起動東九龍 擬設專責辦事處 [Energizing Kowloon East plans to set up dedicated office]," *Oriental Daily,* October 29, 2011, https://orientaldaily.on.cc/cnt/news/20111029/00176_044.html.

236 **posed as a concertgoer:** Elson Tong, "Video: Hong Kong Indie Music Venue Hidden Agenda Raided by Police and Officials," *Hong Kong Free Press,* March 8, 2017, https://hongkongfp .com/2017/03/08/video-hong-kong-indie-music-venue -hidden-agenda-raided-police-officials/.

246 **managed by the government:** One year, Clockenflap organized a subsidiary show at an East Kowloon venue that was boycotted by the band scene as a protest against the government's policies of "revitalizing" the scene; its artistic director has also said, when asked whether the festival would have a protest stage during the Umbrella Movement, "Clockenflap was still a rather new festival, and they did not want to appear to have a strong political stance."

252 **rather than just anger:** Ahkok Wong, *caak3 seng1* 拆聲 (Hong Kong: Soundpocket, 2016).

261 **never signed to a major record label:** Kim Ruehl, "Carissa's Wierd: The Band That Got Away," *No Depression,* August 30, 2010, https://www.nodepression.com/carissas-wierd-the -band-that-got-away/.

## A City in Purgatory

266 **the gunfire scorched the night:** " 'Why Is the Army Shooting People?' Tiananmen in 1989, 1999 and 2009, as Seen by *The Globe,*" *The Globe and Mail,* June 4, 2019, https://www .theglobeandmail.com/world/article-why-is-the-army -shooting-people-tiananmen-in-1989-1999-and-200/.

266 *People Will Not Forget:* 《人民不會忘記》(Hong Kong: Hong Kong Journalists Association, 2014).

267 **"understand the culture of their motherland":** 家長教師 會會訊 *Parent-Teacher Association Newsletter 2012*年4月, April 2012. "We should be alert to our primary mission in education: to have our students understand the culture, history, and development of the motherland, so that they would be willing to draw on their strengths and serve the people of Hong Kong and China."

268 **shelve a plan to introduce a pro-Chinese, patriotic curriculum:** Stuart Lau, Amy Nip, and Adrian Wan, "Protest
Against National Education to End After Government Climb-
down," *South China Morning Post,* September 9, 2012, https://
www.scmp.com/news/hong-kong/article/1032535/protest
-against-national-education-end-after-government-climbdown.

269 **building a small protest village:** "何雪瑩, 金鐘村民, 困住
記憶的烏托邦 [The Villagers of Admiralty: A Memory-Trapping
Utopia]," *The Initium,* September 26, 2015, https://theinitium
.com/article/20150924-hongkong-umbrellamovementtrauma02/.

269 **political change eluded the city:** Jeffie Lam, "Four Years On
from Failed Occupy Protests, What Next for Hong Kong's De-
flated Democracy Movement?" *South China Morning Post,* September 28, 2018, https://www.scmp.com/news/hong-kong
/politics/article/2166075/four-years-failed-occupy-protests
-what-next-hong-kongs.

270 **shadow district councils:** Karen Cheung, "Beyond Politics:
The Sai Wan 'Shadow District Council' That Closed Its Doors,
but Lives On in Spirit," *Hong Kong Free Press,* August 20, 2017,
https://hongkongfp.com/2017/08/20/beyond-politics-sai-wan
-shadow-district-council-closed-doors-lives-spirit/.

270 **pro-Beijing council refused a top job:** Kris Cheng, "Jo-
hannes Chan Appointment to HKU Key Position Rejected, 12
Votes to 8," *Hong Kong Free Press,* September 29, 2015, https://
hongkongfp.com/2015/09/29/johannes-chan-appointment
-to-hku-key-position-rejected/.

271 **eighty-seven rounds of tear gas:** Isabella Steger and Chester
Yung, "Hong Kong Protesters Mark Month After Police Fired
Tear Gas," *The Wall Street Journal,* October 28, 2014, https://www
.wsj.com/articles/hong-kong-protesters-mark-anniversary-of
-police-firing-tear-gas-1414510036.

271 **turnouts were often abysmal:** See, for instance, Ng Kang-
chung et al., "Annual July 1 Pro-Democracy March in Hong
Kong Draws Record Low Turnout: Police," *South China Morning Post,* July 1, 2017, https://www.scmp.com/news/hong-kong
/politics/article/2100860/hong-kong-pro-democracy-march
-sets-anniversary-citys. However, during this period, there were
also spontaneous protests on Chinese New Year in 2016, which
eventually saw Edward Leung jailed for six years; protests out-

side the China Liaison Office over the disqualification of law-makers in late 2016; and a massive turnout for the march when Joshua Wong, Alex Chow, Nathan Law, and thirteen land activists were jailed in 2017.

273 **A pro-Beijing politician is later seen shaking hands:** Jennifer Creery, "Video: Office of Hong Kong Pro-Beijing Lawmaker Junius Ho Trashed as Dozens Protest Response to Yuen Long Attacks," *Hong Kong Free Press,* July 22, 2019, https:// hongkongfp.com/2019/07/22/video-office-hong-kong-pro -beijing-lawmaker-junius-ho-trashed-dozens-protest-response -yuen-long-attacks/.

276 **placing a ban on face masks:** "Hong Kong: Anger as Face Masks Banned After Months of Protests," BBC, October 4, 2019, https://www.bbc.com/news/world-asia-china-49931598.

279 **pepper-sprayed for singing:** "Hong Kong Protests: Police Use Tear Gas and Pepper Spray as Christmas Demonstrations Turn Ugly," *Young Post,* December 26, 2019, https://www .scmp.com/yp/discover/news/hong-kong/article/3070129 /hong-kong-protests-police-use-tear-gas-and-pepper-spray.

279 **Paramedics wear reindeer headbands:** Zhang Jiamin, "網民發起到商場示威 防暴警提早到場戒備 [Netizens Organize Protest at Mall, Anti-Riot Cops Show Up Earlier as Precaution]," *HK01,* December 25, 2019, https://www.hk01.com /社會新聞/414134/聖誕節-網民發起到商場示威-防暴警提 早到場戒備, and "香港示威：商場示威、催淚彈襯出烽煙 四起的聖誕節 [Hong Kong Protests: Mall Demonstrations, Tear Gas, and the Smoky Christmas]," BBC, December 25, 2019, https://www.bbc.com/zhongwen/trad/chinese-news-50909392.

282 **"For many people they don't have this choice":** Michael Forsythe, "Q. and A.: Anson Chan on Beijing's Pressure Tactics in Hong Kong," *The New York Times,* June 12, 2014, https:// sinosphere.blogs.nytimes.com/2014/06/12/is-now-the-time -for-hong-kong-to-stand-up-to-beijing/.

284 **arrested for holding up signs:** "Eight Arrested Over CUHK Protest Last Month," *The Standard,* December 7, 2020, https:// www.thestandard.com.hk/breaking-news/section/4/160522 /Eight-arrested-over-CUHK-protest-last-month.

284 **"Liberate Hong Kong" stickers:** "Man Arrested for 'Sedition' Over Stickers Outside Own Flat," *The Standard,* June 28,

2021, https://www.thestandard.com.hk/breaking-news/section /4/175575/Man-arrested-for-alleged-%E2%80%98sedition%E2 %80%99-over-stickers-outside-own-flat.

287 **"going into exile is not emigration":** Tom Grundy, "Hong Kong Democrat Ted Hui Confirms He Will Go into Exile and Not Return from Denmark," *Hong Kong Free Press,* December 3, 2020, https://hongkongfp.com/2020/12/03/breaking -democrat-ted-hui-confirms-he-will-go-into-exile-and-not -return-from-denmark/.

289 **has been put onto a wanted list:** Clifford Lo, Kanis Leung, and Stuart Lau, "National Security Law: Hong Kong Police Seek Activist Nathan Law and 5 Others for Inciting Secession and Collusion, Insider Says," *South China Morning Post,* August 1, 2020, https://www.scmp.com/news/hong-kong/law -and-crime/article/3095615/national-security-law-hong -kong-police-said-seek.

289 *Stand News* **did a video interview:** "刀鋒下的政黨 解散之 後 好好活著的責任 [The Political Party Facing the Axe; the Responsibility to Live Well After Breaking Up]," *Stand News,* December 30, 2020, https://www.thestandnews.com/politics /2020-全家福-9-刀鋒下的政黨-解散之後-好好活著的責任.

292 **when they say they love a place:** Inspired by podcast episode 15 of 唔好意思我倒瀉咗酒 [Sorry, I Spilt the Alcohol], featuring Sampson Wong, Eric Tsang Tsz Yeung, and Kitty Ho, hosted by Chan Yu Hong.

292 **a crowd gathers in Tsim Sha Tsui:** "尖沙咀除夕倒數 市 民高叫「光時」唱《榮光》 警衝向人群截查市民 [Tsim Sha Tsui Countdown, Residents Chant 'Liberate' and Sing 'Glory to Hong Kong,' Police Conduct Stop and Search]," *Stand News,* January 1, 2021, https://www.thestandnews.com/society /尖沙咀除夕倒數-市民高叫-光時-唱-榮光-警衝向人群截 查市民.

## ABOUT THE AUTHOR

KAREN CHEUNG is a writer and journalist from Hong Kong. She has written about politics, music, and books for *The New York Times, Foreign Policy, The Rumpus, This American Life, The Offing,* and others. She was formerly a reporter at *Hong Kong Free Press,* and currently works as an editor at an arts archive. She lives in Hong Kong with her partner. *The Impossible City* is her first book.

Twitter: @karenklcheung

This book was set in Bembo, a typeface based on an old-style Roman face that was used for Cardinal Pietro Bembo's tract *De Aetna* in 1495. Bembo was cut by Francesco Griffo (1450–1518) in the early sixteenth century for Italian Renaissance printer and publisher Aldus Manutius (1449–1515). The Lanston Monotype Company of Philadelphia brought the well-proportioned letterforms of Bembo to the United States in the 1930s.